ORIENTALISM, ISLAM, and ISLAMISTS

NOTES ON CONTRIBUTORS

Bryan S. Turner is at present Professor of Sociology at Flinders University in Australia. His principal publications are *Weber and Islam* (1974); *Marx and the End of Orientalism* (1978); *The Dominant Ideology Thesis* (1980) and *For Weber* (1981); *Religion and Social Theory* (1983) and *Capitalism and Class in the Middle East* (1984).

□

Professor Ziya-ul-Hasan Faruqi is the author of a number of books and articles in English and Urdu. He is also the editor of *Islam and the Modern Age* (English quarterly), *Islam Aur Asr-i-Jadeed* (Urdu quarterly), and the *Jamia* (Urdu monthly) published by the Jamia Millia Islamia in New Delhi, India. He is the Director of the Zakir Husain Institute of Islamic Studies.

□

Professor Aziz al-Azmeh is the author of *Ibn Khaldun in Modern Scholarship*; *Ibn Khaldun: An Essay in Reinterpretation*; *Historical Writing and Historical Knowledge*; *The Principles of Historical Craft*, and *Conception in the Arab-Islamic Middle Ages* (in Arabic). He is currently at the Department of Arabic and Islamic Studies at the University of Exeter.

□

Gordon E. Pruett's field of interest is religious studies with special concern for Islam. His essays have appeared in several learned journals, including *Sociological Analysis*, *Studies in Religion/Science Religieuses*, *The Journal of the American Academy of Religion*, and *Arab Studies Quarterly*. He is currently an Associate Professor of Philosophy and Religion at Northeastern University, Boston.

□

Sulayman S. Nyang is an Associate Professor of Political Science and Public Administration at Howard University, Washington, D.C. He is the author of *Seminar Papers in African Studies* (1974); *Ali A. Mazrui: The Man and His Works* (1981); *Islam, Christianity and African Identity* (forthcoming). He has contributed chapters in many volumes and his papers have appeared in *Presence Africaine; L'Afrique et Asia Modernes; Islamic Culture; Africana Research Bulletin; Pakistan Historical Review; Nigerian Journal of Social and Economic Studies; African Studies Journal; The Search: Journal of Arab-Islamic Studies; Indian Journal of Political Science; Phylon; Journal of Asian and African Studies; The French Journal of African Political Studies.*

◻

Dr. Samir Abed-Rabbo is the President of the Center for Arab and Islamic Studies and the Editor of *The Search: Journal for Arab and Islamic Studies.* He has contributed a number of articles on Islamic and Arab affairs, and is co-author, with Mohamed El-Khawas, of *American Aid to Israel: Nature and Impact* (Brattleboro, Vermont; Amana Books, 1984).

◻

Robert Olson is the author of *The Seige of Mosul and Ottoman-Persian Relations, 1718-1743: A Study of Rebellion in the Capital and War in the Provinces of the Ottoman Empire* (Indiana University Press, 1975), which was translated into Arabic in 1983 as *Hisar-ul 'Mawsil wa alakat il-Uthmaniyyat il'Farsiyyat 1718-1743* (Riyadh, Saudi Arabia) and *The Ba'th in Syria 1947-1982: The Evolution of Ideology, Party and State from the French Withdrawal to the Era of Hafiz al-Asad* (The Kingston Press, Inc., Princeton, New Jersey, 1982). He is also the co-editor of *Iran: Essays on a Revolution in the Making* (Lexington, Kentucky: Mazda Press, 1981). He is Associate Professor of Middle East History at the University of Kentucky.

◻

Dr. Jamil Qureshi has taught in Oxford and is currently a Research Fellow at the Islamic Foundation, Leicester.

◻

Asaf Hussain has contributed a number of articles to *Asian Survey; Strategic Studies* and *The Developing Economies.* He is the author of *Elite Politics in an Ideological State: The Case of Pakistan* (1979); *Islamic Movements in Egypt, Pakistan and Iran: An Annotated Bibliography* (1983); *Political Perspectives on the Muslim World* (1984); *Islamic Iran: Revolution and Counter-Revolution* (forthcoming) and *The United States and Israel: The Politics of a Special Relationship.* He is currently teaching at Moat Community College, Leicester.

TABLE OF CONTENTS

INTRODUCTION

Orientalism as a discipline is still held in high esteem, and many of its practitioners are still holding forth in various prestigious institutions and universities of the West. Many of their non-Western students, equipped with their doctoral degrees from some university in the West, are continuing the same tradition in their own countries. The network is therefore still very strong and Orientalists still claim to be the experts on Islam. Hence the title of this book: *Orientalism, Islam and Islamists*. But this false mask is cracking, for some Western and non-Western scholars have dealt it severe blows and exposed the facade of its supposed 'academic' objectivity and value-free assumptions.

Among the various criticisms made of Orientalism, none was so severe as Edward Said's devastating critique: *Orientalism*. Said's splendid study worked with strategies of analysis advanced by Michel Foucault. It was a comprehensive account of the relation between the West's intelligent discussion of the Islamic Orient and its received notions about it. Foucault's theory that discourse is inevitably a function of power relations was amply demonstrated. Although Edward Said is a single author covering a large field, he passionately exposed the West's abuse of its cultural power.

But there is need for more such studies and this book is another contribution to the growing literature performing the post-mortem of Orientalism. The collection of essays offered here expresses the response of different authors (Muslims and non-Muslims) to Orientalism in general, and to the work of particular Orientalists. Any collection of this kind is open to the complaint that in some respects the essays are repetitive, in others too diverse and unrelated. But this advantage should be offset, first, by the variety of tone and approach as well as variety of diagnosis, and, second, by the closer attention of differently committed critics to the work of individual Orientalists.

There is good reason for lumping Orientalists together in order that their work offer a solid unity of effect. Orientalists do not all set out at the same distance from Islam nor travel to exactly the same point in it: the two parts of this collection should reflect the unity and the difference.

Any binding editorial line would obviously have negated the point of inviting the contributors' views; nevertheless, after the event, it seems to us perfectly proper to state briefly the line that has emerged to bind the book.

Asaf Hussain's introductory essay shows how the ideology of Orientalism worked in the service of imperialism. Orientalism helped to legitimize imperialist policies devised to control the colonized. In his essay Hussain stresses the overall view of these essays: the Orientalist is really addressing the West. If he fails to find the Orient as it is properly constituted in its own history and in its own cultural and societal norms, it is not important because that is not, finally, what he values nor what interests him.

Utilizing Michel Foucault's analysis of discourse, Bryan Turner continues the theme of Asaf Hussain's argument that Orientalism also served the interests of imperialism and the West by stressing the absence of a 'civil society' in Islam: an absence which resulted in Islamic decay and decadence and in Western vibrance, democracy and dynamism. His analysis of the frequently alleged absence of civil society in Islam concludes that the allegations were a response to the need to find despotism in the Orient so that its contrary, democratic institutions, could be located in the West as an affirmation of the European spirit's natural inheritance from classical Greece. Although 'Western' and 'Oriental' could be convincingly applied in certain respects to either or both Islam and Christianity, only the differences were observed. The contributions of Muslim scholarship to European thought were slighted, the continuity of institutions under Christian-Muslim-Christian rule in Spain neglected. On inspection, Oriental despotism turns out to have been a caricature of Western monarchy, the debate about it reflecting the anxieties about how, and if, to extend political rights to the few or to all.

Gordon Pruett's essay also selected change and reform in Islam as the key issue. Orientalism, hopelessly insensitive to the feelings of Muslims, ignores as of no consequence the historical fact of Muslim belief in Islam; whatever the Orientalists' belief, their belief remains a fact. In insisting, first, that 'Islam' is a cultural artifact, and then judging it against Western norms, the Orientalists miss the central fact that, for Muslims, Islam is primarily an ongoing concern to live in submission to the will of God, and they miss, too, an occasion to contribute intelligently to that concern. Pruett then demonstrates from the work of three Orientalists why the view that Islam (being 'Islam') is incurably resistant to reform, or that its best is past and unrecoverable, or that it must reform on Western lines to meet modern times, is in each case insulting and useless to Muslims. It refuses the abundant historical evidence of Muslim reform of Islam, and denies to Muslims, past or present, any capacity of constructive response to occasions of threat to their Islam. Ultimately, the Orientalist claim is that reforming is an active element of only Western culture, of its humanism, of its search for truth, of its commitment to the development and welfare of the individual.

In "Articulation of Orientalism," Aziz Al-Azmeh describes the rigid conceptual structure by means of which Western criticisms of Islam are generated. The structure is mechanical, the generation a repetitive re-copying: it is noted that every predicate about Islam is negative, but that it is the negative corresponding to an affirmative proposition about Christian/Western civilization. The key affirmative is that the West is capable of invention, of dynamic change, therefore the Orient is stuck. This justifies the specifically enumerative, accumulative character of the discipline, at the same time obliging the Orientalist to represent any 'un-sticking' or positive element in Islam as: (1) the consequence of Western influence and thus, (2) a transitory aberration unassimilable by mainstream Islam.

In the second section of the book on individual Orientalists, Gordon Pruett addresses the Christian attitude to the Prophet in the work of Duncan Black Macdonald. Macdonald was an energetic inspirer of mission, a zealous Victorian, convinced of his good intentions and determined to rescue the Muslims from their heathen confusion. The Prophet was not a fake, but a geniune, mad poet, the best of his Arabian kind, muddled in his recollections of the Jewish and Christian faiths, carried away by the simplicity of believing in the one 'Allah', and perhaps too quick to abuse for political purposes his gifts as seer-poet. Muslims themselves, Macdonald felt, are childlike in their disposition to mendacity, irrelevance, fantasy, superstition, incapable of organized thought, of systematic life in general, and accept only at endless elaboration of a single intuition. They should be kindly treated, however, if they are to be converted, their naive confidence in their own spirituality should not be disturbing. Ziya-ul-Hasan Faruqi's tribute to the scholarship of the late H.A.R. Gibb's knowledge of Islam and his contributions to it was a useful reminder of how much Muslims owe to Orientalism which, for all its faults, rediscovered and presented in a scholarly fashion a sizeable body of information which Muslims themselves had, as it were, 'forgotten.' More particularly, Gibb actually liked at least two Muslims, Ibn Khaldun and Salah Ad-Din; his biography of the latter is, Faruqi acknowledges, as objective and sympathetic a study as any Muslim scholar might have produced. Gentle academic though he was, Gibb was also committed to Christianity as the "ultimate in religious experience:" his 'Islam' was therefore 'Mohammedanism,' a viewpoint consciously adopted and, as the essay illustrates, consciously provocative to Muslims and manifestly wrong on matters of faith of the utmost centrality — on, for example, the role of the Prophet.

Bryan Turner criticizes the intellectual poverty of Gustave von Grunebaum's approaches to his subject — despite gestures towards cultural/sociological analysis, he in fact depended upon a fairly naive application of Hegelian idealism. He saw Islam as a society trapped in sacred law that could not be adapted to changed historical circumstances, any and every detail of it confirming for him this notion of its rapid and inescapable degeneration. One is forced to conclude that much of von Grunebaum's prolific output on Islam was repetitive and redundant.

By contrast, Bernard Lewis is complimented by Sulayman S. Nyang and Samir Abed-Rabbo for the zest of his quite different polemic. Careful biographical notes explain the sequence and timing of his publications: Lewis' responsibilities to the needs of British intelligence, or of Western diplomacy, generally, in the Middle East and Turkey, or, later on, his studious association with Israel. Much of his work is in fact journalistic while claiming academic authority.

Jamil Qureshi's essay discusses Kenneth Cragg, whose writings have focused on various aspects of Islam. Cragg is not interested in the study of Islam for its own sake but attempts to show how near 'alongside' it comes to the Christian view, how near and yet (since Islam is deficient) so far. Cragg's writings, as perhaps could be expected from a Christian clergyman, suffer from the intrinsic limitations of his own world views.

In the end it is hoped that this volume will inspire and initiate more investigations into the works of other Orientalists not included in this study.

The Editors

1

THE IDEOLOGY OF ORIENTALISM
Asaf Hussain

Until the arrival of Islam, Christianity had no rival to compete with in the world. After Judaism, its status as a revealed religion was institutionalized through an established church and priesthood. When Islam emerged on the scene in the Middle East, both Judaism and Christianity felt threatened and did not want to accord it the status they enjoyed. But the dynamic message of the new religion soon spread from Arabia to China and various Muslim empires have left their imprint on the history of the world. Christians soon realized that Islam had come to stay.

Why did Christianity and Judaism feel threatened by Islam? It seems it was because Islam had come to complete the message brought by many prophets, including Moses and Jesus. Islam claimed that the revelations of Jesus Christ had not been retained but compromised in the Bible. Judaism and Christianity, however, did not accept this contention. They attacked Islam; and no strategy, including the Crusades, was left untried to destroy the credibility of Islam as a revealed religion. The ferocity of attacks launched against Islam not only exposed the sensitivity of Christians when dethroned from their elitist pedestal but also questioned whether they were really in possession of God's revelation. Their lack of confidence was demonstrated by their dislike towards Muslims who also believed in the same God.

The polemical writings of early Christian religious writers considered that the Prophet of Islam was an imposter and the Qur'an a fabrication. On such literature the Crusaders were nourished and the direct encounter of the Christian West with the Muslim East took place on the battlefields of Palestine.

But even crusading knights full of hatred towards Islam had mixed feelings when confronted with a Muslim general such as Saladin Ayyubi (1137-1193 A.D.) the defender of Islam during his times. His generosity and his kindness towards Christian prisoners, including knights whom he captured, were proverbial. When he captured Jerusalem in 1187 A.D. from the Christians he forbade his troops to massacre and loot Christians. This shocked his Christian enemies, who had considered

Saladin a barbarian. The crusaders were "fascinated by a Moslem leader who possessed virtues they assumed were 'Christian.' "[1]

Saladin's reputation travelled to the West and captured the imagination of writers from Dante to Sir Walter Scott and Orientalists like H.A.R. Gibb and Stanley Lane-Poole.

The conquest of Spain and Sicily brought Christians and Muslims into close interaction with one another and Christian reconquests of these places evoked an interest in Islam. These relationships widened the sources of knowledge regarding Muslims which Christian theologians, who had greatly distorted Islam,[2] were able to utilize. They had "built up the picture of Islam as an odious and malignant force with its Prophet depicted either as an idol or tribal god and therefore false and spurious, or else equated with Satan or Antichrist." By no stretch of imagination were they concerned with objective truth. One of these polemicists, Guibert de Nogent, freely admitted that he used no written sources for his polemics against Islam, but only hearsay, adding, "It is safe to speak evil of one whose malignity exceeds whatever ill can be spoken."[3]

Saladin's death however, did not remove the threat posed by Islam to Christianity and Judaism regarding the authenticity of their scriptures. Furthermore, even though Umayyad rule had faded from Spain by the twelfth century, the image of the Muslim warrior with the sword in one hand and the Qur'an in the other haunted the West even as the Turks captured Constantinople in 1453 and established the foundations of the Ottoman empire. Their empire spread into Eastern Europe and negative images of Islam were reinforced, inflaming once again Christian fanaticism. Fear of Islam and the Ottoman Empire spread in the West. It was assumed that such an empire stood for the perpetuation of Islamic misrule and tyranny. Such assumptions remained unquestioned throughout the nineteenth century.[4]

The discovery of a sea route to India by Vasco da Gama in the 15th century incited the interests of the British, French, Portuguese and the Dutch. Rivalry among them for expansion of their trade across new frontiers necessitated conquests of these new lands. Since the two major empires (the Mughal and Ottoman) were under Muslim rulers, it ignited a renewed interest in Islam. Chairs of Arabic Studies were established in Cambridge (1632) and Oxford (1636). William Bidwell (1561-1632), known as the father of Arabic Studies, wrote that Arabic was "the only language of religion and the chief language of diplomacy from the Fortunate Isles to the China Seas."[5] The university authorities considered that Arabic would prove useful "to the good service of the King and State in our commerce with the Eastern nations, and in God's good time to the enlargement of the borders of the Church, and the propagation of Christian religion to them who now sit in darkness."[6]

The study of Arabic and other languages of Muslim countries like Persian and Turkish laid the foundations for the study of the literature of those countries. These studies in the initial stages were motivated more by commercial and missionary than political reasons.

Christian missionaries laid the foundation for the development of Orientalism. This interest reached its peak during the first half of the nineteenth century and early twentieth centuries and missionaries from Belgium, France, Britain, Holland, Spain and the United States were all involved. Such names as S. Zwemmer, H. Lammens, D.B. Macdonald, M.A. Palacious, C. De Faucoult, M. Watt to K. Cragg, have all produced studies which created doubts about Islam or relegated it to an inferior status.

Duncan Macdonald believed that Muslim societies were going to suffer from a collapse of Islam from the onslaught of European civilization. So as soon as the "legend of Muhammad" crumbles and "his character be seen in its true light" then the "entire fabric must go," as such Christian schools and preachers should "save these people . . . for Christianity."[7] The most effective way to achieve missionary objectives was not "to attack Muhammadanism directly but to let new ideas eat away its foundation."[8]

Others like Montgomery Watt believed that "Muhammad appears to have tried to mould Islam as the older religion."[9] The old religion was Judaism and, since the first *Qiblah* was to face towards Jerusalem, it initiated a desire on the part of the Prophet to be accepted by the Jews. Montgomery Watt speculates that, had the Jews come to terms with the Prophet Muhammad, Islam could have become "a sect of Jewry."[10] In fact the missionary Orientalists had one objective and that was "to deny and disprove the Prophet's status as such and the Qur'an as revelation."[11] In other words, they did not study Islam to understand it but to discredit it.

Side by side with missionary interests, commercial interests had begun to develop during the seventeenth century. Trading companies had been established by a number of European countries like Britain,

France, Germany, Portugal, Holland and Spain both in Muslim and non-Muslim countries. Muslim countries were of major interest, however, for the whole of India was under Mughal rule, while the Middle East was ruled by the Ottomans. It did not take long for European trading to develop political interests. The untapped resources of these countries soon gave way to exploitation and monopolization over territorial controls for ensuring its continuity and maximization of profits from new materials.

While the economic and political interests of the Europeans in non-Western countries were beginning to make inroads in these far off lands, interests in the culture, literature and religion of these lands had also begun to develop. There was a rapid turnover of such literature by travellers and scholars; the Orient was considered exotic and mysterious and scholars like Abraham-Hyacinthe Anquetil-Duperron and Sir William Jones translated the *Avesta* texts of Persian Zoroastranism, the *Upanishads* of Hinduism and founded the Asiatic Society of Bengal in 1784. What has been labelled as "scientific Orientalism" is considered to have started at this time when Silvestre de Sacy opened the Ecole des Langues Orientales in Paris in 1795.[12] It is not surprising that during his conquest of Egypt Napoleon had taken with him a number of scholars who wrote 23 volumes of studies on Egypt, initiating Egyptology as a field of study in order to "restore a region from its present barbarism to its former classical greatness; to instruct (for its own benefit) the Orient in the ways of the modern West; to subordinate or underplay military power in order to aggrand the project of glorious knowledge acquired in the process of political domination of the Orient; to formulate the Orient, to give it shape, identity, definition with full recognition of its place in memory, its importance to imperial strategy, and its natural role as an appendage to Europe . . ."[13] Such earlier interests led to the production of a number of translations, dictionaries, travelogues, etc., all designed to explain the Orient or make its study easier through the knowledge of its languages and literature. But by the nineteenth century these haphazard and independent pursuits had given way to more vigorous methods in keeping with the developing scientific consciousness of the times. A general consensus of how to approach Oriental studies was developing among scholars of the Orient.

The status of Orientalism began to be recognized as a discipline. It must also be remembered that in the milieu in which the discipline was born there was a growing demand for it. This demand was generated by the expanding conquests and interests of colonialism. As new colonies were established the colonialists were faced with new cultures, religions and ideas which were alien to them. In order to control these non-Western people more knowledge about their cultures and religions was needed. This need was fulfilled by secular Orientalism. It opened a new front against Islam in which both Christian as well as Jewish scholars participated. Orientalism was becoming "an integral part of western culture."[14] The scholarly studies of Silvestre de Sacy, Ernest Renan, Edward William Lane "made Orientalism effective and congruent with the interests and political concerns of imperialist rulers."[15] Said therefore offers the most appropriate definition of Orientalism: its function was "To understand, in some cases to control, manipulate, even incorporate, what is a manifestly different world."[16]

Orientalism helped the imperialist to legitimize his conquests. Some Orientalists were directly involved in aiding colonial administrations by providing interpretations of how to dispute the natives' perceptions of Islam. Louis Massignon worked with the Ministry of Foreign Affairs and for the French administration in Morocco. According to him, "the curve of evolution is inclining more and more towards Paris and it is to it and not to the East that the great mass of North Africans are turning their eyes."[17] For the French and British colonialists who colonized Muslim countries many times larger than their own, Arabic and Islamic studies became a guide for the "pacification of the colonized territories as a means to achieve their colonial objectives."[18]

It must also be mentioned that Orientalism was not the only direction which had sought to subvert the civilizations of the eastern peoples. Another discipline which worked hand-in-glove with colonial interests was anthropology. It was considered to be another "child of imperialism."[19] Anthropologists' studies aided colonial administrators as well as others, such as missionaries, in understanding the customs and lifestyles of the peoples. Social anthropology, "became important to ... colonial administration, in the context of direct coercive rule and in the context of reforms from above."[20] The colonialists did not know the different cultures of the various peoples. The cultures of the non-Western peoples were as different from each other as they were from their new ruler's. At any rate the study of the cultures of the non-Western peoples was taken over by anthropologists. In the colonialists'

hands such data was extremely useful. The more the colonialist understood the culture of the ruled, the more he began to comprehend their
strong and weak points, which enabled him to manipulate them. The
motive for the study of non-Western peoples was not to produce
knowledge for knowledge's sake but to help the colonialists to exploit
non-Western nations. Funding was easily available in areas where there
was a dearth of studies or the area was difficult to study. Numerous
studies were therefore done on Asia, Africa and the Middle East under
academic garb and considered objective. But as Talal Asad observes, "it
is worth noting that virtually no European anthropologist has been won
over personally to the subordinate culture he has studied."[21] Objectivity
was therefore a myth to sanctify the fundings of anthropology.

Orientalism and anthropology both served colonialism but in different ways. Anthropology evolved much later than the former at a time
when colonialism had spread far and wide into the non-Western world
and colonialists needed concrete methodologies as to how to bring
about political, economic and social changes among the colonialized.
Anthropologists provided the imperial countries the relevant theoretical model known as "structural-functionalism." This theory exercised
the most powerful influence not only academically through the writings
of anthropologists and sociologists like Bronislaw Malinowski and Tal-
cott Parsons but also introduced new theoretical methodologies of
political change into non-Western societies. Structural functionalism
posited that every society contains structures devised according to the
history and traditions of the indigenous people. Functionalism posits
these structures have political, economic and social functions to perform. In order to change any society its structures must be altered or
demolished and new ones created or substituted. Its functions would
then automatically change. The colonialists took full advantage of these
ideas and through coercion, appropriation, negotiation, persuasion and
education initiated new political and economic structures in colonized
societies. In varying degrees resistance was offered to change by different societies, but these attempts were overwhelmed by force or by legal
means. Concepts of "culture" and "ethnicity" were put to good political advantage by colonialists. Sometimes imperialist countries did not
have to engage in battle with subjugated groups but accomplished their
purposes by setting one group against the other, by employing the now
famous 'divide and rule' tactics. In these efforts they had local

collaborators. In some colonized societies like the Indian subcontinent, it was easy to set two communities, such as Hindus and Muslims, against each other. In the Middle East this proved difficult; structural function-alism faced a strong obstacle in the unifying force of Islam and its political culture.

One of the dynamic pillars of Islamic political culture was ensconced in the concept of *umma* (community of believers). The ideal *umma* transcended the national, tribal and ethnic boundaries among Muslims. All Muslims were part of this *umma* and it was considered the duty of every Muslim to strengthen and consolidate it and not weaken it. But in the contextual realities, Muslim rulers often deviated from Islam and did not prove to be ideal in their rule over their subjects or in their political relationships with other Muslim countries such as that which existed between the Turkish Ottomans and the Safavid Iranians. There were many reasons for this which are beyond the scope of this paper. Suffice it to state that the colonists found such weaknesses easy to exploit by introducing westernized notions of ethnicity and nationalism.

Men like T.E. Lawerence were instrumental, for example, in inciting the Arabs against the Turks. They could just as well have acted on the reverse principle, that is, of reconciling the political differences between Arabs and Turks, but this would not have served colonial objectives in the Middle East. Nationalism then became a potent new political force in the Middle East, separating the Arabs from the Turks but dividing the former among themselves. The irony was that when political consciousness dawned upon them, exposing colonial intrigues and exploitation, nationalist forces threw off the yoke of colonialism. This sometimes entailed a heavy cost in human lives, as in the Algerian struggle against the French.

Another Islamic principle was the inseparability of religion from politics. The selection of Islamic political leadership was directed towards those considered through consensus in the *umma* to possess a high degree of commitment to Islam. Each Muslim ruler was considered to be competent to rule the *umma* and implement the principles of the Qur'an and Shari'ah in their own societies. But Muslim rulers often fell short of this criteria as dynastic rule was institutionalized in the political systems of Muslim countries. Few members of any dynasty, if any, possessed the degree of Islamic commitment expected of them by their subjects.

The colonialists were quick to take advantage of this opportunity and introduced secularist doctrines which sought to separate the sphere of religion from politics. This approach appealed to the ruling dynasties, for Islam did not legitimize such rule, and they did not want Islamic approval or disapproval of their political and personal behavior. The colonialist secular doctrines reflected norms from their own political culture which had subordinated to the Monarchy of Parliament. Such ideas of secularism found many new advocates not only among Arab, Turkish and Iranian intellectuals but also among the various political leadership groups. The new ideas regarding formulation of a "constitution" and implementation of the liberalized western doctrines of a "democracy" which functioned through elected representatives in "parliaments" reformed and radically altered the political structures in the Middle East. Orientalism therefore became a valuable tool for the subversion of Islam. The main task of such subversion was to pull out the "claws" of Islam which could impede colonial exploitation of Muslim lands. It gave a Westernized interpretation of Islam and distorted the real meaning of Islamic concepts like *jihad, umma, tawhid,* etc. Departments of Islamic studies were opened at western universities which conferred doctorates in Islamic studies on Muslims themselves. To be an Islamic scholar was not to be committed to Islam but academically qualified in the theories of Orientalism. In fact, in the oral examinations of post-graduate students in Islamic studies, students were questioned on the theories of Orientalism and "the student, in order to pass has not only to know the theories but to accept them essentially as correct."[22] Such training and interpretations created an Orientalist's Islam parallel to the real Islam.

The colonialists derived enormous benefits from such "Westernized" Islam and ridiculed concepts of *umma* as a far-fetched notion or referred to *jihad* as "holy war" which had faded with the Crusaders and not as an ongoing struggle and individual striving. For example, some Orientalists like Snouck Hurgronje, another Orientalist employed by his government, devised policy guidelines for the Dutch government's colonial rule in Indonesia. Hurgronje articulated the objectives of Orientalism very well in serving colonialism for he considered that "the more intimate the relations of Europe with the Muslim East became, the more muslim countries fall under European suzerainty, the more important it is for us Europeans to become acquainted with the intellectual life, the religious law and the conceptual background of Islam."[23] A number of studies were produced by the Orientalists and their motives were merely reflections of Hurgronje's view.

In the political dimensions of Islam, "the orientalist image" of repressive relations between Islamic rulers and their subjects was "rooted not only in the historic christian experience of aggressive Islam ... but more importantly, in the bourgeoisie European evaluation of 'progressive' and 'fanatical' Islam that required to be directly controlled for reasons of empire. As rulers of vast Muslim populations, the imperialists could attempt to legitimize their own governing position with arguments supplied by Orientalists that Islamic rule (colonial rule is by contrast humane), that Islamic political theory recognizes, the legitimacy of the effective *de facto* ruler (colonial rule is manifestly better than the corruption, inefficiency and disorder of pre-colonial rule), that political domination in Muslim lands is typically external to essential articulation of Islamic social and religious life (therefore no radical damage has been done to Islam by conquering it as its central political tradition remains unbroken)."[24] Such deductions from Orientalism reinforced the ideology of colonialism.

But such studies contained a serious flaw which misperceived Islam. Muslim history was considered as a projection of Islam. Dynastic and patrimonial leadership was taken as political behavior. Islam was confused with folk culture. These were not expressions of Islamic political behavior. In fact, Muslims themselves identified with Islamic history as only that which was practiced during the lifetime of the Prophet. His discussions and judgements were emulated by his four companions (who later became caliphs of the Islamic empire) after which Islamic was usurped by dynastic considerations in which individual and not Islam power became the prime consideration.

Orientalists did not make such fine distinctions between Islamic history of the *Rashidun* period (the first four Caliphs) and Muslim history dating from the ascension to power of the Umayyad dynasty in 661 A.D. Orientalists perceived history on a single time continuum. Muslims, however, regarded the *Rashidun* period as the proof that an Islamic state could be established based on the principles of the political system established during this period. The Kerbala tragedy in 680 A.D. in which the grandson (Husayn) of the Prophet tried to defy the unIslamic regime established by the Umayyad rulers was another event from history singled out by Muslims. The principle of *jihad* in action against an un-Islamic ruler legitimized revolt against tyranny. The effect of this incident on Muslims is still evident, as it was a strong mobilizing factor in the Islamic revolution in Iran in 1979. Orientalists created history according to western concepts which totally ignored Islamic history and how it was meaningful to Muslims themselves. In order to diffuse and distort the meaning of divine history through which, as Muslims believe, God tried to demonstrate the *Sirat al-Mustiqim* (the straight path), they found fault. Their common targets were the life of the Prophet, the Qur'an and the Hadith (traditions) of the Prophet.

During the second half of the nineteenth century, a number of major Orientalists wrote books on the Prophet's life. Some of the major contributions were Muir's *The Life of Mohamet* (in 4 volumes 1858); Sprengler's *Das Leben und die Lehre des Muhammed's* (in 3 volumes 1861-1865); Noldeke's *Das Leben Muhammed's* (1863); Wellhausen's *Muhammed in Medina* (1882); Krehl's *Das Leben des Muhammed* (1884); Grimme's *Mohammed* (in 2 volumes 1892-95); Buhl's *Muhammed* (1903); Margoliouth's *Mohammed and the Rise of Islam* (1905); Caetani's *Annali dell'Islam* (1905); Tor Andrae's *Mohammed, the Man and His Faith* (1936); Blachere's *Le Probleme de Mahomet* (1952); and Watt's *Muhammad at Mecca* (1953) and *Muhammad at Medina* (1956). Most of these books focused on some common themes concerning the Prophet's life. Some considered that he came from humble origins, suffered from epileptic fits, doubted his divine mission, behaved like a Prophet at Mecca and a politician at Medina; that he was worshipped by the Muslims as an idol; that he had knowledge of the Bible; that he tried to mould Islam from imitating other religions like Judaism and Christianity.[25] The aim of all this was the character assassination of the Prophet Muhammad. If this could be achieved, the validity of the Prophet would be discredited. Such unsubstantiated generalizations were believed in the West and used by missionaries.

It is not surprising to find, as among anthropologists, hardly any Orientalist who was sympathetic to Islam. Scholars looked down upon 'subjective' attitudes and pretended to be 'objective'. But in spite of such a facade their deep-seated prejudices could not remain hidden. It could often be easily detected by questions the Orientalists posed and in the selection of methodology utilized in their studies. On studies of the

Qur'an, quite often it is noticeable that the main preoccupation of the Orientalists was either to prove that it had borrowed ideas or that it was a forgery from pre-Islamic Arab ideas and customs, or evolved from Judaism or Christianity. A translator of the Qur'an in the eighteenth century commented that the Prophet "was really the author and chief contriver of the Qur'an is beyond dispute."[26] This unsubstantiated assumption was upheld by a number of other Orientalists except that different reasons were attributed to it. Some considered that it was "nothing else but a pure creation and concoction" and that it was the "fire of his genius" and a "reflection of his energy."[27]

Other Orientalists, like J.W. Stobard, considered that the Prophet possessed some "poetic fire and fancy." Stobart reinforced the views of Robert Bell and of Maxime Rodinson, who considered the Qur'an as a poem of the Prophet's unconscious mind.[28] Some Orientalists were not convinced by such reasons and assumed that the Qur'an was the "result of wishful thinking" which was expressed by his subconscious mind.[29] On the other hand, others, like Montgomery Watt, were more subtle and considered that Muhammad may have been mistaken, for "what seems to a man to come from outside himself may actually come from his unconsciousness" and as such the Qur'an was "the product of creative imagination."[30]

But the Qur'an still remained a puzzle for many Orientalists who considered that no creative imagination could put together such a work. Many Orientalists remained convinced that it was composed with the help of Jewish and Christian sources. The Prophet, it was contended, was a widely travelled man from his youthful days when he used to go on trips with his uncle. In these travels he is considered to have met some Christian monks. Some considered that he met some bishops and monks in Mecca while others consider that he met a Christian convert to Islam.[31] They argued that he must have learned about Judaism from some unnamed teacher because the "long rambling accounts of Jewish patriarchs and prophets (in the Qur'an) corresponded in so much detail with the Talmud that of their essentially Jewish origin there can be no doubt."[32] Some even considered that the Qur'an had been put together by Jews and Christians "especially employed for this purpose . . . in order to satisfy popular demands."[33] But an even more ludicrous assertion was the belief that the Prophet was possessed of demons and the Qur'an was expressed through him.[34] The important point to note is that the Orientalist was not ready at any cost to believe that the Prophet was the messenger of God and the Qur'an was a revelation. At the same time they acceded that there was a God and that Moses and Jesus were sent by Him.

Studies of Hadith fared no better at the hands of the Orientalists, who considered them to suffer from serious defects. Muslim scholars, however, were aware of those defects and had already established three categories of Hadith: *sahih* which were considered genuine after verification procedures had been applied; *hasan* which were acceptable but considered inferior in authenticity to the former and, lastly, *da'if* which were considered weak and not reliable. The latter were subdivided further into categories according to their continuity or discontinuity of their *isnad* (chain of transmitters).

Orientalists, however, tried to prove that the Hadith literature in general was considered to have been arbitrarily devised, influenced by history and carelessly put together. Studies in this area done by Ignaz Goldziher and Joseph Schacht created a number of doubts regarding their authenticity.[35]

As stated earlier, the objectivity of the Orientalists was deceptive. It started with an *a priori* assumption that the Qur'an was not revealed by God but was the work of a man. But any scientific method must take the claim of the subject of study, for example that the Qur'an is a revelation of God, and then try to prove that it is not. In other cases, the analogy of Christianity in Western civilization was applied to Islam. They argued that if there was reform in Christianity then there should be reform in Islam and, if not, why not? The answer supplied was that, since Islam does not lend itself to change with the times, it is primitive. Such false assumptions are again described through the use of Western terminology of what is 'progressive' or 'reactionary,' what is 'holy war' or who is 'fundamentalist.' All these words have meanings in the Western historical experience and if applied to non-Western civilizations impose meanings not relevant in their context or deliberately distorting, as in the Islamic context.

Through such studies the Orientalists had posited the inferiority of the Muslims and the superiority of the West. Furthermore, Muslim civilizations were considered to be decadent while Western civilization was considered dynamic. In this sense colonization was considered necessary to 'civilize' these people and their institutions. In fact, as

Albert Hourani correctly states, "there was a tendency to view Islamic history in terms of 'rise' and 'decline': Muhammad plants a seed, which grows to its full height under the early Abbasids, in terms both of political power and cultural renaissance; after that, political fragmentation and cultural stagnatiion lead to a long decline from which the Muslim world does not begin to awaken until the nineteenth century, with the impact of Western civilization and the stirrings of national spirit."[36]

With the fading of colonialism in the Middle East, Orientalism started falling from its high pedestal because its utility to the colonial powers lessened. But its influence did not diminish entirely, for after World War II, United States imperialism emerged as the new force in the Middle East and the knowledge of the Orientalists regained importance. A new generation of scholars was created to fulfill this need. Numerous departments in United States universities became authoritative centers of what was labelled as Middle Eastern or Islamic Studies. Apart from the universities, many American foundations (Carnegie, Ford, Rockefeller), Councils (American Council of Learned Studies) and corporations (Rand), etc. provided funds for research. The United States government itself was the largest surveyor of such research as the State Department and Defense Department required such data for policy making. The Middle East Institute was founded in 1947 in Washington and its quarterly publication, *The Middle East Journal* became the main channel for communication for scholars.

In 1951 the Social Science Research Council set up a 'Near and Middle East Committee' which later merged with the Joint Committee of the American Council of Learned Societies and encouraged research in the Middle East. A survey of its work over the past two decades indicated that their purposes in serving United States national interests in the Middle East were not different from the old school of Orientalists who had served colonialism. The survey revealed that in the initial stages it had depended on the Orientalists who saw in it a new opportunity to work for neo-colonial United States interests while at the same time it recruited new scholars who also envisaged a new role for their discipline which related to the power of the United States to maintain its political and economic hegemony in the region.

As these political and economic interests increased, the powerful Middle East Studies Association was founded in 1966 and built a network of scholars in Middle Eastern Studies. Its statement of purpose in 1967 stated that the Middle East Studies Association was organized to "promote high standards of scholarship and instruction in the area, to facilitate communication among scholars through meetings and publications and to foster cooperation among persons and organizations concerned with the scholarly study of the Middle East."[37]

Such linkages were not only created within the United States but extended abroad in association with the American University of Beirut, the American University of Cairo, the American Research Center in Egypt, and American Research Institute in Turkey and the American Institute of Iranian Studies in Iran before the Islamic Republic was established.

In these new developments, the Orientalists were not left behind but quickly adjusted themselves to the new area studies programs. Orientalists like Bernard Lewis joined Princeton University while H.A.R. Gibb went to Harvard. The latter soon promoted area studies by pointing out its four functions of providing knowledge to undergraduates, training graduate students with a scholarly understanding of complex cultural factors, the necessity of taking a multicultural approach and coordinating various disciplines within a given area to stimulate interest in these areas of study. This was necessary because "in the increasingly close interrelations of the modern world and the insistent need for Western man to live with and to communicate with men of non-western societies and traditions, it has become necessary to enlist the cooperation of the social scientist in the task of interpreting the structure and motivations of contemporary Asian and African societies. It is a well established maxim that economics is much too serious a matter to be left to the economists, and we too have to admit, with whatever misgivings, that the Orient is much too important to be left to the Orientalists."[38]

People like Gibb and his generation may have faded but were farsighted enough to lay the foundations of contemporary Middle East Studies. Social and political scientists have drawn from their work and the misconceptions and misperceptions are evident in their studies of Islam and the Middle East. These studies, despite claims to be objective, still project Western centered approaches which distort reality as it is in the context and fail to perceive the point of view of the subjects of the study. The result is that such studies have covered the political and economic realities of the subjects under study with Western ideologies.

In fact, "Modern day orientalists who write about Islam have shed the overt hostility of the 19th century missionary scholar who viewed Islam as a heathen religion, unworthy of respect. Tolerance and intercultural understanding have been actively cultivated in Islamic studies in keeping with the accommodation and avoidance of conflict that characterized U.S. actions in its first ventures in the Middle East, but beneath the facade of understanding, most orientialists basically view Islam as an under-developed religion, just as the Middle East is an underdeveloped area."[39] The ideology of the Orientalists has not changed and still persists and functions in the same manner but under new labels.

Such flaws were evident in studies done on Iran. None could detect the revolutionary potential of Islam. When the Islamic forces erupted in 1978 and established the Islamic Republic in 1979, the whole field of Islamic studies received a rude shock. Particularly the United States was taken by surprise as it suffered heavy political and economic losses. The revolution stimulated much rethinking about what has been labelled as "resurgent" or "fundamentalist" Islam, but hardly any new ground has been broken in terms of the real nature of Islam. Western scholars are still groping to understand the complex facets of Islam and its political potential. But they are aware that Islam is a force to be reckoned with and can impede the extension of Western imperial interests in the Muslim countries.

NOTES

1. Philip H. Newby, *Saladin in His Time* (London: Faber and Faber, 1983), p. 212.

2. Norman Daniel, *Islam and the West: The Making of an Image* (Edinburgh: University of Edinburgh, 1960); also see, R. W. Southern, *Western Views of Islam in the Middle Ages* (Cambridge: Harvard University Press, 1962).

3. C.E. Bosworth, "Orientalism and Orientalists," in D. Grimwood, *Arab Islamic Bibliography* (Sussex: Harvester Press, 1977), p. 148.

4. Norman Daniel, *Islam, Europe and Empire* (Edinburgh: University of Edinburgh Press, 1966).

5. A.J. Arberry, *British Orientalists* (London: William Collins, 1933), p. 16.

6. Quoted in A.J. Arberry, *The Cambridge School of Arabic* (Cambridge: Cambridge University Press, 1948), p. 8.

7. Duncan B. Macdonald, *Aspect of Islam* (New York: 1911), pp. 12-13.

8. *Ibid.*, p. 13. For a comprehensive exposition of Macdonald's views see Gordon Pruett's chapter in this book.

9. Montgomery Watt, *Muhammad at Medina* (Oxford: Clarendon Press, 1956), p. 199.

10. *Ibid.*, p. 219.

11. Muhammad Benaboud, "Orientalism and the Arab Elite," *The Islamic Quarterly*, XXVI:1 (1982), p. 7.

12. Bosworth, "Orientalism and Orientalists," p. 150.

13. Edward W. Said, *Orientalism* (New York: Vintage Books, 1978), p. 86.

14. Stuart Schaar, "Orientalism at the Service of Imperialism," *Race and Class*, XXI:1 (1979), p. 68.

15. *Ibid.*, p. 69.

16. Said, *Orientalism*, p. 12.

17. Benaboud, "Orientalism and the Arab Elite," p. 6.

18. *Ibid.*, p. 9.

19. K. Gough, "Anthropology: Child of Imperialism," *Monthly Review* (April 1968).

20. S. Feuchtwang, "The Colonial Formation of British Social Anthropology," in Talal Asad, ed., *Anthropology and the Colonial Encounter* (London: Ithaca Press, 1975), p. 93.

21. Talal Asad, "Introduction," in Talal Adad, ed., *Anthropology and the Colonial Encounter*, p. 17.

22. Hamid Algar, "The Problem of Orientalists," *Islamic Literature*, XVII:2 (1971), p. 35.

23. Said, *Orientalism*, p. 256.

24. Talal Asad, "Two European Images of Non-European Rule," in Talal Asad, ed., *Anthropology and the Colonial Encounter*, p. 117.

25. M. Siddigi, "The Holy Prophet and the Orientalists," *Islamic Studies*, XIX:3 (1980), pp. 143-165.

26. George Sale, *The Koran* (London: Frederick Warne, 1899).

27. F.J.L. Menezes, *The Life and Religion of Mohammed, the Prophet of Arabia Sands* (London: 1911); G. N. Draycott, *Mohemet: Founder of Islam* (London: Martin Secker, 1916).

28. J.W. Stobard, *Islam and its Founder* (London: SPCK, 1876), p. 108; Robert Bell, *The Origin of Islam in its Christian Environment* (London: Macmillan, 1926); Maxime Rodinson, *Mohammad* (Hammondsworth: Penguin Books, 1977.

29. J.N. Anderson, ed., *The World Religions* (London: Frank Cass, 1965), p. 56.

30. Montgomery Watt, *Muhammad: Prophet and Statesman* (Oxford: Oxford University Press, 1961), p. 15.

31. Muhammad Khalifa, *The Sublime Quran and Orientalism* (London: Longman Group Ltd., 1982), p. 14.

32. Anderson, *The World Religions*, p. 57.

33. Khalifa, *The Sublime Quran*, p. 10.

34. *Ibid.*, p. 12.

35. M.M. Azmi, *Studies in Early Hadith Literature* (Indianapolis, Indiana: American Trust Publications, 1978).

36. Albert Hourani, *Europe and the Middle East* (London: The Macmillan Press, 1980), p. 18-22.

37. Lynne Barbec *et al*, "Middle East Studies Network," *MERIP Reports*, 38 (1975), p. 11.

38. *Ibid.*, pp. 6-7.

39. *Ibid.*, p. 19.

2

ORIENTALISM AND THE PROBLEM OF CIVIL SOCIETY IN ISLAM

Bryan S. Turner

While the problems of understanding, comparison and translation are critical issues in philosophy, language and social conscience, they arise in a particularly acute fashion in sociology. In addition to the technical difficulties of bias, distortion and misrepresentation in the methodology of the social sciences, there are the more profound questions of relativism, ethnocentrism and ideology which call into question the whole basis of comparative analysis. It is difficult to imagine what would count as valid sociology without the comparative method and yet there are numerous methodological and philosophical difficulties which often appear to invalidate comparative sociology. There is major disagreement over the issue of whether, following the position adopted by Max Weber, a 'value-free sociology' is either possible or desirable.[1]

In more recent years, social scientists have become increasingly sensitive to the fact that, in addition to these technical and philosophical issues, the structure of power politics is profoundly influential in shaping the content and direction of social science research. In short, the existence of exploitative colonial relationships between societies has been of major significance for the theoretical development of anthropology and sociology. The role of imperial politics has been especially decisive in the constitution of Western images of Islam and the analysis of 'oriental societies'.[2]

In the conventional, liberal perspective, there is the assumption not only that power and knowledge are antithetical, but that valid knowledge requires the suppression of power. Within the liberal history of ideas, the emergence of science out of ideology and common sense beliefs is thus conjoined with the growth of individual freedom and with the decline of arbitrary political terror. This view of the contradiction of reason and power has been recently challenged by the French philosopher Michel Foucault, who argues that the growth of bureaucratic control over populations after the eighteenth century required more systematic forms of knowledge in the form of criminology, penology, psychiatry and medicine. The exercise of power in society thus presupposes new forms of scientific discourse through which deviant groups are defined and controlled. Against the liberal tradition, we are, through an analysis of the Western rationalist tradition, forced to admit

> that power and knowledge directly imply one another; that there is no power relation without the correlative constitution of a field of knowledge, not any knowledge that does not presuppose and constitute at the same time power relations.[3]

The growth of scientific discourse does not, therefore, inaugurate a period of individual freedoms, but rather forms the basis of more extensive forms of institutionalized power through an alliance of the prison and penology, the asylum and psychiatry, the hospital and clinical medicine, the school and pedagogy. Discourse creates difference through classification, tabulation and comparison. The categories of 'criminal', 'insane', and 'deviant' are the manifestations of a scientific discourse by which the normal and sane exercise power along a systematic dividing of sameness and difference. The exercise of power over subordinates cannot consequently be reduced simply to a question of attitudes and motives on the part of individuals, since power is embedded in the very language by which we describe and understand the world. Valid comparisons between deviants and normal individuals, between the sane and insane, between the sick and healthy cannot be achieved by simply reforming attitudes and motives, since these distinctions themselves presuppose a discourse in which conceptual differences are expressions of power relations.

The analysis of knowledge/power in the work of Michel Foucault provides the basis for Edward Said's massive study of Orientalism as a discourse of difference in which the apparently neutral Occident/Orient contrast is an expression of power relationships.[4] Orientalism is a discourse which represents the exotic, erotic, strange Orient as a comprehensible, intelligible phenomenon within a network of categories, tables and concepts by which the Orient is simultaneously defined and controlled. To know is to subordinate.

The Orientalist discourse was thus a remarkably persistent framework of analysis which, expressed through theology, literature, philology and sociology, not only expressed an imperial relationship but actually constituted a field of political power. Orientalism created a typology of characters, organized around the contrast between the rational Westerner and the lazy Oriental. The task of Orientalism was to reduce the endless complexity of the East into a definite order of types, characters and constitutions. The chrestomathy, representing the exotic Orient in a systematic table of accessible information, was thus a typical cultural product of Occidental dominance.

In Said's analysis of Orientalism, the crucial 'fact' about the Orientalist discourse was that we know and talk about Orientals, while they neither comprehend themselves nor talk about us. In this language of difference, there were no equivalent discourses of Occidentalism. The society from which comparisons are to be made has a privileged possession of a set of essential features — rationality, progress, democratic institutions, economic development — in terms of which other societies are deficient. These features account for the particular character of Western society and explain the defects of alternative social formations. As an accounting system, Orientalism set out to explain the progressive features of the Occident and the social stationariness of the Orient.[5] One of the formative questions of classical sociology — why did industrial capitalism first emerge in the West? — is consequently an essential feature of an accounting system which hinges upon a basic East/West contrast. Within the broad sweep of this Occidental/Oriental contrast, Islam has always represented a political and cultural problem for Western accounting systems.

Unlike Hinduism or Confucianism, Islam has major religious and historical ties with Judaism and Christianity; categorizing Islam as an 'Oriental religion' raises major difficulties for an Orientalist discourse. While the issue of prophetic uniqueness is a contentious one, there are strong arguments to suggest that Islam can, along with Judaism and Christianity, be regarded as a variant of the Abrahamic faith.[6]

Furthermore, Islam has been a major cultural force inside Europe and provided the dominant culture of many Mediterranean societies. While Islam is not ambiguously Oriental, Christianity is not in any simple fashion an Occidental religion. Christianity as a Semitic, Abrahamic faith by origin could be regarded as an 'Oriental religion' and Islam, as an essential dimension of the culture of Spain, Sicily and Eastern Europe, could be counted as Occidental. The problem of defining Islam has always possessed a certain urgency for the discourse of Orientalism; thus in Christian circles it was necessary to categorize Islam as either parasitic upon Christian culture or a sectarian offshoot of the Christian faith.

The point of Foucault's analysis of discourse is to suggest that the same rules governing the distribution of statements within a discourse may be common to a wide variety of apparently separate disciplines.[7]

Thus, the Orientalist problematic is not peculiar to Christian theology, but is a discourse which underlines economics, politics and sociology. If the basic issue behind Christian theology was the uniqueness of the Christian revelation with respect to Islam, the central question behind comparative sociology was the uniqueness of the West in relation to the alleged stagnation of the East. In an earlier publication I have suggested that sociology attempted to account for the apparent absence of capitalism in Islamic societies by conceptualizing Islam as a series of gaps.[8] Western sociology characteristically argued that Islamic society lacked those autonomous institutions of bourgeois society which ultimately broke the tenacious hold of feudalism over the Occident. According to this view, Islamic society lacked independent cities, an autonomous bourgeois class, rational bureaucracy, legal reliability, personal property and that cluster of rights which embody bourgeois culture. Without these institutional and cultural elements, there was nothing in Islamic civilization to challenge the dead hand of pre-capitalist tradition. The Orientalist view of Asiatic society can be encapsulated in the notion that the social structure of the Oriental world was characterized by the absence of a civil society, that is, by the absence of a network of institutions mediating between the individual and the state. It was this social absence which created the conditions for Oriental Despotism in which the individual was permanently exposed to the arbitrary rule of the despot. The absence of civil society simultaneously explained the failure of capitalist development outside Europe and the absence of democracy.

The Concept of Civil Society

There is in Western political philosophy a set of basic categories, which can be traced back to Aristotle, for distinguishing between government in terms of monarchy, democracy or despotism. While it is possible to approach these categories numerically, that is, by the one, few or many, one central element to the problem of government is the relationship between the state and the individual. Typically, for example, the notion of 'despotism' involves a spatial metaphor of the social system in which there is an institutional gap between the private indi-

individual and the public state. In despotism, the individual is fully exposed to the gaze of the despotic ruler because there are no intervening social institutions lying between the ruler and the ruled. The individual is completely displayed before the passion, caprice and will of the despot and there are, as it were, no social groups or institutions behind which the ruled may hide. The distance between the despot and the subject may be considerable, but that social space is not filled up with a rich growth of social groupings which could encapsulate the individual and within which separate interests could develop in opposition to the unified will of the despot. By way of a preliminary definition, we may argue that despotism presupposes a society in which 'civil society' is either absent or underdeveloped. A 'civil society' is that prolific network of institutions — church, family, tribe, guild, association and community — which lies between the state and the individual and which simultaneously connects the individual to authority and protects the individual from total political control. The notion of 'civil society' is not only fundamental to the definition of political life in European societies, but also a point of contrast between Occident and Orient.

In the Scottish Enlightenment tradition, the emergence of civil society was regarded as a major indication of social progress from the state of nature to civilization. The theory of civil society was part of the master dichotomy of nature/civilization, since it was within civil society that the individual was eventually clothed in juridical rights of property, possessions and security. In Hegel's social philosophy, civil society mediates between the family and the state; it is constituted by the economic intercourse between individuals. The Hegelian conceptualization of 'civil society' in terms of economic relationships was the germ of much confusion in subsequent Marxist analysis in that it became difficult to locate civil society unambiguously in metaphor of economic base and superstructures. For Marx,

> Civil Society embraces the whole material intercourse of individuals within a definite stage of the development of productive forces. It embraces the whole commercial and industrial life of a given stage and, in so far, transcends the State and nation, though, on the other hand again, it must assert itself in its foreign relations as nationality and inwardly must organise itself as a State.[9]

Since Marx was primarily interested in the theoretical analysis of the capitalist mode of production, it has subsequently been difficult for Marxists to determine the precise relationship between civil society/ state, on the one hand, and to analyze such sociological concepts as 'family', 'church', 'community', or 'tribe', on the other. One solution, of course, is to treat this area of social life as explicable in purely economic terms; the primary divisions within society are those between classes, which in turn are explained by the mode of production.[10]

The difficulties of locating civil society in relation to the economy and the state are exemplified by some recent debates over Antonio Gramsci's analysis of the concept.[11]

In a famous passage, Gramsci commented that,

> Between the economic structure and the state with its legislation and its coercion stands civil society.[12]

In Gramsci's writing, civil society is the area within which ideological hegemony and political consent are engineered, and it therefore con- trasts with the state, which is the site of political force and coercion. Such a conception complicates the more conventional Marxist dichot- omy of base/superstructure, but there is much dissensus over exactly where Gramsci places his theoretical emphasis.[13] While there is much disagreement over the extent of hegemonic consent in modern capital- ism, it is interesting to note that Gramsci's conceptualization of 'civil society' was important for his view that political strategies were rele- vant in relation to the extent of coercion and consent in society.[14] Gramsci made a basic distinction between the West, in which there is widespread consensus based on civil society, and the East, where the state dominates society and where coercion is more important than consensus. Speaking specifically of Russia, Gramsci argued that

> the state was everything, civil society was primordial and gelatinous; in the West, there was a proper relation between state and civil society, and when the state trembled a sturdy structure of civil society was at once revealed. The state was only an outer ditch, behind which there stood a powerful system of fortresses and earthworks . . .[15]

Where civil society is relatively underdeveloped in relationship to the state, political coercion of individuals is the basis of class rule rather than ideological consent which characterizes the bourgeois institutions of Western capitalism.

Liberal political theory, while clearly fundamentally different in outlook and conclusions, has often approached the East/West, coercion/consent contrasts in somewhat similar terms, especially in terms of the notion of constitutional checks and balances. In *The Spirit of the Laws* written in 1748, Montesquieu distinguished between republics, monarchies and despotisms in terms of their guiding principles which were respectively virtue, honor and fear.[16] The main differences between monarchy and despotism were that (1) while monarchy is based on the inequality of social strata, in despotism there is an equality of slavery where the mass of the population is subject to the ruler's arbitrary will; (2) in monarchy, the ruler follows customs and laws, whereas a despot dominates according to his own inclination (3) in despotism there are no intermediary social institutions linking the individual to the state. In an earlier work, *Considerations on the Causes of the Greatness of the Romans and Their Decline,* Montesquieu had been particularly concerned with the problems of centralization in the Roman empire and with the transformation of republics into monarchies.[17] Montesquieu, who was profoundly influenced by Locke and British constitutional history, came to see the divisions of powers and constitutional checks on centralized authority as the principal guarantee of political rights. His *Persian Letters*[18] permitted him to write a critical review of French society through the eyes of Oriental observers; it has subsequently not been clear whether Montesquieu's definition of and objections to the despotism of the East were, in fact, directed against the French polity, especially against the absolute monarchy.[19]

Emile Durkheim, whose Latin dissertation on Montesquieu and Rousseau was published in 1892, came to see the problem of modern political life not in the effects of the division of labor on common sentiments but in the absence of regulating institutions between the individual and the state. The decline of the church, the weakness of the family, the loss of communal ties and the underdevelopment of occupational and professional associations had dissolved those important social relations which shielded the individual from the state. Unlike Herbert Spencer, however, Durkheim did not believe that the extension of state functions in contemporary society necessarily resulted in political absolutism. Durkheim, in 'Two laws of penal evolution', defined absolutism in the following terms:

what makes the central power more or less absolute is the more or less radical absence of any countervailing forces, regularly organized with a view toward moderating it. We can, therefore, forsee that what gives birth to a power of this sort is the more or less complete concentration of all society's controlling functions in one and the same hand.[20]

While Durkheim does not specifically employ the term, in the light of his reference to the importance of 'countervailing forces', it is not illegitimate or inappropriate to suggest that Durkheim's argument is that the weakness of civil society lying between the individual and the state is a condition for political absolutism.

This French tradition in the political sociology of absolutism from Montesquieu to Durkheim cannot be properly understood without some consideration of the debate which arose in France over the nature of enlightened government. What we now refer to as 'enlightened despotism' or 'enlightened absolutism' first arose as an intellectual and political issue in France in the 1760's partly as the result of the doctrines of the Physiocrats.[21] The terms favored by the Physiocrats were 'Despotisme eclaire' and 'Despotisme legal,' so, for example, T. G. Raynal provided a definition of good government as *'Le gouvernement le plus heureux serait celui d'un despote juste et eclaire'* in his history of trade with the West and East Indies. In their economic doctrines, the Physiocrats adhered to *laissez-faire* policies to free the economy and the individual from the unnatural fetters which constrained efficiency and economic output. However, society was not free from such artificial constraints and it was necessary for radical changes to be brought about by 'Despotisme eclaire.' The Physiocrats took for granted that such a despotism would be in the hands of an hereditary monarchy which would rationally sweep aside the artificial clutter of the past to restore the natural order of individual freedom. The despot had the duty to force people to be free by a rational policy of education and social reform.

The debate about the virtues of forms of government was generated not only by absolutism in the late eighteenth century but also by the rise of colonialism in the nineteenth. Colonial administrators were forced to decide upon schemes of imperial control for the new dependencies. Raynal's use of the notion of legal despotism is interesting in the context of a discussion of colonies. Utilitarian discussions of political organization in Britain were similarly set in the context of criticisms of British government by an hereditary aristocracy and in terms of colonial administration in India. The utilitarians were concerned both with the problem of the working class and parliamentarian government in Britain and with the government of Indian natives.[22] Thus, James Mill's *The History of British India* was particularly concerned with the question of native despotism and government reform. He observed that,

> Among the Hindus, according to the Asiatic model, the government was monarchical, and, with the usual exception of religion and its ministers, absolute. No idea of any system of rule, different from the will of a single person, appears to have entered the minds of them, or their legislators.[23]

For Mill, there was a social hiatus between the traditional, all-embracing life of the Indian village and the outer, public world of kingdoms. The constant break-up of the latter contrasted with the social isolation and stagnation of the former. The principal political solution to this static despotism was a dose of 'Despotisme eclaire,' that is, strong central government, benevolent laws, modernized administration and a redistribution of land rights. In many respects, John Stuart Mill followed his father's line of argument both about political reform in Britain and colonial government. J.S. Mill's basic fear was focused on the effects of majority rule in popular democracies on the life and conscience of the educated and sensitive individual. This fear had been greatly confirmed by the more pessimistic aspects of Alexis de Tocqueville's analysis of American political institutions in *Democracy in America*, which Mill read in 1835.[24] According to de Tocqueville, majority rule on the basis of universal franchise could result in a sterile consensus which was inimicable to individuality and individual rights. The only check to the despotism of the majority would be the existence of strong voluntary associations (that is, civil society) protecting the individual from majority control and protecting diversity of interests and culture. Without safeguards, democracy would produce in Britain the same sterility which tradition had brought about in Asia, namely social stagnation. Mill's fears were consequently:

> not of great liberty, but too ready submission; not of anarchy, but of servility; not of too rapid change, but of Chinese stationariness.[25]

In the case of colonial rule, however, the choice was between two types of despotism, native or imperial. Native despotism was always arbitrary and ineffectual, while the enlightened despotism of 'more civilized people' over their dominions was firm, regular and effective in promoting social reform and political advancement.

   John Stuart Mill (1806-1873) and Karl Marx (1818-1883) were contemporaries. In formulating their views on Asiatic society, they were influenced by similar contemporary events and by a similar range of documentary evidence. It is not entirely surprising, therefore, to find that they also shared some common assumptions about Asiatic society, despite very different evaluations and expectations of British rule in India. While Marx's concept of the Asiatic mode of production was primarily formulated in terms of economic structures and processes (or the absence of them), the Asiatic mode is also a version of the conventional political notion of 'Oriental despotism.' In Marx's journalistic writing, Oriental society was characterized by ceaseless political changes in ruling dynasties and by total economic immobility. Dynastic circulation brought about no structural change because the ownership of the land remained in the hands of the overlord. Like James Mill, Marx also emphasized the stationary nature of village life, based on self-sufficiency. No civil society existed between the individual and the despot, between the village and the state, because autonomous cities and social classes were absent from the social system.

   While Weber acknowledged a debt to Marx's analysis of Indian village life in his *The Religion of India*,[26] Weber's various elaborations of political forms — patriarchalism, patrimonialism — concentrate more on the problem of military organization than on the economic bases of political life. In fact, it is possible to see Weber's sociology as the analysis of the interconnections between the ownership of the means of production and the ownership of the means of violence. He thus established an abstract continuum between a situation where independent knights own their own weapons and provide military services for a lord, and another context in which the means of violence are centralized under the control of a patrimonial lord. Empirically, Weber recognized that these 'pure types' rarely occurred in such simplified forms, but the contrast was important in Weber's analysis of the tensions between centralizing and de-centralizing processes in political empires.

   In feudalism, where knights have hereditary rights to lands and provide their own weapons, there are strong political pressures towards localism and the emergence of autonomous petty-kingdoms. The crucial political struggles in feudalism are thus *within* the dominant class, not between lords and serfs, because the crucial question is the preservation of the feudal king's political control over other landlords who seek extensive feudal immunities from their lord. In patrimonialism, one method of controlling aristocratic cavalries based on feudal or pre-bendal rights to land is to recruit slave or mercenary armies. Such armies have little or no attachment to civil society — they are typically foreigners, bachelors or eunuchs and detribalized. Hence, slave armies have no local interests in civil society and are, formally at least, totally dependent on the patrimonial lord. As Weber points out, patrimonialism can only survive if the patrimonial lord enjoys a stable fiscal liquidity or access to other resources by which to pay off his armies. Patrimonial empires suffer from two perennial crises: (1) revolts by slave armies and (2) instability of political succession. While Weber does not use the feudal/prebendal distinction as a necessary criterion for distinguishing the West from the East, he does regard patrimonial instability — or 'sultanism' — as a major problem of Oriental society, especially of Turkey.

The debate about Oriental empires in European social thought found its classic expression in the twentieth century in Karl Wittfogel's *Oriental Despotism*.[27] Characteristically subtitled 'a comparative study of total power,' Wittfogel presented an essentially technological account of Oriental empires. The climatic aridity of Oriental regions gave rise to the need for extensive hydraulic systems which, in turn, could be organized only on the basis of centralized political power. The difficulties of hydraulic management could be solved only on the basis of bureaucratization, general slavery and centralized authority. The hydraulic state was forced to obliterate all countervailing social groups within society which could threaten its total power. These 'nongovernmental forces' included kin groups, independent religious organizations, autonomous military groups and owners of alternative forms of property.[28] Oriental despotism thus represented the triumph of the state over society and Wittfogel saw the absence of 'civil society' in hydraulic empires as a necessary basis for total power. In Europe, absolutism was always faced by countervailing forces in civil society:

> the absence of formal constitutional checks does not necessarily imply the absence of societal forces whose interests and intentions the government must respect. In most countries of post-feudal Europe the absolutist regimes were restricted not so much by official constitutions as by the

actual strength of the landed nobility, the Church and the towns. In absolutist Europe all these nongovernmental forces were politically organized and articulated. They thus differed profoundly from the representatives of landed property, religion or urban professions in hydraulic society.[29]

To summarize, the political problem of Oriental society is the absence of a civil society which will counterbalance the power of the state over the isolated individual.

Although the notion of the absence of civil society in Oriental Despotism was formulated by reference to Asia as a whole, it has played a particularly prominent role in the analysis of Islamic societies; it is an essential feature of the Orientalist discourse. Furthermore, the theme of the missing civil society cut across political and intellectual divisions in the West, providing a common framework for Marxists and sociologists. Marx and Engels in their articles for the *New York Daily Tribune* observed that the absence of private property in land and the centralization of state power precluded the emergence of a strong bourgeois class. The dominance of the bureaucracy and the instability of urban society meant that

> the first basic condition of bourgeois acquisition is lacking, the security of the person and the property of the trader.[30]

A similar position was adopted by Max Weber in *The Sociology of Religion* where he suggested that the effect of Islamic expansion had been to convert Islam into a "national Arabic warrior religion;" the result was that the dominant ethos of Islam

> is inherently contemptuous of bourgeois–commercial utilitarianism and considers it as sordid greediness and as the life force specifically hostile to it.[31]

In Western sociological accounts of Islamic societies, it has been argued that, because of the absence of a 'spirit of capitalism' in the middle class, trade in most Islamic societies was dominated historically by minorities (Greeks, Jews, Armenians and Slavs.) Recent sociological studies of Islam have continued this tradition by suggesting that the absence of the entrepreneural spirit and achievement motivation is linked to the underdeveloped nature of the middle class in Islam.[32]

The absence of a civil society in Islam and the weakness of bourgeois culture in relation to the state apparatus have been associated, in the

Orientalist problematic, not only with the backwardness of economic development, but also with political despotism. There is a common viewpoint among political scientists that there is no established tradition of legitimate opposition to arbitrary governments in Islam because the notions of political rights and social contract had no institutional support in an independent middle class.[33] However, the Orientalist theme of the absence of a civil society extends well beyond the area of economics and politics. The scientific and artistic culture of Islam is treated as the monopoly of the imperial court which, within the 'city camp,' patronized the emergency of a rational culture in opposition to the religion of the masses. The union of science and industry which was characteristic of the English Protestant middle classes in the nineteenth century was noticeably absent in Islamic culture. Thus, Ernest Renan, in a forthright commentary on Islam and science, suggested that, "the Mussulman has the most profound disdain for instruction, for science, for everything that constitutes the European spirit."[34]

For Renan, science could only flourish in Islam in association with heresy. While Renan's highly prejudicial attitudes are rarely articulated in an overt fashion in contemporary Oriental scholarship, the same arguments concerning elitist patronage of arts and sciences in the absence of a middle class are constantly repeated. This perspective is normally conjoined with the notion that science in Islam was merely parasitic on Greek culture and that Islam was simply a vehicle transmitting Greek philosophy to the Renaissance in Europe.[35] The deficiences of Islamic society, politics, economics and culture are, in Orientalism, located in the problem of an absent civil society.

Alternatives to Orientalism

In the period following the second World War, Orientalism has shown many symptoms of internal crisis and collapse,[36] but the alternatives to Orientalism have been difficult to secure, since Orientalism retains substantial intellectual and institutional supports. Orientalism is a self-validating and closed discourse which is highly resistant to internal and external criticism. Various attempts at reconstruction have been presented in, for example, *Review of Middle East Studies* and by the *Middle East Research and Information Project* (MERIP). One problem in the transformation of existing paradigms is that Marxist alternatives have themselves found it difficult to break with the Orientalist perspective which was present in the analyses of Marx and Engels.[37]

Although there have been major changes in Marxist conceptualization of such basic notions as 'the mode of production,' much of the theoretical apparatus of contemporary Marxism is irrelevant in the analysis of Islamic societies. Those Marxists who have adopted the epistemological position of writers like Louis Althusser are, in any case, committed to the view that empirical studies of the Orient will not be sufficient to dislodge the Orientalist perspective without a radical shift in epistemology and theoretical frameworks. An entirely new paradigm is required, but in the present theoretical climate there is little to suggest the presence of radical alternatives. While Edward Said has presented a major critique of the Oriental discourse, the conceptual basis on which that critique is founded, namely the work of Michel Foucault, does not lend itself unambiguously to the task of reformulating perspectives. A pessimistic reading of Foucault would suggest that the alternative to an Oriental discourse would simply be another discourse which would incorporate yet another expression of power. In Foucault's analysis there is no discourse-free alternative since extensions of knowledge coincide with a field of power. We are thus constrained to

> the patient construction of discourses about discourses, and to the task of hearing what has already been said.[38]

At one level, therefore, Said is forced to offer the hope that "spiritual detachment and generosity"[39] which will be sufficient to generate a new vision of the Middle East which has jettisoned the ideological premises of Orientalism.

There may, however, exist one line of development which would be compatible with Said's employment of Foucault's perspective on discourse and which would present a route out of Orientalism. By its very nature, language is organized around the basic dichotomy of sameness and difference; the principal feature of the Orientalist discourse has been to emphasize difference in order to account for the 'uniqueness of the West.' In the case of Islam and Christianity, however, there is a strong warrant to focus on those features which unite rather than divide them, or at least to examine those ambiguous areas of cultural overlap between them. Historically, both religions emerged, however antagonistically, out of a common Semitic-Abrahamic religious stock. They have been involved in mutual processes of diffusion, exchange and colonization.

In this sense, as I have already suggested, it is permissible to refer to Islam as an Occidental religion in Spain, Malta, Yugoslavia and the Balkans and to Christianity as an Oriental religion of North Africa, the Fertile Crescent and Asia. This obvious point has the merit of exposing the fundamental ambiguity of the notion of 'the Orient' within the Orientalist discourse. In addition to these mutual contacts in history and geography, Islam and Christianity have, for historically contingent reasons, come to share common frameworks in science, philosophy and culture. Despite these areas of mutual contact, the general drift of Orientalism has been to articulate difference, division and separation. One important illustration of these discursive separations can be found in conventional histories of Western philosophy.

Islam and Christianity are both grounded in prophetic revelation and were not initially concerned with the philosophical articulation of orthodox theology. Both religions were confronted by the existence of a highly developed system of secular logic and rhetoric which was the legacy of Greek culture. Aristotelianism became the philosophical framework into which the theologies of Islam and Christianity were poured. Eventually the formulation of Christian beliefs came to depend heavily on the work of Islamic scholars, especially Averroes (Ibn Rushd), Avicenna (Iba Sina), Al-Kinda and Ar-Razi. Here, consequently, is an area of mutual development in which medieval Christianity was parasitic on the philosophical developments which had been achieved in Islam. However, the Orientalist response to this situation has been to claim that Islam simply mediated Hellenism, which subsequently found its 'true home' in the universities of medieval Europe. Thus, we find writers like Bertrand Russell in his *History of Western Philosophy* following the tradition of Renan and O'Leary in simply denying that Islam made any significant contribution to European philosophy.[40] The attraction of connecting Western philosophy with Hellenism is obvious; it provides the link between Western culture and the democratic traditions of Greek society. Greek rhetoric grew out of public debate in the political sphere where systematic forms of argument were at a premium. On this basis, it is possible to contrast the closed world of Oriental Despotism with the open world of Greek democracy and rhetorical speech. One difficulty with this equation of Hellenism and political democracy is that it remains largely silent with respect to the slave economy of classical Greece. The majority of the Greek population was excluded from the world of logic and rhetoric by virtue of their slave status.

The philosophical and scientific legacy of Greek civilization passed to Europe through the prism of Islamic Spain, but here again Orientalism treats the impact of Islam on Spanish society as merely regression or, at best, repetition. In Wittfogel's view, the particular combination of population pressure and climatic conditions created the context within which Muslim colonialists in Spain created the despotic polity of hydraulic society. Under Islam, Spain

> became a genuinely hydraulic society, ruled despotically by appointed officials and taxed by agromanagerial methods of acquisition. The Moorish army, which soon changed from a tribal to a 'mercenary' body, was definitely the tool of the state as were its counterparts in the Umayyad and Abbasid caliphates.[41]

Prior to Islamic influence, Spain had, according to Wittfogel, been a de-centralized feudal society, but, with the introduction of the hydraulic economy, was rapidly transformed into a centralized, despotic state. In other words, within an Occidental setting, Islam still carried the essential features of an Oriental despotic culture. Similarly with the *reconquista,* Spain reverted to a feudal rather than despotic polity. The reestablishment of Christianity 'transformed a great hydraulic civilization into a late feudal society.'[42] Contemporary scholarship on Islamic Spain presents a very different picture, emphasizing the continuity of agricultural and irrigation techniques between Christianity and Islam. A complex and regulated irrigation system requires considerable economic investment over a long period. While the Spanish irrigation system was considerably improved under Muslim management, this was on the basis of a system which was already in operation from classical times. It is the continuity of technology and polity in Spain rather than the difference between Islamic and Christian management which is the important issue.[43]

The conservation of civil society and economy in Spain under Islam and Christianity thus pinpoints the Orientalist fascination with difference, a difference constituted by discourse rather than by history.

Conclusion: The Individual and Civil Society

The concept of 'civil society' forms the basis of Western political economy from the Scottish Enlightenment to the prison notebooks of Gramsci; while the concept has been frequently discussed in contemporary social science, the fact that it has also been a major part of the Orientalist contrast of East and West has been seriously neglected. In simple terms, the concept has been used as the basis of the notion that the Orient is, so to speak, all state and no society. The notion of 'civil society' cannot be divorced from an equally potent theme in Western philosophy, namely the centrality of autonomous individuals within the network of social institutions. Western political philosophy has hinged on the importance of civil society in preserving the freedom of the individual from arbitrary control by the state. The doctrines of individualism have been regarded as constitutive, if not of Western culture as such, then at least of contemporary industrial culture. It is difficult to conceive of the nexus of Western concepts of conscience, liberty, freedom or property without some basic principle of individualism and therefore individualism appears to lie at the foundations of Western society. The additional importance of individualism is that it serves to distinguish Occidental from Oriental culture, since the latter is treated as devoid of individual rights and of individuality. Individualism is the golden thread which weaves together the economic institutions of property, the religious institution of confession of conscience and the moral notion of personal autonomy; it serves to separate 'us' from 'them.' In Orientalism, the absence of civil society in Islam entailed the absence of the autonomous individual exercising conscience and rejecting arbitrary interventions by the state.

Underlying this liberal theory of the individual was, however, a profound anxiety about the problem of social order in the West. The individual conscience represented a threat to political stability, despite attempts to argue that the moral conscience would always conform with the legitimate political authority. In particular, bourgeois individualism — in the theories of Locke and Mill — was challenged by the mob, the mass and the working class which was excluded from citizenship by a franchise based on property. The debate about Oriental Despotism took place in the context of uncertainty about Enlightened Despotism and monarchy in Europe. The Orientalist discourse of the absence of civil society in Islam was thus a reflection of basic political anxieties about the state of political freedom in the West. In this sense, the problem of Orientalism was not the Orient but the Occident. These problems and anxieties were consequently transformed onto the Orient which became, not a representation of the East, but a caricature of the West. Oriental Despotism was simply Western monarchy writ large. The crises and contradictions of contemporary Orientalism are, therefore, to be seen as part of a continuing crisis of Western capitalism transferred to a global context. The end of Orientalism requires a radical reformulation of perspectives and paradigms, but this reconstitution of knowledge can only take place in the context of major shifts in political relations between Orient and Occident; the transformation of discourse also requires a transformation of power.

NOTES

1. Alvin Gouldner, "Anti-Minotaur: the Myth of Value-free Sociology," in *For Sociology,* ed., Alvin Gouldner (London: Harmondsworth, 1973), pp. 1-26.

2. See Norman Daniel, *Islam and the West, the Making of an Image* (Edinburgh: Edinburgh University Press, 1960) and R. W. Southern, *Western Views of Islam in the Middle Ages* (Cambridge: Harvard University Press, 1962).

3. Michel Foucault, *Discipline and Punish, the Birth of the Prison,* trans. from the French by Alan Sheridan (New York: Pantheon Books, 1977).

4. Edward W. Said, *Orientalism* (New York: Vintage Books, 1978).

5. Bryan S. Turner, "The Concept of Social Stationariness: Utilitarianism and Marxism," *Science and Society,* 38 (1974), pp. 3-18.

6. Marshall G.S. Hodgson, *The Venture of Islam* (Chicago: University of Chicago Press, 1974), in three volumes.

7. As discussed in Michel Foucault, *The Archeology of Knowledge* (New York: Pantheon Books, 1972).

8. Bryan S. Turner, *Marx and the End of Orientalism* (London: George Allen & Unwin, 1978).

9. Karl Marx and Frederick Engels, *The Russian Menace in Europe* (London: George Allen & Unwin, 1953), p. 76.

10. Nicholas Poulantzas, *Political Power and Social Classes,* trans. from French and edited by Timothy O'Hagen (London: NLB, Sheed and Ward, 1973).

11. For this discussion see Perry Anderson, *Lineages of the Absolutist State* (London: NLB, 1974): N. Bobbio, "Gramsci and the Conception of Civil Society," in Chantal Mouffe, ed., *Gramsci and Marxist Theory* (London: Routledge & Kegan Paul, 1979) and John Urry, *The Anatomy of Capitalist Societies: The Economy, Civil Society and the State* (London: Macmillan, 1981).

12. Antonio Gramsci, *Selections from the Prison Notebooks,* trans. and edited by Quintin Hoare and Geoffrey Nowell Smith (New York: International Publishers, 1971).

13. Perry Anderson, "The Antinomies of Antonio Gramsci," *New Left Review,* No. 100 (1977), pp. 5-78.

14. Nicholas Abercrombie, Stephen Hill and Bryan Turner, *The Dominant Ideology Thesis* (London: George Allen & Unwin, 1980).

15. Gramsci, *Selections,* p. 238.

16. Charles Montesquieu, *The Spirit of the Laws,* trans. from French by Thomas Nugent (New York: Hafner Pub. Co., 1949).

17. Charles Montesquieu, *Considerations on the Causes of the Greatness of the Romans and their Decline,* trans. from French by David Lowenthal (New York: Free Press, 1965).

18. Charles Montesquieu, *Persian Letters,* trans. from French by John Davidson (London: G. Routledge & Sons, 1923).

19. In this regard see Louis Althusser, *Politics and History: Montesquieu, Hegel and Marx (London: NLB, 1972)* and Anderson, *Lineages.*

20. Emile Durkheim, "Two Laws of Penal Evolution," in M. Trangott, ed., *Emile Durk-*

41

heim on Institutional Analysis (Chicago: University of Chicago Press, 1978), pp. 153-180.

21. Fritz Hartung, *Enlightened Despotism* (London: Routledge & Kegan Paul, 1957).

22. Turner, "The Concept of Social Stationariness," pp. 3-18.

23. James Mill, *The History of British India* (London and New Delhi: Associated Publishing House, 1972), pp. 212-13.

24. Alexis de Tocqueville, *Democracy in America,* ed., Philip Bradley (New York: A.A. Knopf, 1946).

25. John Stuart Mill, *Dissertations and Discussions* (London: John W. Parker and Son, 1859 in two volumes), p. 56.

26. Max Weber, *The Religion of India,* trans. from German and edited by Hans. H. Gerth and Don Martindale (Glencoe, Ill:, Free Press, 1958).

27. Karl Wittfogel, *Oriental Despotism* (New Haven: Yale University Press, 1957).

28. *Ibid.,* p. 49.

29. *Ibid.,* p. 103.

30. Marx and Engels, *The Russian Menace,* p. 40.

31. Max Weber, *Economy and Society: an Outline of Interpretative Sociology,* trans. from German by Ephraim Fischoff, edited by Guenther Roth and Claus Wittich (New York: Badminister Press, 1968).

32. See especially Alfred Bonne, *State and Economics in the Middle East* (London: Routledge & Kegan Paul, 1960); Daniel Lerner, *The Passing of Traditional Society: Modernizing the Middle East* (Glencoe, Ill., Free Press, 1958) and David Clarence McClelland, *The Achieving Society* (Princeton: Van Nostrand, 1961).

33. P.J. Vatikiotis, ed., *Revolution in the Middle East and Other Case Studies* (London and Totowa, New Jersey: Rowman and Littlefield).

34. Ernest Renan, ed., "Islamism and Science," in *Poetry of the Celtic Race, and Other Studies* (London: W. Scott, 1896), p. 85.

35. Lacy de O'Leary, *How Greek Science Passed to the Arabs* (London: Routledge and Kegan Paul, 1949).

36. Abdallah Laroui, *The Crisis of Arab Intellectuals, Traditionalism or Historicism?* (Berkeley University of California Press, 1976).

37. Turner, *Marx and the End of Orientalism.*

38. Michel Foucault, *The Birth of the Clinic,* trans. from French by A.M. Sheridan Smith (New York: Pantheon Books, 1973), p. xvi.

39. Said, *Orientalism,* p. 259.

40. Bertrand Russell, *History of Western Philosophy* (New York: Simon and Schuster, 1945).

41. Wittfogel, *Oriental Despotism,* p. 215.

42. *Ibid.,* p. 216.

43. Thomas F. Glick, *Irrigation and Society in Medieval Valencia* (Cambridge: Harvard University Press, 1970) and N. Smith *Man and Water: A History of Hydro-Technology* (Cambridge: Belknap Press of Harvard University Press, 1970.

3

"ISLAM" AND ORIENTALISM

Gordon E. Pruett

In reviewing the writings of those Orientalists who, as non-Muslim scholars, are committed to interpreting the nature and role of Islam, we can see an impressive divergence on such questions as the sources of Islamic faith and belief, the influence of Hellenic culture, the importance of Sufism, the relationship between religion and culture, and the viability of Islam in the modern age. But from a Muslim perspective a more striking pair of conclusions emerges: that the Orientalists address each other rather than the Muslim community;[1] and that what they say of Islam is offensive and repugnant. In fact, debates among the Orientalists rest upon assumptions which are quite unacceptable to Muslims themselves. Islam is viewed by the Western Orientalists as, variously: a powerful enemy; an exotic and deviant growth of the Near East; a semi-inert, introverted mass; a failed civilization in need of restoration and revision; a mission field; and a fanatical, even suicidal, reaction against the trends of modern time. Some Orientalists are content to speculate on the fate of Islam on the basis of their identification of the driving forces within it; others, some conservative, others liberal, urge reform and revision in accordance with their notion of what the essential Islam may be said to be. None seems to feel that it will simply go away or, less simply, be destroyed. But it constitutes a problem which requires explanation, especially in the context of geopolitical concerns regarding the Third World, oil and petrodollars. Whether the assumptions and motivations of the Orientalist are theological, political, social, or economic, what he says is more or less distasteful to the Muslim, and suggestive of condescension and denigration.

I wish to focus on one highly significant aspect of the Orientalist tradition which I believe explains its attitudes and the intense resistance to it by the people about whom the Orientalist writes. This aspect is that of thinking about Islam as an historical movement and cultural development *only*, rather than as a dynamic effort to do what the very name of the tradition demands, to submit to God. The Orientalist and the Muslim share one assumption, at least — that the history of Muslims is a history of change, success, failure, ignorance, insight, courage, and

cowardice. Seen thus, that history may be from time to time the object
of attempts to understand what went wrong and what went right. Both
groups have accepted this challenge. But there is a great difference
between them: the Muslim assesses his past and present in light of the
will of Allah, Whose Judgment is final; the Orientalist judges by other
standards, none of which is that of the Muslim. Islam for the Orientalist
is a cultural movement of great significance in the history of the human
race. For the Muslim, Islam is the command to submit to Allah in every
aspect of his life. Only Allah can judge. In contrast, the Orientalist has
dismissed this fundamental consideration from his reading of Islam.
That is to say, he fails to see the transcendent truth and good in the
Muslim tradition and thinks of it as a cultural artifact only.

Now it may be thought that this difference is inevitable and that it is
not subject to change; for, it might be argued, the Orientalist is not a
Muslim in the sense that he is not a member of the Ummah, the
community of Islam, and therefore does not accept the Muslim's belief
that the history of the Islamic community is a history of expressions of
faith or of efforts and attempts to submit to the will of Allah. This does
not prevent him from saying that Muslims believe this of their history;
but that is not at all the same thing. *He*, the Orientalist, does not believe
it. He is, in short, an outsider, and thus bound to interpret Islam as an
historical object, to judge it in terms of its success or failure in the
context of cultural and historical forces. He will not reflect upon Islam
as he will upon his own tradition, whether Christian, Jewish, Marxist,
humanitarian, or other. Further, the Orientalist is likely to object to the
notion that he should participate in the Muslim's view of the latter's
history, on the grounds that his scholarly objectivity would be eroded.

I wish to argue (1) that unless the Orientalist accepts the truth of the
assertion that the history of Islam is indeed the history of attempts to
submit to Allah, he will both misunderstand that history and, as a matter
of course, fail to contribute anything worthwhile to the ongoing task of
the Muslim, (2) that the concern for "objectivity" as the Orientalist
defines it is a misguided goal based on the prior reification or objectifica-
tion of Muslim faith — an act which is possible or desirable only for one
who begins with the unquestioned assumption that Muslim history is *not*
a history of attempts to submit to Allah, whatever Muslims may
believe — and (3) that it is indeed possible to adopt a perspective from
which to view Muslim history as Muslims view it, by accepting the

truth of the transcendent orientation of the tradition and not merely the "truth" that Muslims believe this. All observations, research and conclusions that follow from this acceptance will be useful, even "right" in the eyes both of those within the Ummah and those without it. One must, I hold, grant this to the traditions of others just as one accords it to one's own.

Before I attempt to describe the remedy just suggested, I would like to describe the disease in greater detail by examining three of its symptoms. The Orientalists whose works I have drawn from are representative of their movement.[2] In their writings we can see three indicators of their predilection for the treatment of Islam solely as an historical and cultural artifact. These are (1) the issue of the "essence" and "definition" of Islam, (2) the issue of cultural borrowing in the history of Muslims (and the implied issue of "originality" in Islam), and (3) the issue of "reform" in Islam, especially in the modern period.

I. The Definition of Islam

H.A.R. Gibb wrote, in the introduction to his influential *Mohammedanism*, that he did not share the view either of those who saw Islam as a corrupt tradition inferior to other religions and incapable of coping with the modern world, or of those apologists for Islam who sought to repel the attacks of its critics. Rather, he wished to present "Mohammedanism" as an "autonomous expression of religious thought and experience, which must be viewed in and through itself and its own principles and standards." He sought, therefore, to expound the principles and ideals of the tradition rather than to lay emphasis upon its failings, which were those of our "our common humanity."[3]

Gibb's mood, then, is one of objective sympathy rather than critical analysis or enthusiastic defense. His view of Islam as an "autonomous expression of religious thought and experience" suggests, however, that he was not himself engaged. Rather, he sought to describe the essential "Mohammedanism", whether or not it was ultimately true or good.

Gibb's works indicate very clearly the element of Muslim history that he regards as the essential Islam: It is Shari'ah, the theological-legal tradition consisting of the learned interpretation of the Qur'an and the *sunna* of the Prophet. It is, he concludes, no exaggeration to say of Shari'ah that it is the "epitome of the true Islamic spirit, the most decisive expression of Islamic thought, the essential kernel of Islam".[4] Islam stands or falls "with the supremacy of the Sacred Law." The Ulama, the learned interpreters and defenders of that law, must be ever vigilant in their task if Islam is to survive.[5] Shari'ah is the sustained expression in history of that experiment in pure monotheism which Muhammad revived from post-Abrahamic corruption and distortion. As such it fulfills the "whole function of Islam," namely "to raise both Arabian and non-Arabian religious conceptions and ethical standards to the levels set by the preaching of the earlier prophets."[6]

However, in thus identifying the Shari'ah and the Ulama as the central institutions of Islam, Gibb is not affirming the transcendent significance of either. Certainly, it could not be said that he really agrees in any fundamental, personal way with either. Rather, he has exercised historical judgment on the question of which element of Muslim history seems most important; but he does not espouse a truly Muslim view, that is, he does not take seriously the possibility that Shari'ah is a continuing effort to obey Allah. He does not hold that it is true. Consider, for example, his treatment of theology in Islam. Islamic thought, he notes, shows none of the nineteenth-century European theological developments. It remains stranded in an absolutist and otherworldly tradition, similar to that of the European eighteenth-century theologians. It would, he says, be impossible to find any Muslim Arab writer who could appreciate such concepts as divine immanence, historical criticism of the Scriptures, or the notion of historical progress.[7]

In fact, he argues, creative theology is clearly the exception to the rule in Muslim history, for the "Arab mind" (an influential tool in Gibb's perception of Islam) is seemingly incapable of the sustained and integrated thought necessary for such theology. Rather, Arab Muslim speculation is atomistic and, frankly, incoherent. Thus, any reliance upon rational theology for the life of Islam would be misguided. On the contrary, the centrifugal forces of the Arab mind have been successfully controlled only by the orthodox religious institutions; and even they suffer from the effects of intuitive reasoning untrammelled by empirical concerns, contributing directly and indirectly to the emergence of a "distinct type of mystical religion."[8]

Nevertheless, despite such predilections, and despite a disturbing tendency toward rigid formalism,[9] the Ulama, in their role as defenders of the Shari'ah, are the hope of Islam's future as they have been the curators of its past. They must respond to three present threats: (1) the introduction of "false gods from the West alongside Allah," that is, the materialism of the West; (2) the "Mahdism" of Pan-Islamic and nationalist movements which falsely believe that truth is served "by the edge of the sword;" and (3) the compromising of Islam's strict transcendentalism by the introduction of "a social and this-worldly outlook and utilitarian ethic."[10] These are threats to Islam as a religion, a cultural artifact, not to the truth; the call to the Ulama to take up their responsibilities must be seen in this light.

Critical to Gibb's notion of the Shari'ah as the essential Islam is its implication for nationalism. Islam has never been nationalistic, he states flatly. Certainly, Arabs have identified themselves with Islam. But the true Islam must never be confused with the nationalistic aims which its followers all too frequently force it to serve. It is understandable that nationalistic leaders have asserted the central role of Islam in their movement, for they must, Gibb argues, "link their policies with the only system of universal ideas congenial to their people, i.e., Islam".[11]

But, there is a significant danger to the purity of Islam in recent Arab socialist and nationalistic movements, such as that of Nasser in Egypt. Gibb's rejection of this use — one can see that he means abuse — of a pristine ideal Islam has attracted the strong criticism of Edward Said, who argues that Gibb has based his critique of modern Muslim and Arab movements on a reified and static Islam which he does not really hold to be ultimately true and which serves as a false standard, one constructed by Gibb and the Orientalists in order to denounce such groups as the Palestinian Liberation Organization.[12] Whatever the truth of such a criticism, it must be said that Gibb's Islam does seem to exist outside history as a virtually static Platonic form. It is difficult to see it as a dynamic tradition striving to render in historical terms the response to the call to submit to God. It is much easier to see it as a "religion," one among many, an artifact defined, whose future is a logical possibility only in the terms of this definition.

Gibb's warnings about the corruption of the Shari'ah and thus of Islam itself — the phrase is significant — differ from the more functional approach taken by other Orientalists. Maxime Rodinson, for example, understands the uniqueness of Islam in terms of its role as ideology. One ought, he argues, to look beyond the "purely religious sphere," for comprehension of the Muslim movement. The attraction of interpreting Islam as a derivative of Christian and Jewish traditions is obvious. But Rodinson insists that Islam's originality lay in the fact that it was an "ideological phenomenon." Islam emerged out of the struggle of the Arabs with their powerful neighbors: "In order to stand up against Byzantium and Persia . . . the Arabs had first of all to form themselves into a state with an ideology of its own, viz. Islam".[13]

The significance of Islam is the sociological identity it provided for the Arabs. But, again, Islam's nature is that of a fixed and static object, if ideological, a *res* which may be grasped or rejected depending upon one's prior convictions. The concept of Islam as a dynamic effort to submit to God is absent.

This perspective is adopted by G.E. von Grunebaum. Islam, he argues, is static and understands itself to be static. The consequences are evident in the Muslim failure to live comfortably in the modern world. He contrasts the Muslim with the Occidental attitude towards change:

> Few culture areas have been subjected to as much and as violent change as that of Islam; none perhaps has as consistently refused to accept the ontological reality of change. The truth of Islam as it has come to be held in some contrast to the more flexible outlook of its origins is not only one and indivisible, it is also immutable; it is neither growing nor shrinking; its understanding may vary in adequacy but it has been changelessly available since it was vouchsafed mankind through the Seal of the Prophets. This goes for doctrine and conduct as well as for their institutionalization. Where the social reality fails to come up to the ideal human heedlessness is at fault; but the ideal needs no revision . . . . Development is still acceptable only either as decline, i.e., as abandonment of divine precept, or as the remedying of some misunderstanding, as the uncovering of some implication of the revealed truth that had hitherto been missed.[14]

For the Muslim, change is always for the worse. The best Islam was in the beginning.[15] All subsequent developments stood or fell in light of the judgment of the past. Islam, then, has always been "traditionalist".[16] It never followed the West in the commitment to the "pursuit of happiness." For the Muslim the ideal of happiness exists apart from human history.[17] Here the stark distinction between Western and Muslim attitudes toward civilization is irresistible. Islam is humanist only in the sense that it is concerned about the salvation of men; it is not, von Grunebaum argues, "interested in the richest possible unfolding and evolving of man's potentialities, in that it never conceived of the forming of men as civilization's principal and most noble task".[18]

It is not creative, then, in the sense that, for example, Greek civilization of the fifth and fourth centuries B.C. was.[19] It has never shown that "overflowing abundance of ideas, that boundless fertility that is the greatness of the Greeks . . . . Islam does not reach to the stars — it is realistic, which is only a euphemism for being timid".[20] It is the last of the nostalgia religions.[21]

Allah reigns and rules; and thus Islam is first of all the community of Allah. As a community, argues von Grunebaum, it seeks to comprehend life in its totality. There is no neutral zone where "religion does not lay claim." In accepting Islam the believer received a "ready-made set of mandatory answers to any questions of conduct that could possibly arise. As long as he obeyed sacred customs, the Muslim's life was hallowed down to its irksome and repulsive episodes, he would be fortified by the assurance of his righteousness".[22] Von Grunebaum understands Islam to be a "religion" in just this way. Thus, he warns Western interpreters against confusing the theological developments from the rigid monothesism of Muhammad with the heart of religion. That heart is the "system which aims primarily at regulating all and everything . . . ."[23] When von Grunebaum writes of Islam as a religion, then, he means its regulating structure, overseen by the Ulama of every age. The very survival of Islam depends, as it has always depended, upon "the existence of an adequate body of *ulama*."[24] When this system has operated at its best, the true strength of Islam is evident, namely its ability to produce a roundedness of personality "amounting to poise and dignity founded on belief in the static conception of the ideal world." In this respect it is to be contrasted with the West's ideal of sacrifice of the present for the future.[25]

Thus, von Grunebaum conceptualizes Islam in terms of a static ideal whose relationship with history and "reality" is problematic and often oppository. Islam hates change; therefore, the hopes of the modern reformers who look for political and spiritual renaissance are, very likely, contrary to the fundamental traditionalism. Their "yearning . . . implies the conviction that human affairs tend to improve, that change tends to be for the better. This belief runs counter to the general feeling of traditional Islam that sees its history as a perpetual decline".[26] The striving for reform is related directly, argues von Grunebaum, to the issues of Westernization and cultural borrowing. His position is clear: Islam must adapt if it is to survive in a Western-dominated world. But this challenge is in fact a dilemma; for Islam's future success would seem to lie in the direction of denying its conception of its self as static ideal. Von Grunebaum's suggestion for resolving this dilemma will be taken up in more detail in a later section; but I see in his view of the dilemma a strong indication of his general thinking about Islam as a static mass. For in order to survive, Islam must distill from its actual history a set of ethical ideals of such flexibility that they present no fundamental conflict with Western values. At present, Islam borrows practical and technological resources only, rather than drawing upon the principles and philosophies which undergird those modern successes.[27] However necessary absorption of occidental optimism about the future may be, it is nevertheless contradictory to Muslim traditionalism, to Islam's very nature as von Grunebaum defines it.

With respect to Islam and cultural borrowing, von Grunebaum observes that such development as may be found in the history of Muslim's peoples is the result of a discriminating incorporation of civilizing forces borrowed from non-Arab sources; for Arabian civiliza-tion itself proved early to be too slim to "carry and unify the legacies of the many pasts which Islam found itself called upon to administer."[28] Von Grunebaum distinguishes, as he believes Muslims distinguish, between the "religious foundation," or the emphasis on religion as the principal bond between people, "and Islam's civilization." Islam, he argues, was careful in its extensive borrowing not to threaten the "religious core," but equally careful to "obscure the foreign character of important borrowings."[29] There is then a "standard Islam," which must be distinguished from the influences of the world of the ancient Orient (including pre-Islamic Arabia) which may be found "below the surface" in the popular beliefs and in sectarian theology.[30]

The "Islamic aspiration" may both mold and be influenced by local traditions; but one must, he argues, be careful to separate them. Thus, for example, Arab nationalism faces the problem of integrating local nationalistic aims with the medieval spiritual basis of its people, namely Islam. The failure to do this continues to present problems for the modern movements, especially with respect to social legislation.

I wish to stress the reifying tendency in the Orientalist view of Islam. In the work of von Grunebaum, Islam is not a continuing and self-critical — but also creative — attempt to submit to Allah in all the paths of life. Rather, it appears to be self-consciously inert and an historical religion, out of step with the dynamic sense of engagement in historical development and change so characteristic of the West. Fazlur Rahman notes that the Orientalist viewed the modern Islam as that of a "semi-inert mass receiving the destructive blows or the formative influences from the West".[31] While there is an explanation for this view — we must concede the political, military and intellectual impingement upon the Muslim world from the West in the past three centuries — it is fallacious to believe that the modern history of Islam is of a community "become internally incapable of reconstituting itself and [that] whatever it might do by the way of reconstruction if at all it can, will be done by influences and borrowings from the West".[32] Rahman points, for example, to the pre-modernist reform movements associated with the name Wahhabi,[33] and to the modernist movements themselves. The false understanding of modern Islam, then, rests upon the assumption that our Orientalists began with, that Islam is a fixed and static entity, facing the dilemma of maintaining its purity — as defined by the Orientalists — while adapting to the presumably irresistible force for change from outside. As though there were not forces of change *within* the history of Islam! So von Grunebaum speaks in the introduction to his *Modern Islam: The Search for Cultural Identity* of his "sustained concern with the structure of the Islamic community and its reaction to the intense contact with the West which, in various forms, has directed its development for the past hundred years." He continues,

> It is the trials as much as, if not more than, the triumphs of each subsequent period which offer a cultural community its chance to realize aspects of its potential which hitherto remained submerged. To uncover such possibilities, tie them to the traditional experience, and attune them to the stimuli, both freeing and threatening, of the West, is the wearisome and intoxicating task of contemporary Islam.[34]

The tenor and the content of this general approach to Islam have been vigorously attacked by A. L. Tibawi. "As a *faith*" he insists, "Islam is of course indivisible; one has to take it or leave it as a whole."[35]

Tibawi's Islam is a faith, or better, faith in the sense that it is a dynamic and historical expression of submission. For example, the Shari'ah has always been in a state of change. This refers not so much to alterations in the legal corpus, but to the constant evaluation of life from

the perspective of the Qur'an as applied by the Hadith and precedent.[36]
Do the Orientalists call for reform? They should see it in abundance; for
Islam persistently has been reforming human life in light of God's
commands.[37]

Tests are constantly applied, and they are old ones: "the consensus of
the community and the approval of the *ulama* in the region concerned."[38]

The outsider can never understand the manner and source of Muslim
life, Tibawi says: "Religious perception is a spiritual, intuitive experience. It cannot be comprehended by analytical or critical methods.
Those outside a *religious system* can never capture the significance of the
experience of those inside it. It is a thing that cannot be learned in
books."[39]

That is the crux of the Orientalists' problem — they cannot see in
Muslim history the effort to know and obey God. Thus to them it is an
historical artifact, a curiosity, requiring explanation. Such an approach
must be offensive to the Muslim. While Tibawi's words may sound
harsh, they are nevertheless the reaction of a devout and learned Muslim
to the Orientalist treatment of Islam and deserve to be taken seriously.
In reviewing essays and entries in three major modern reference works,
viz. the *Cambridge Modern History, The Legacy of Islam,* and the *Encyclopedia
of Islam,* he concludes:

> Enough examples have been given . . . to show that there are two
> versions of Islam as a religion and as a civilization. The one version
> derives from love, faith and tradition, and the other from hatred, scepti-
> cism and speculation. There is complete divorce between the one and the
> other on almost all essentials. Islam is perhaps the only religion to be thus
> maltreated by outsiders.[40]

Here is eloquent and troubling testimony to the effects of reification of
the Muslim tradition into a religion, a thing virtually invented by
outsiders, and a thing for which they have no ultimate care.

II. *The Issue of Cultural Borrowing*

Our Orientalists took up the question of the manner in which and the
degree to which Islam has depended, and may continue to depend, upon
external cultural sources of inspiration for its beliefs and practices. But
let us inquire first of the Muslim community whence came the Qur'an,
and to what source we should attribute the prophetic career of Muham-

mad. The answer, too widespread and deeply rooted to require citation, is that the Qur'an is of Allah and Muhammad is the Prophet of Allah. Any reply which contradicts that response is *eo ipso* false. In sharp contrast, one need only briefly consult the work of the Orientalists to discover that they do not answer the questions in this way; and they do not do so because they are either unwilling or unable to link Muslim history with Allah or, in English, with God. Therefore, they must necessarily look to the historical, social, political, and cultural history of Islam — whose essence they have already established — for answers. Thus, not only do they refuse or ignore the link between Muslim history and Allah, but also (with some exceptions, whom I shall address) they hold that fundamental aspects of Islam are borrowed from other cultures and traditions. Islam, then, is neither transcendentally significant nor historically authentic. At times one gets the impression from our Orientalists that Islam is an incoherent pastiche of vaguely remembered, misunderstood, borrowed ideas, sustained as well as could be expected by an analogously incoherent social grouping or groupings. Such a view enables the Orientalist to explain the "problems" of Islam — for that is the underlying tone, that Islam *is* or at least *has* a problem — and to suggest directions which Islam must take in order to survive, if it is to survive at all.

A. Muhammad

The issue of borrowing arises for the Orientalists at the beginning of the tradition, with Muhammad and the Qur'an. For example, Gibb argues that Muhammad's "conception" — the word is significant — of a "primitive undistorted monotheism constantly revived by a succession of Prophets," of whom he himself was the last, was sustained by an appeal to Abraham as the original *hanif*. A legacy of the indigenous Arabian prophetic tradition, of which only vague suggestions have survived to us, may have provided precedent for Muhammad's declaration. Certainly, says Gibb, the only distinctly Arabian institution extant in Islam is the pilgrimage to the Ka'ba, now sanctified through the person of Ishmael and "given an ethical significance altogether foreign to its original Arabian character."[41] The Qur'anic proclamation by Muhammad, furthermore, is not original. Later Muslims agreed; for the Qur'an is uncreated. Muhammad was simply recalling the pristine recitation of God's will for man. No claim for originality, given these views, is therefore appropriate, says Gibb, nor would it be "appropriate in any case in a monotheistic tradition." But the "Mohammedan" religion is nevertheless constituted in a unique fashion. It may be seen as a logical "if not philosophical" development of monotheism, in that it combines the universalism of Christianity with absolute and unconditioned monotheism, and is underlaid by the stark contrast between man and God which constitutes "the original tension of Islam." It is not a nationalist movement, such as Judaism, nor does it permit the relics of nature cults found in the history of the Christian church.[42]

Despite his neutrality on the Muslim claim that the Qur'an is of God, Gibb chooses to describe Muhammad's prophetic career and the religion which emerged in terms of the prior Christian and Jewish traditions: without them Islam would be incomprehensible. Von Grunebaum takes the same view, but is more explicit concerning Islam's historical sources. Indeed, his interpretation of the origins of Islam contradicts any claim for transcendent origins. Like Gibb he finds originality in Islam; but it lies in its tone; "flavour," and "spirit," rather than content or structure.

Jewish and Christian patterns were, von Grunebaum concludes, "instrumental in the formation of the Prophet's ideas; Biblical and Haggadic lore permeate the Koranic narratives. His monotheism was developed at least partially in controversy with Christian trinitarianism".[43] However, the "ideas" of the Qur'an are Muhammad's. The problem is to identify the sources and explain these ideas as they occurred to Muhammad — who von Grunebaum obviously assumes is the author of the Qur'an.

To be sure, significant aspects of Muhammad's teachings are Arab: " . . . the way of life imposed by Muhammad, the ritual of the pilgrimage, and, on the level of verbalization and argumentation, a certain prephilosophical crudeness — all this was genuinely Arab . . . ."[44]

But Muhammad lifted his people out of their primitive ignorance and undeveloped self-understanding. When he declared that Abraham had founded the Ka'ba at Mecca he "gave greater depth to Arab historical consciousness, he prolonged the memories of his people back to the day of Creation, and he gave them a spiritually significant tradition of holy history to supplement their ill-kept records of events of local importance . . . ."[45] "[Muhammad's] appropriation of biblical history . . . put the Muslims at the end of one great development".[46] Von Grunebaum examines pre-Muslim Arabian civilization for any clues of "original aspects of Islam." But he looks in vain. "The utter emptiness of Arabic paganism forced the dissatisfied thinker, the believer in quest of a god to believe in, to fall back on alien notions and alien sentiments if he wished to express his longings at all. Any documentation of religious growth had to assume traits of Christian or Jewish teaching simply because his own background had left him without any pattern for a life in God".[47] The desert-like aridity of Muhammad's religious background, with its lack of conceptual tools, forced him to borrow. "No wonder Muhammad was fond of using sonorous vocabulary".[48] Muhammad's insistence upon the Arabizing of the faith meant a "huge advance" for his people. Yet, Jewish and Christian inspirations are the deepest roots of Islam.[49]

The picture von Grunebaum draws of Muhammad is of a remarkable man struggling to assemble a language that could express what was in his mind and heart. He found so little in his own tradition that he was forced to construct his words and thoughts out of gleanings from other fields. What was in fact in his mind and heart we cannot tell, von Grunebaum implies. What Muhammad says — for there is no doubt that the Qur'an is the word of Muhammad only — is derivative. Other Orientalists have addressed themselves to this question of whether Muhammad borrowed "his ideas," i.e., the Qur'an, from Jewish and/or Christian sources. Alfred Guillaume could see no reasonable objection to the assertion that the Qur'an is derived from Jewish and Christian traditions. Muhammad, "disappointed and disgusted as he was with the heathenism of Mecca . . . was originally awakened to the existence of the God of Jews and Christians, and when he appeared openly as a prophet he looked to them for support." As his prophetic career developed, he came increasingly to depend upon the tradition of the Old Testament and of Jesus and his apostles.[50]

Guillaume asks, what connection could we understand to exist between Muhammad's listeners and such heroes of the Old Testament as Abraham, Moses, Noah, and Joseph? Among his audience only Jews and Christians, especially the former, would have recognized them. In Medina, the Jews and Muhammad came to a dramatic parting of the ways. But by this time Muhammad had formulated his theory of Abraham as the original Muslim, and of Ishmael's link with the Meccan Ka'ba. That this novelty is Muhammad's idea is indicated by the complete absence of corroborating records outside the Qur'an. Moreover, Muhammad, if the Qur'an is to be believed, used Aramaic and Greek forms of the Old Testament names, which means that they can only have been borrowed. The point is important, says Guillaume: for "the Qur'an claims to be an Arabic Qur'an and a revelation to the Arabs in plain unequivocal language." It might be true that Muhammad's non-Jewish and non-Christian hearers may have recognized the vocabulary and names from association with Christians and Jews. But the derivative nature of the Qur'an cannot be gainsaid.[51]

The contradiction between the fact of Christian and Jewish inspiration of the Qur'an and the Muslim belief concerning the Qur'an remains unresolved:

> . . . it must always be remembered that to the Muslims the Qur'an is a faithful and unalterable reproduction of the original scriptures which are preserved in heaven, and this in spite of the fact that the Qur'an teaches, and almost everyone holds, that a large number of verses are superceded and abrogated by later revelations. The Muslim world has not yet come to grips with the problem which Christian Europe faced after the Renaissance, but signs are not wanting that thoughtful Muslims are seeking a way out of the impasse.[52]

(The reference to the problem of the historical roots of scripture suggests the lines Guillaume will take in his admonition to Islam to reform. Like von Grunebaum, Gibb, and Rodinson, he is impressed with the almost total lack of an historical sense, and the Muslim resistance to historical analysis of the Qur'an and Hadith.)

Maxime Rodinson seeks to interpret the rise of Muhammad, and of Islam in general, as an ideological awakening to the social and economic needs of Arabia. While it is patently inaccurate, he observes, to conclude that Islam was "born in a sealed container in an environment sterilized against the germs of other ideologies," as most contemporary Muslims believe, many Orientalists have ventured too far in the opposite direction.[53] They have ignored the originality of Islam, an evident fact seen in the historical success of Muhammad and his followers. One must never forget, he argues, the importance of a "structural analysis which takes into account the functional necessity of the new theology. After all, Muhammad became neither a Jew nor a Christian."[54]

In Rodinson's view, Muhammad, because of a "personal, psychological solution," became an instrument "capable of formulating and communicating an ideology that corresponded to the needs of the time and the milieu." His emergence is of a type found in similar conditions in other socio-economic settings.[55] Thus, while Rodinson admits to the significance of the non-Muslim sources in the rise of Muhammad and the Qur'an, he insists that both emerge in response to socio-economic problems and are explicable according to classic sociological categories of interpretation of Marxist coloring. Muhammad is a product of those forces as well as a focus for the shifting of their balance. Such a socio-economic interpretation has little room for an appreciation of the personal experience of Muhammad as one to whom Allah spoke and called to prophethood. While one may have "respect for the faith of sincere believers," Rodinson writes, the work of the historian must not be blocked by misplaced sympathy. "Passing directly from the plane of the coherence of religious ideas or of respect for the religious life to the plane of objective reconstruction of past religious consciousness is inadmissible".[56] Thus the life of faith in history may be a reality to the believer — however self-deceived he may be — but it is not material to the historian, whose concerns must be guided by strict empirical attention to the social and economic setting. The implication is clear: the historian may not ascribe Muhammad's significance to his faith. For Rodinson, Muslim self-interpretation of Muhammad and the Qur'an fails by definition, for its view is precisely that. Only those Muslim historians who follow the Western tradition of historiography as Rodinson understands it can succeed in their task. They must become outsiders; they may not accept the view that Allah commands the obedience of those who obey (*muslims*) and that the response is what is properly known as Muslim history.

J. Fueck takes a position on Muhammad rarely defended by Orientalists. Over and against such scholars as C. C. Torrey, who held that Jewish influences were dominant in the Qur'an and thus in Muhammad's prophetic career, and others, such as W. Ahrens, who awarded Christian influences the prize, Fueck rejects any explanation based on borrowing, but he underscores the methodological lesson to be learned. The usual approach to the issue of borrowing is a version of *post hoc, propter hoc*; that is, because there was contact between Jews, Christians and Muhammad, the former must have influenced the latter. That there were contacts no one, least of all Muhammad, denies. The claim that the Qur'an is a melange of Christian and/or Jewish concepts is, however, quite a different matter. Fueck writes:

> Every attempt to prove [dependence] leads inevitably to insoluble diffi-
> culties and contradictions. Now it might seem that the actual solution to
> this problem could be found if (putting aside all partiality) one explained
> the various contacts as just so many stimuli, so that the Qur'an could be
> represented as the product of Christian, Jewish, and numerous other
> impulses . . . . Such investigations, however, tend to dissolve the Qur'an
> into a mosaic of countless individual stones of various origins which have
> no inner connection linking them together . . . . Studies based on rational
> and scientific method will never completely succeed in lifting the veil of
> mystery that surrounds the personality of [Muhammad].[57]

No scientific study of influences and sources, Fueck argues, can reveal
"what it was that enabled him to find his way through difficult experiences to the certainty that God had appointed him to be a warner and
an apostle." "It belongs to the essence of all great men of the spirit to
make generous use of material transmitted to them while impregnating
it with new life".[58]

Thus, Muhammad's deepest motives and driving ambition arise from
sources not available to the objective historian. His teachings, furthermore, show elements of originality which could not have been derived
from contemporary non-Muslim influences. Fueck gives us his chief
example: the doctrine of cyclical revelation. This, he says, "cannot be
derived either from Judaism or from Christianity." There is a parallel
notion in Manichaeism, but as of Fueck's writing there was no evidence
of direct historical connection. Nevertheless, even if a connection were
established, "the special form of this doctrine as it appears in the
Qur'an, particularly the inclusion of early Arabian prophets, would be
seen to be Muhammad's own creation."[59]

Furthermore, the remarkable fact of the persistent influence of
Muhammad on the history of Islam points to a truly unique, charismatic, individual. He is not simply a borrower and twister of tales.
Indeed, as if to prove his case, Fueck observes that Muslims have always
rallied to the *sunna* of the Prophet whenever foreign influence posed a
threat to Islam.[60]

However unique, charismatic and inscrutable Muhammad may have
been, however independent of direct influence from Jews and Christians, in Fueck's view, the most that can be said is that Muhammad came
to the conclusion that he was a *rasul*, that in acting in accordance with
the requirements of that office he created several original notions and

that he played a role which no one else had played before. The Muslim explanation for all this is quite clear: *Muhammad rasul allah.* Fueck is bound to object to the simplistic versions of other Orientalists such as Torrey and Ahrends. But his conclusions are still those of the Orientalist. The Qur'an is Muhammad's work, however remarkable a person Muhammad may have been. He *thought* he was a prophet. Fueck has replaced dubious explanation of foreign influence with agnosticism.

Just how far the attitudes of our Orientalists are from the Muslim view of Muhammad and the Qur'an may be illustrated by now asking them whether there is any sense in which they would accept the truth of the Muslim declaration that the Qur'an is of Allah, and Muhammad is the Prophet of Allah. I see no alternative to a negative response. It is true that they did not ask the question in the first place, choosing rather to seek among the historical sources for explanations of the content, style, and intent of the Qur'an and of the behavior of Muhammad. By implication, then, the issue of the truth of the Muslim claim for Muhammad and the Qur'an is resolved indirectly: only the cultural setting may be cited to explain them.

As for what is original and what is borrowed, the historical context provides the answers. Thus the debate is joined on what for the Muslim is an irrelevant and blasphemous matter, viz. how much Muhammad took from the Arabian tradition and how much from the Christian and Jewish. From the Muslim perspective, this is no mere academic issue, for by implication it constitutes an attack on the core of Muslim tradition. It is a provocative and unnecessary challenge, writes Tibawi, to occupy oneself with this question. For what is implied is that Muhammad is a false Prophet and that the Qur'an is a melange of derived quotations. The position is precisely that of the medieval polemicists.[61] Further, while none of our Orientalists has challenged the sincerity of Muhammad's beliefs, or has accused him of distorting what he knew to be true for his own ends (that would make him a *kafir*), they agree that he drew his proclamations, and thus the Qur'an, from available cultural sources, and expressed them according to his own intentions. One cannot have it both ways, Tibawi argues. If Muhammad is a true Prophet, a sincere Prophet, then the content of his message is not derived or borrowed. He is either a borrower, and thus not a true Prophet, or he is a true Prophet, and not a borrower. The Orientalists attempt to hold both positions; and that is an untenable stance. At least, Tibawi concludes, the extremists who deny Muhammad's role as a Prophet are comprehensible.[62] Finally, the presence of apparent similarities among the traditions does not bear the weight of the argument for borrowing; and only one who did not accept the truth of the statement that Muhammad is the Prophet of God would feel the need to resort to such an explanation.

B. Islam and Cultural Borrowing

In the judgment of our Orientalists, Muhammad's assembling of the core of Islam from available cultural sources proved paradigmatic for the history of Islam up to the present day. The relationship between Muhammad's tradition and the contending cultural pattern is seen to be one of resistance and incorporation; it was precisely these confrontations that shaped the face of Islam. As Gibb, for example, notes with respect to one of the formative episodes in the history of Islam, the conflict between Greek speculative philosophy and intuitive thought for control of the Muslim mind "not only conditioned the formulation of the traditional Muslim theology but set a permanent stamp upon Islamic culture." The modern contact with Western thought is ambiguous as a result.[63]

The impact of cultural borrowing upon Islam received considerable attention in the work of von Grunebaum,[64] particularly the borrowing from Greek civilization. This borrowing was characterized on the one hand by resistance to Greek philosophical categories and on the other by the "Islamicizing" of those categories for theological purposes. Hellenistic influence succeeded only insofar as it was integrated into the Islamic tradition, especially in devotional circles where its distinct character was obscured by its resemblance to traditional forms. Hellenistic categories on the other hand were in fact resisted by the people and the Ulama.[65] A distinction was drawn between the "ancient" sciences and the "religious" sciences in order to account for the presence of useful philosophy, notably Greek, not found in the Qur'anic tradition. The distinction accepted by Islam, von Grunebaum argues, is not between "foreign and native" but between "religiously praiseworthy and blameworthy." The standard against which all knowledge was to be judged was that of utility, for this world or the next. The "semi-independent" strands of thought, ancient and religious, were cultivated side by side in line with this standard, "with the ancient science slowly losing out in the perpetual struggle between the theological and the philosophical-scientific approach."[66]

The "ancient" sciences never lost the taint of alien origin and possible godlessness,[67] *falsafa* thus took on a distinctly Muslim face. Whereas Greek philosophy roamed free, Muslim *falsafa* was fragmented by the need to reconcile verification by reason with verification by faith, i.e., by the Qur'anic tradition. It was, in short, barred from independent treatment of the Muslim life.[68] Greek philosophy *per se* was gradually eliminated from the Muslim tradition, but not before many of its contributions had been absorbed.[69] Islam was not fortunate in the level of philosophical discourse that it imitated: "Instead of Plato, Neo-Platonism, instead of Plotinus, Porphyry and Proclus, and Aristotle mostly as seen through the commentaries of the epigone." But "it was under the impact of Hellenism on every area of thought, be it philosophy, the sciences, or literary theory . . . that Islamic civilization passed through that glorious era of the ninth and tenth centuries whose colorful intensity and diversity will always astound and enchant the spectator."[70]

Muslim civilization's debt to cultures other than the Greek is also large. From the Greeks and Romans, Muslims learned abstract thinking; but from the Persians they learned statecraft and imagery. The Persian tradition "showed its power in molding the forms and ethics of civic life . . . . It furnished the Muslim mind with a great deal of imaginative and moralistic subject matter." The spectacle of Islam's progress from the "compartively poor" background of Arabian civilization through the increasingly sophisticated incorporation of foreign cultures to the "fully rounded" facade it presents now is one of the most fascinating of historical tales, says von Grunebaum. Islam may seem "omnivorous"; it welcomed Greek dialectics, Persian allegorical interpretations, Christian asceticism. It appreciated and rewarded the Persian administrator, the Christian physician, the Indian mathematician. It even accepted the prejudices of its teachers; the dislike for pictorial representation, the worship of the saints, and the system of the harem and homosexuality were allowed to exist or in some cases encouraged.

But this borrowing, von Grunebaum argues, was in fact highly selective. Nothing survived within the Muslim community which appeared to challenge "the religious foundation." Moreover, Muslims ensured as far as they could that the foreign sources of their civilization were obscured.[73] It is possible to distinguish that which was kept from which was rejected in the process of obscuring the act of borrowing: the former consisted entirely of information and techniques, the latter of philosophies and formative ideas. "Elements of material civilization as well as political institutions and administrative techniques were welcomed, ideology, whenever possible, rejected. Usefulness remained the ultimate criterion of acceptability. The individual result was taken over, the system that justified it neglected."[74] Further, what Islam borrowed it did not improve (with the express exception of the study of optics), but simply put to its own use with no real concern for development.[75] It was, von Grunebaum says, the "fascination with the useful" which blinded Islam to the fact that it was not the technical achievements of, for example, the Greeks that made their culture great but its spirit; and even now, he notes, "the pressure of politics reinforces the appeal of the immediately practical and makes the impatient Easterner forget that the power of the West does not spring from its technical accomplishments but from the spirit that brought them about."[76]

Finally, the deliberate obscuring of foreign sources in the history of Muslim civilization has an ironic effect: "More than anything else," says von Grunebaum, "does this hiding of the foreign influence and the concomitant increase in its power of stimulation contribute to the apparent uniformity and roundedness of Muslim civilization."[77] This obscurantism is worked on the Muslim as well as the external world. For example, in his discussion of nationalism among the Muslims von Grunebaum points to what he thinks is an inescapable contradiction to which Muslims seem to be stubbornly insensitive between the Western concept of nationalism and its expression in Islam. As purveyors of "nativist movements of foreign kindling," the apostles of nationalism can succeed only by denying the cultural achievements of their community, that is, precisely those borrowed but nevertheless definitive characteristics of Muslim culture.[78] Yet, the Muslim solution to all problems of incorporation of foreign elements into Islamic culture has been to make "the heterogenetic appear as orthogenetic wherever possible."

> The borrowed element is envisaged as something bestowed on the West many a century ago and now come home, as it were, modified perhaps yet of Muslim origin. Or it is found adumbrated or even enjoined in the Holy Book. Or it is accounted for as a legitimate, a logical development

from Muslim presuppositions correctly interpreted. Parliament and monogamy are intimated in the Qur'an; equality was practised during the early period of the empire; the devotion to pure science is characteristic of the Muslim legacy; so is tolerance to minorities; and concern with social ills.[79]

This attitude toward cultural borrowing has always posed serious problems for Islam. Von Grunebaum is far from sanguine about their solution. First, the claim that Islam bestowed culture on the West is untenable: It is "preposterous so much as to ask" whether any of the essential elements of occidental civilization arise from Muslim inspiration. Except, possibly, for Averroism, "it would seem that never did original Muslim thought influence Western thought so as to remain a live force over a prolonged period of time completely integrated and indispensable to its further growth."[80] Second, Muslim self-understanding is hampered severely by self-deception. This is especially true for the modernist movement; but the following observation is illustrative of the entire Muslim attitude toward its cultural borrowing. Von Grunebaum writes:

> One psychological difficulty impeding the Muslim modernist would be removed if he could assume a less twisted reaction to the phenomenon of cultural borrowing. All too frequently the reaction resembles that of Haikal to the idea of evolution: he rejects it politely but then shows with pride that it is indigenous to Islam, having been developed by Ibn Khaldun. Innovation still has to be made palatable by tracing it in the early days of the faith. Affected by this spirit, even Taha Husain in his study of Ibn Haldun tried to demonstrate the harmony of modern philosophy both with the traditional belief of Islam and with Arab medieval philosophy.[81]

What von Grunebaum fails to appreciate is that we can distinguish between a reaction to Western incursions upon Muslim civilization which is at times defensive and the firm conviction that Allah works and has worked in the history of Muslim life. Failing to appreciate the second fact of Muslim history, he focuses solely on the former phenomenon as though it revealed something of the essence of Islam. As I have already argued, von Grunebaum's vision of Islam is obscured by his implied rejection of its role as a *din,* that is, as a tradition through which the truth of Allah may be seen and by which the Muslim may attempt to live up to his calling as the servant of Allah. As for the Muslim's "twisted reaction" to cultural borrowing, von Grunebaum's conclusions arise naturally from his blinkered focus on what is obvious and superficial, external, and evident to the outsider only. The more significant element of the faith of Muslims, that is their capacity for seeing, undeceived, Allah's hand in history in much the same manner as Muhammad saw it, has no bearing on the issue, in his thinking. He thus fails to appreciate what is significant about so-called cultural borrowing; that it is a secondary phenomenon dependent upon the primary phenomenon of faith.

A.L. Tibawi has observed that von Grunebaum's conclusions rest upon a skewed view of the history of Islam; this view is nowhere more evident than in the latter's conclusion concerning the failure of Muslims to acknowledge on the one hand the fact of borrowing and, on the other, the "concomitant increase in its power" within the tradition. One must, Tibawi insists, see clearly the distinction between faith and its expressions, and between culture or civilization and what drives it. He writes of von Grunebaum:

> If by Islam is meant civilization or culture, then neither the fact of absorption of foreign elements nor their source has ever been denied. On the other hand, if by Islam is meant its dogma and creed, the writer of that statement [i.e., von Grunebaum's conclusion with respect to cultural borrowing] hardly needs a reminder that if Islam were to remove the cause of his complaint it would cease to be itself and would have to renounce the explicit teaching of its holy book.[82]

III. Reforming Islam

Thus far I have argued that the Orientalists discussed here limit their analysis of the Muslim tradition to its external facts, to its "cultural history." What gives that tradition power in the first place, faith, is ignored or allowed to disappear behind the cultural forms of Islam. I do not think it surprising, then, that our Orientalists also conclude that Islam is in serious need of reform. But their thinking is confused. For, if we understand the notion of *islam* as *muslims* do, there is no "thing" to reform. On the one hand, as Muhammad Abduh said, there is nothing wrong with Islam, only with Muslims. That is to say, the ideal of submission (*islam*) to Allah can never be reformed — the notion is inconceivable given the absolute nature of Allah and His commands. On the other hand, that Muslims have failed more or less and from time to time to submit to Allah was never in question within the Muslim community. Thus, reform, if that is the proper word, is the perceptual goal of the tradition — indeed, one may define the tradition as the ongoing historical attempts to "reform," that is to submit; and it should be remembered that it is the attempt we are discussing when we speak of *islam*. An outsider's call for reform is therefore gratuitous.

But if we accept the Orientalists' position that Islam is a religion, a cultural artifact only, the meaning of "reform" quickly is clarified. Whereas the Muslim seeks to reform in order to live according to the commands of Allah, the Orientalist urges reform for the purpose of political, economic and social survival in the conflict of contemporary trends and forces. If Islam is to be successful, they say, it must alter or abrogate this or that practice, belief or political structure. Success means cultural success, survival in the contemporary world that is dominated by Western values. The Orientalists are not in complete agreement on how this might be achieved. Some hold that Islam should hold fast to its medieval heritage of Shari'ah; others contend that "liberalization" of the social practices of Islam is essential. Most think that Islam is incapable of accomplishig such necessary reforms. My point, however, is that the call for reform is directed to the preservation of a cultural artifact, not to the perfection of faith, the ever-maturing understanding of God's Word and the institution of the just and good society. The distinction is, I think, essential; for it helps to explain how Orientalists can come to those conclusions about Islam which Muslims find so very offensive. Finally, the assumption supporting this somewhat perverted notion of reform, to my thinking anyway, is quite clear. They simply do not believe that the Muslim tradition is a tradition of faith, that God is working through it. Rather, it is simply a fascinating, influential, and somewhat perplexing force in the history of cultures. There is no sense in which they hold that it is true or good. They seek to explain, I am arguing, rather than to understand or participate.

What, then, do our Orientalists conclude about the need for the reform of Islam? As will be evident, this matter is intimately tied to the general issue of Westernization, the purported crisis caused by the need to adjust to occidental hegemony in the areas of education, historiography and philosophy (as opposed to technology, which Islam is more or less willing to borrow). Let us risk this generalization: that the perceived need for reform is, for the Orientalists, primarily a function of the perceived Muslim relationship to the West.

One observation is widespread: the Muslim attitude toward the Qur'an and the *sunna* of the Prophet is uninformed by any historical sense such as is found in Christian theology. Alfred Guillaume writes that "The Muslim world has not yet come to grips with the problem which Christian Europe faced after the Renaissance, but signs are not wanting that thoughtful Muslims are seeking a way out of the logical impasse".[83] The "impasse" is the logically absurd claim that the Qur'an is an unalterable reproduction of scriptures preserved in heaven, a claim made in the teeth of the facts of abrogation and supercession of texts evident in the Qur'an itself. The modern Christian historical sense of the Word Incarnate permits and, at times, encourages interpretation and even textual revision and editing of scripture. This, notes Guillaume, is largely impossible among Muslims. True, there are exceptions. Those few thinkers who have been students at Western universities understand the benefits of historical criticism as it might be applied in Qur'anic scholarship. But they, he says, will not speak for fear of the power of the Ulama. Their professional standing would be threatened were they to question in any way the position that the Qur'an is literally the Word of God. He cites the case of Taha Husayn, hounded by the authorities because of a modification he proposed in the traditional beliefs concerning the uncreated status of the Qur'an.[84]

Nevertheless, the very presence of such persons is, in Guillaume's view, a good sign. Perhaps, he writes, Islam stands at the leading edge of a Reformation not unlike that which occurred in Europe.[85] The position taken by Shaykh Muhammad Ashraf, for example, for the reform of the Hadith, is surely heartening. Ashraf's call for the development of "fresh principles of historical and rational criticism" and the re-examination and recodification of the Hadith selected according to these principles is cause for hope; "In this formidable task all men of good will would wish the Muslim community an abiding success".[86] Moreover, "liberalization" in the practice of Shari'ah has been documented, notably by Guillaume's colleague J.N.D. Anderson. Whether this reform movement, based as it is upon modern scholarly and historical sensitivities not found in the Muslim community at large, will succeed is very difficult to know; for there is conflict between reactionary and liberal forces. The former hold to the old ways with tenacity and power. The great danger to reform, says Guillaime, "is that the old forces of reaction will be too strong for the new spirit of liberalism, armed as they are with the shibboleths and anathemas which can rouse the ignorant masses and terrorize men of vision. Only time can show which party will gain the upper hand".[87]

However this struggle evolves, Guillaume insists that Islam must bring its beliefs and practices into line with modern historical criticism, modern philosophy and modern science.[88] It need hardly be said that all of this modernism has a Western structure; "liberal reform" means Westernization. What is missing from Guillaume's view is the Muslim perspective; that reform seeks to move Islamic life closer to the will of Allah, not to the powers and principalities of the times.

H.A.R. Gibb's call for reform resembles Guillaume's. The contrast and implied conflict between historical thinking (for example, the recognition that the Qur'an is a product of historical forces and human decision), and the classic Muslim position on the Qur'an as the Uncreated Word of God impresses him greatly. True reform, he argues, will come "through the cultivation of historical thinking. Only historical thinking can restore the flexibility demanded by this task, in proportion to its success in freeing the vision of the great overriding movement of the Eternal Reason for the frailties, the halting interpretations, and the fussy embroideries of its human instruments and agents".[89]

The need for reform is apparent to Gibb; what, then, is his view of those who have attempted it recently? The modernists (to begin with them) have found the conflict between the medieval/classic Islamic world-view and the burgeoning secularization of knowledge and social structures to be a critical challenge which simply cannot be overlooked. It is this conflict which justified their endeavour. However, in striving toward a modernized formulation of Islamic principles and doctrine, the reformers ". . . outstripped the great body of the learned, not to speak of the masses." Their influence is thus limited to their own kind, among whom only a few Muslims may be numbered.[90]

Furthermore, the modernist faces a dilemma which Gibb believes is finally insoluble. "The Koran must be true and final. And yet he is uneasily conscious that there is something amiss in the current Muslim social ethic. At the same time, it deeply wounds his feelings as a Muslim and his self-respect as a man to find that the only thing which the average Westerner knows about Islam is that a Muslim may have four wives," and so forth. The modernist attempts to cut this Gordian knot by the assertion that the Islam constructed by the medieval doctors is in some significant sense a departure from the pure Islam of the earliest days, a pristine tradition which must be recovered. This task, Gibb observes, is simply impossible and a delusion.[91] The fact is that the modernists are responding to superimposed Western principles, not to the heart of Islam.[92] Concludes Gibb, any successful reform will "be practical and realistic and far removed from the intellectual confusions and the paralyzing romanticism which clouds the minds of the modernists of today".[93]

Yet, he says, the fact that the modernist movement arose at all suggests that something must be done," . . . that re-formulation cannot be indefinitely shelved".[94] That reformulation must be carried out by the Ulama. First, however, it is important to identify the source of the disease. That source is, of course, Western influence on the Muslim community. Although other Orientalists were more forthright in saying so, Gibb agrees that the impetus for change and reform came from outside Islam, from the West. Western power and influence could not be ignored; "but to relate them to bases of his own life and thought called for an effort of comprehension and adjustment which he [the Muslim] was not ready to undertake." Yet the effort had to be made and, unfortunately, made without any clear indication from the West as to the best directions to take. "To distinguish the effect from the cause, the secondary and superficial from the essential, the instrument from the motive, the false from the true" — in this task the Western advisor to the Muslim was of little assistance and caused much confusion.[95]

Gibb describes two alternatives. The Ummah could "start from the basic principles of Islam and . . . restate them in the light of the contemporary situation. Or, it could start from a preferred Western philosophical base and translate it into Muslim terms. Neither approach has been acceptable to the Ulama, for whom, after all, the need for "restatement" is far from proven. Further, among those who took seriously the need to respond, only a few addressed the fundamental issues of Muslim thought; the rest sought to defend Islam from the encroachments of Western influence either by apologetics or by cosmetic reforms of organization and practice. As for the few who addressed the real need to rethink Islamic beliefs, their influence has been almost negligible.[96]

In sum, although Islam has responded, sometimes energetically, to the prodding of the West, its activity seems to have been for the sake of activity, or can be seen as a symptom of some underlying anxiety. If true reform occurs, it will be the work of the Ulama, in their role as protectors and interpreters of the Shari'ah. It is, after all, the Ulama who will resist the three great temptations that face Islam in its anxious relationship with the West: the substituting of a social and profane attitude for uncompromising transcendentalism; the borrowing of the "false gods" of the West, such as materialism and communism; and the rejection of "all those hard-won positions by which Islam consolidated its claims in the intellectual life of mankind and from which it must start in the new effort to establish their validity in the modern world".[97] (This third temptation is revealing: it calls on the Ulama to establish the validity of Islam in the modern world — a task which Gibb regards as fundamental and pressing. Therefore, his concern is not with Muslim history as obedient to Allah, but with the problems for Islam as a religion trying to survive as a cultural artifact under the pressures of a modern, westernizing, world.

The Ulama have not succeeded. Their formulations are out of touch with the realities of the lives of the people, and certainly out of touch with the intellectuals. "It is not Islam that is petrified," Gibb concludes, "but its orthodox formulations, its systematic theology, its social apologetic. It is here that the dislocation lies, that the dissatisfaction is felt among a large proportion of its most educated and intelligent adherents and that the danger for its future is most evident".[98] But it is not all hopeless. One cannot help but be impressed, Gibb wrote in 1965, by the revision and rethinking ("which are not the same thing, however") taking place in Muslim countries. He points to such legal reforms as the new laws regarding marriage, divorce and inheritance, which will alter the practice of the Ummah. The Ulama, further, have shown some willingness to adjust Qur'anic principles to the modern situation, especially in the area of social law. They have done so, quite properly, in the manner of earlier generations who sought to mediate between the principles of Shari'ah and political innovations.[99] Thus, if there is to be any success in the crucial task of responding to the West, it will be accomplished by the Ulama, and without leaving the masses behind.

Whether such success can be achieved is far from clear. For Gibb the pristine Islam has been identified; but the implacable forces of Westernization may not permit it to survive. Gibb's notion of reform places

Islam, by his own understanding, athwart the irresistible trends of the times. The efforts of the Ulama may not be enough, even if they are the only legitimate "reformers." Nowhere is this pessimism more obvious than in Gibb's assessment of the nationalist movements among Muslims.

It was the failure of the Ulama to control and, when necessary, suppress nationalism among Muslim countries that encouraged a development which Gibb regrets intensely, the rise of "Arab Socialism." Like von Grunebaum, Gibb is cognizant of the weakness of Muslim political rule, a weakness resulting from the traditional role of the state as the defender of the faith but as essentially unconcerned with the creation of a stable political structure. Chronic political apathy has been the historical consequence. In recent times the weakness of nineteenth-century Muslim rule created a vacuum that was filled by the power and expansionist policies of the West. It was perhaps inevitable that Western models of politics, systems of laws and administration were instituted, and with little opposition. When it was realized finally that such developments were disruptive of traditional Muslim ideals, a rearguard action was fought against Muslim groups (notably the Sufi establishments) which seemed opposed to a new, anti-Western, Muslim structure. Nevertheless, what transpired was an identification of purported Muslim ideals with the local, that is "national," political aspirations, as in the case of Egypt under Nasser. The traditional sense of Muslim unity was thereby seriously threatened. More, traditional Muslim institutions, notably the Shari'ah, were weakened, in some cases to the point of extinction. The Ulama were superceded by the new breed of nationalist leaders, who sought to implicate the unity of Islam, falsely, "in the rivalries and ambitions of secular political forces".[100]

A fundamental dilemma emerged; for the nationalist forces appealed on the one hand to the unity of Islam under the traditional rubrics of Muslim life, and on the other substituted nationalist and socialist aims of Western origin for traditional goals of the Muslim life. What emerged then was not a true nationalism[101] (as in nineteenth-century Europe), but a frantic political rebellion against Western hegemony which sought also to extirpate the non-competitive elements of Islam itself. The Arab nationalists and socialists are heirs to the earlier liberal and modernist attacks on stagnant traditionalism, but refuse any identification with traditional Western democracy, which is to say with Western imperialism. "It can be said that they are gambling with the future, in the expectation or hope that out of the confrontation with the modern world and a reconstructed social order there will emerge a new and acceptable interpretation of Islam, patterned on the lines of their experiment and furnishing emotional support for it".[102]

This movement threatens the core of Muslim tradition, Shari'ah and the Ulama. In Egypt, for example, it disturbed Gibb to see the Ulama act simply as "ad men" for the socialist governments. They had not measured the goals of Arab socialism against the traditional Muslim standards. Fortunately, says Gibb, Egypt under Nasser does not hold the future. In the end, Islam will survive only so long as it is anchored to the Ulama and the Shari'ah. Reformulation and re-interpretation cannot be put off; but they will succeed only insofar as they remain within the boundaries of the tradition.[103]

Von Grunebaum's treatment of reform in Islam is the most extensive, especially with respect to Westernization. In his discussion of medieval Muslim literature, von Grunebaum focuses upon what he holds to be an essential weakness in Islam's attitude toward reform, namely its failure to address the realities of political life. There is, he argues, a clearly discernible trend in this classic period toward literary stereotyping, toward the construction of ideal types, whose chief and only virtue is their literary value. He dubs this tendency "literarization;" its concomitant development is depersonalization. With literarization came the supremacy of the notion of reform of the self, so that it conformed to the literary ideal regardless of the exigencies of history. Of this Muslim ideal he writes:

> Depersonalization naturally entailed a restriction of the interest in reform to an interest in reforming one's self. The ego has to be changed to fit the pattern, to become responsible to, and worthy of, the supreme vision. Their illuminatus is kind and charitable; he may wish to open the high road to God to as many as he can reach, but social conditions as such, the fate of the multitude as such, are none of his concern. The social reformer, unless disguised as prophet or heretic, is not provided for in the scheme of patterns; and the best minds are not interested in his task nor do they feel too keenly the sting of the evils that rouse the socio-political innovator.[104]

It is rhetoric, not justice, he argues, which moves the Muslim. The modernist may decry this fact, but it is irresistible.[105]

Therefore, only the impact of external forces could explain the

modern concerns for reform.[106] Left alone, Muslim civilization would
dream itself to death.[107] This stimulus prompts a painfully ambivalent
response. Whenever some measure of independence has been achieved
or when political ambition "has become a conscious motive of action . . .
a sense of backwardness and the painful realization of the intellectual
impoverishment of the traditional patterns hasten the drive toward
modernization." An ominous logic appears: the drive toward modernization cannot be resisted; and the more powerful that drive the more
obvious the weaknesses of the ancient tradition on which the culture is
founded. The incongruity is overwhelming and the anxiety
appropriate.[108]

The crucial issue here is the distribution of power. The idea that the
people should engage in government, so significant in Western political
theory, is contrary to the Muslim tradition. (It would be better to
compare the rise of democratic aspirations in the Muslim world to the
primitive European movements of 1789 rather than to those of 1918, so
indigestible is the concept.)[109] The conflict is severe, for it pits the
Western view of the state, with its burgeoning participatory ideals
leading to nationalism, against the traditional indifference to the state,
apart from its role of protector of the faith. Traditional Islam left the
state to its own devices and salvation to the individual in his attempt to
conform to the will of Allah. The new and troubling ideals of the
nationalist movements demur from this tradition. Von Grunebaum
writes:

> Ideally, the modern Arab has to be a citizen of the state before being a
> member of his group. This shift in his primary loyalties, accompanying
> the change in the social-economic setting, adds to his freedom in terms of
> social and cultural mobility. It tends to lift him out of the group life and
> to impose full and individualistic independence on him. But, simultane-
> ously, it replaces or at least supplements his individualistic conception of
> personal fulfillment by enjoining cooperation toward the new collective
> goals of community advancement and community power. He is becom-
> ing responsible for the continuance and the progress of an entity whose
> operation he does not yet quite comprehend and whose demands he can,
> for the time being, meet only by the emotional outburst of extreme
> nationalism.[110]

The modern Arab, caught in the logic of this dilemma of Westernization and loyalty to Islam, is forced to choose between Islam and
secularism, or conservatism and modernism, or some Western habits

over others. "He will be aware of the indispensability of foreign assistance but will fall a prey to xenophobia, and in general he will in the same breath hate and love, admire and despise, the West, whose spiritual structure he has no means of understanding, which reveals itself to him most obviously through its technology and political aggressiveness." This marriage of the modern national state and medieval Islam is a "dream of contradictions".[111]

The modern Muslim attempts at self-interpretation in the context of Westernization reveal another fundamental difficulty. For orthodox Islam there is one truth, that of the Qur'an and the Prophet. But while orthodoxy may pronounce on the Islamic way of life, von Grunebaum observes that it is not really concerned with Islamic civilization, that is, does not think of it as a civilization among others. Self-interpretation, then, means only that the "Muslim scene needs scrutiny with respect to its harmony with the unalterable divine ordinance, but not with respect to its cultural elements and the forces responsible for its birth and growth".[112] Let us note in passing that those "forces" do not include, in von Grunebaum's list, faith and the operation of Allah, as the Muslim believes. In contrast, what counts in responsible scrutiny are those insights attainable by "scientific research methods" which "have not yet found universal acceptance." The Muslim, then, is "lamentably ignorant of the origin, development, and achievements of [his] civilization".[113] Thus the Muslim setting out upon the course of self-interpretation will fail; for he does not understand what it is that he is examining, namely Islamic civilization as one civilization among others whose roots are in history only. And, at least according to von Grunebaum, that is the crucial issue of self-interpretation for the Muslim world *vis-a-vis* the West.

That Muslim interpreters are not willing to play the game this way is suggested in von Grunebaum's lament that

> Whatever the modern Near Easterner has to say about his own background and about the West is primarily a political judgment. His presentation is meant to influence rather than describe. A vision of this world as it ought to be, not cognition of this world as it is, is mainspring and goal of his analytical endeavors. Pride and sensitivity not infrequently provide additional temptations to swerve toward semiconscious distortion of the facts.[114]

Moveover, this vision of the ideal Islam clashes with the very notion of progress which the modernists champion. Following a review of Muslim modernists such as Iqbal, Abduh, Qasimi, Kurd Ali, Ali Abdarrizaq, and Haikal, von Grunebaum concludes that the commitment to the paradigm of pristine original Islam forces them to acknowledge, even as they preach progress, an irreversible decline in Muslim history. "The 'best' Islam was that obtaining in the days of the Prophet Muhammad, the next best that practiced by his immediate successors. The world deteriorates and Islam with it . . . . [The] obvious advances registered here or there in a later age do not refute this 'cultural primitivism' in the view of the Muslim".[115]

A further problem for Muslim self-interpretation is the oft-cited Muslim fascination with the technical and mechanical in the West. Von Grunebaum frequently underscores this point: Muslims want to imitate the West in these respects, but refuse to understand, and certainly to incorporate into their own thinking, the philosophical assumptions which underlie science and technology. Although seeking to emulate Western technology, Islam is nevertheless "afraid of accepting the fundamentals of the occidental development lest it lose its center of gravity".[116] The one exception to this rule is the concept of evolution. But even here application of evolutionary thinking is in the service of hope for a resurgence of Muslim power and grandeur. "The belief in evolution is not a result of scientific deliberation; it is the rationalization of the deepest longing of the contemporary East".[117]

Von Grunebaum concludes that Muslim attempts at self-interpretation are flawed by their continued loyalty to a transcendent ideal — that is, if one may put it thus, by their being Muslim. He offers this suggestion for meaningful reform:

> . . . an Islam inspired by a revelation re-interpreted as a Book of humanist directives stressing morality and not legality as the ethical aim of religion and relegating the obsolete legal, social, economic precepts to the background, will be rid of its two paralyzing dilemmas: whether to adopt the attitude of the West to reality, which is at the bottom of its scientific control of nature, or reject it as materialism; and whether to adopt or reject its attitude that holds criticism permissible in the face of any authority.[118]

Von Grunebaum's admiration for Qasimi's book, *Hadi hiya'l-aqhlal* ("These Are The Chains"), is noteworthy. Qasimi's call for reform rests upon a "fiery belief in man." Here is a sign of hope — but for what? At present the process of Westernization in the Muslim world is mired in dilemmas of the sort already described. To extract themselves, Muslims must sweep away those commitments and assumptions that still stand between them and the acceptance of Western culture. The present imitation, says von Grunebaum, may have produced higher rationalization of thought and coordination of economic and political forces; but it will not take up the underlying principles of Western culture. Qasimi's humanism, however, gives a sign of hope for the emergence of just these principles in the Muslim world; ". . . he may well be the harbinger of a genuine and general reversal of the Muslim outlook on man that may, as in the Western Renaissance five centuries ago, release dormant resources of creative energy. It is the revaluation of man that has at all times presaged a cultural renewal".[119] Islam would not lose itself to the West in this movement, but would accept the fundamental structures of thought and action that the West has already established. Islam will cease to be in conflict, then, with the great Western principles of culture; "and therein lies its salvation".[120]

To accomplish this goal the gap between Muslim political self-awareness and cultural self-awareness must be closed. The Muslim world has made no significant contribution to humane scholarship. Even in the study of Muslim culture itself the dominant force is Western in origin and method. One should not, furthermore, "expect any sudden changes".[121] Islam's cultural development lacks a metaphysics "to jus-tify its existence and to encourage its progress in a Westernized world." But the adjustment to the Western model of culture will be hindered by loyalty to the ancient tradition. That is not necessarily a bad thing, von Grunebaum observes; for in the period of cultural lag caused by this conflict a slower but steady adjustment to the Western-dominated world will occur, perhaps staving off the cataclysms inevitable in abrupt change.[122]

What is lacking in the present situation is "not the study of foreign culture, but self-construction, self-manipulation, in the light of the Western phenomenon that must be mastered, whether by a partial assimilation or by purposive recourse to the past".[123] Muslim peoples must Westernize; but von Grunebaum, whose concern is not with the truth of Islam but the academic question of whether Islam can survive in the modern world, is not sanguine.

Westernization is above all an act of the will. Its consummation is eminently adapted to increasing self-confidence once the justification for collective action is perceived (for example, according to the Turkish model) in modernization as such and in the resultant participation in the Western cultural community. And yet this attitude presupposes the belief in the primacy of culture. The duality of the Arab world, which —as one feels tempted to formulate it — recoils before its intrinsic difficulty into politics, impedes that adjustment between a self-view and action, which, experienced as peace and composure, constituted the traditional Muslim mood of life . . . . For without self-confidence sure of its possibilities, a quiet acceptance of the West on the Arabs' part is unthinkable.[124]

I will conclude this presentation of von Grunebaum's views by observing that in demanding the acceptance of the primacy of culture he asks nothing less than a sacrifice of the religious life prescribed and encouraged by the Qur'an and Muhammad. Why would he require it as a condition of survival? The answer is quite obvious: he does not see any fundamental human and saving power in *islam*, i.e., submission to Allah, whatever his views of Islam the religion, the cultural artifact.

After reading our Orientalists' views, we might be tempted to believe that the issue of reform did not arise within the Muslim Ummah until the impact of Western power was felt — from the time, say, of Napoleon's entrance into Egypt. Further, it might seem that reform cannot be separated from some type of Westernization, if we follow von Grunebaum and Guillaume, or from some conservative resistance to Western forces which threaten to corrupt an ideal religion, if we follow Gibb. In either case, we might never suspect that "reform" had ever played any telling part in the history of the Muslim community. As Fazlur Rahman notes, an external observer might conclude —and at times some Muslims concluded — "that Islam has become internally incapable of reconstituting itself and whatever it might do by way of reconstruction, if at all it can, will be done by influences and borrowings from the West." That this conclusion is patently untrue is obvious.[125] Furthermore, the existence of controversialist and apologetic literature, which our Orientalists hold up for criticism, is testimony not so much to the vacuity of Muslim self-interpretation and attempts at reform, but to the pathos of the Muslim response to desperately unfair attacks on the community. "Our contemporary Orientalists," states Rahman, "who complain against these trends do not recognize fully the inner poverty and the superficial logic of the initial Western stand".[126]

The "real challenge that the Muslim society has had to face and is still facing is at the level of social institutions and social ethic as such".[127] This challenge may be traced from Muhammad's time to the present day, and may be expected to continue for so long as there are Muslims. If there is a difference between present and past versions of this challenge, or, to use the Orientalist vocabulary, evidence of a "need for reform," it is certainly not that social institutions in the past have been wrong or irrational. Rather, whereas in the early centuries the community began *ab initio,* so to speak, from a clean slate and created the medieval Muslim society, the present and future issue is how much of that slate is to be wiped clean preparatory to a new entry.[128] This is the perpetual challenge of any religious community. The impact of the West, while not utterly irrelevant, is clearly inferior in importance to this primary challenge to live one's life as a Muslim. The Orientalist will perforce fail to see the issue of "reform" in this way; for he is not concerned with living his life as a *muslim,* but simply with explaining the perceived troubles of Muslim society in a Western-dominated world.

This is not to deny that the Muslim attitude toward the state is culturally problematic. The ambivalence toward the state is inherent in the history of the Ummah. But we should construe the matter as a challenge of faith; for the relationship between the state and the Muslim life will always be as it always has been, one of tension, and for the most part of creative tension. If, for example, the Muslim attitude of our time is that the public must participate in government, then of course some sort of democratic structure must be maintained. But this issue has little if anything to do with the supremacy of Western models, *a la* von Grunebaum. Rahman writes:

> But it is imperative that the Muslims decide the issue *from the inside,* keeping free from external pressures both direct and indirect (in the form of external propaganda), although drawing lessons from the experience of other peoples. They will find the Islamic principles broad enough to admit a varying range of constitutions, within a democratic framework, depending on social and political climates actually obtaining.[129]

In the end the entire notion of reform and the need for it as presented by our Orientalists rests, at best, upon a misunderstanding of the nature and history of the Muslim Ummah and, at worst, upon a deliberate rejection of its true orientation, toward Allah. In the view of A.L. Tibawi, the call for reform from the West has both characteristics. Islam, he argues, consists of two parts: "Apart from being a civilization and a culture, Islam has a creed and laws. Reform of the Creed is, clearly, out of the question because it is utterly unnecessary, whatever an outsider may hold to be true. The laws, on the other hand, have been in a constant state of reform." Thus, to call for reform is to require of Muslims what they have always required of themselves. The demand is, then, both gratuitous and insulting.[130]

Only the Islamic community may judge what is good for it, in light of its faith. In practice and in theory that judgment should be conducted now as it always has been: "The essential test of validity in our own time is still the old one: the consensus of the community and the approval of the *ulama* in the region concerned".[131] This is, to repeat, no innovation, but the way in which Islam has conducted its self-examination from the beginning. That outsiders fail to understand this is the inevitable consequence of failing to appreciate, and certainly to share, the fundamental religious perceptions of the Muslim life, not just in the superficial sense of not being members of a given group but in the more profound sense of failing to know what submission to Allah implies for any person, for any *Muslim*.[132]

The testing for validity in light of the truth has been the constant preoccupation of the Muslim community. In this it has not, insists Tibawi, been too rigid — by whose standards? — in its historical understanding of religious law, as the Orientalists frequently claim. What it has done is to constantly apply the test of purity of life. This is precisely the intention and purpose of its institutions. It is not too much to say, then, that "reform" is a permanent feature of Muslim institutions.[133]

Two final comments concerning the Orientalists' call for reform are appropriate. First, in more recent times (as Tibawi noted in 1979) that call has virtually died away.[134] The reason lies, in part, in the second comment that the Orientalists' "reform" actually meant a combination of secularization and Westernization. The Orientalists who called, or continue to call, for reform "seem unconsciously to reduce the present impact of modern European thought on Islam to a one-way process. Islam must come into line with that thought, but there is no question of modern thought adapting itself to Islam. That is an arrogant assumption which has a built-in reason for its failure to materialize. Hence, the fainter voices of its advocates".[135] For the fact is that Muslims not only have not moved in the direction of secularization but have experienced a rejuvenation of loyalty to their own tradition and have openly rejected those values which the Orientalists insisted were indispensable to the future of Islam. Again, the call for reform was perceived to be both gratuitous and insulting. It cannot be said that the faintness of the call for reform is due to Orientalists' coming to share with the Muslim the sense of Muslim history as a striving for purity in light of the will and truth of Allah. Rather, Orientalists have simply taken note of the fact that Muslims have resisted actively their imposition of non-Muslim values on the interpretation of Islam. They have, in short, simply backed off. There is no sign of a growth in understanding. As noted above, Tibawi's review of the major general sources and treatments of Islam, such as the *Legacy of Islam*, the *Encyclopedia of Islam*, etc., indicated to him that their authors and editors treat Islam with hatred, scepticism and speculation. Redress, he holds, is virtually impossible; for it requires a transformation of the Orientalist into one who loves the Muslim tradition, who knows its faith and tradition to be true. The possibilities for such a transformation, he believes, are virtually nil.[136]

Conclusion: Islam and "islam"

I have attempted to suggest that the Orientalists' critique of Islam rests on a fundamental assumption, that Islam is a cultural artifact requiring interpretation by outsiders. This assumption — which is, so far as I can determine, never defended or discussed despite its significance — means that it is not important to recognize in the tradition any transcendent truth. The Orientalists know, of course, that Muslims believe this; but that is a far different matter than whether the Orientalists believe it. Only in light of this assumption, I am arguing, are their concerns with identifying the essential Islam, with the question of cultural borrowing, and with the need for reform comprehensible. It is, furthermore, highly significant that Muslims themselves find these issues irrelevant and irreverent. The stark contrast between agendas suggests very powerfully, to me at least, that the Orientalists do not believe that the Muslim tradition is an attempt to express and live with, in and for, transcendent truth. The effect of this "atheism" or, perhaps, "agnosticism", is that Orientalists interpret Islam in a specious and self-serving manner, creating an "Islam" consisting entirely of externals. But if the Orientalists were to share in the act of *islam*, of submission to God, or truth, that is to be *Muslims*, the issues which concern them would appear in an entirely different light.

Let me develop this point.

In the first place, Islam would cease to be seen as a "religion" in the sense of being a cultural artifact. As the very word suggests *islam* — a verbal noun — means an ongoing, dynamic process of submission, in history, to Allah. As a process, then, it is not static, but new every day, a tradition living in creative tension with the World of Allah and the exigencies and demands of human history. We may go further: since it is not merely a cultural artifact, it must be a tradition and a life of faith from which no one is barred — on the contrary, it demands (literally) that everyone accept the truth when it is presented to them, that everyone live, as rigorously as they are able, in accordance with that truth. The fact that *islam* is an Arabic term is, of course, highly significant; but what it conveys is more so. It conveys a truth open to all, a truth to which all are called to attest to in word, thought and deed.

The proper study of Islam, then, should be directed toward the understanding, at the very least, of the problems and possibilities of the Muslim community in light of Allah's command, and, at best, toward the involvement of the student in that truth and the tradition that embodies it. Such a study cannot be conducted on the assumption that Islam is a cultural artifact of a "religious type." That is precisely, however, what the Orientalist is attempting to do, when he reduces Islam to its historical and cultural expressions. If one must speak of the "essence" of Islam at all, it is in the word's meaning, submission to Allah, to God, to Truth. That act is limited neither to the historical "religion" nor to outsiders. We are all, one hopes, *muslim*. The study of *islam* is, in the final analysis, a study of the faith of other men *and* our own faith. The proper study of Islam, then, calls for participation in the truth of the tradition, and thus for understanding of its daily renewal of the command to submit in every respect to God. Is "Islam" true? The Orientalists must say no, I think, and we should agree with them — insofar as they refer to the cultural artifact of their own creation. But the question of truth must be referred to God; *islam*, as submission to God, must then be true by definition, although *Muslims*, Arab-speaking and others, fail from time to time to submit fully. Abduh's famous comment that there is nothing wrong with *islam*, only with *Muslims*, must then apply to us all, not only to the others whom we hope to understand. *Islam* is true both in the sense of submission and in its role as the *din*, the tradition, which is the way, the path for *Muslims*. How could it be false?

Second, if we can accept this approach, the "issue" of cultural borrowing as the Orientalists define it must be abandoned as a meaningful question in the interpretation of Islamic history. As I have tried to show, the Orientalist sets himself the goal of discovering what Muhammad and Islam owe, and how much, to other traditions, and how this borrowing has determined the nature and face of Islam. This method is wholly consistent with the assumption that Islam is a cultural artifact requiring an exploration of its origins and history.

Now, it is obvious to all, especially *Muslims*, that *islam* means submission in human history — thus, *pace* von Grunebaum, history is sanctified as the context in which *islam* may be achieved. Indeed, the emergence of Muhammad and the proclamation of the Qur'an is miraculous in Muslim eyes precisely because it occurred in history, in a community, among other communities. The absolute was manifested, revealed, in time. Nor was it an invention, but by nature that which was true at all times and before "time." The miracle of the Qur'an, then, is to be understood to require a cultural, historical setting.

From the Orientalists' perspective, Muhammad and the Qur'an pose a problem: where did these ideas and thoughts come from? Similarities are sought, causal sequences established, influences weighed. Orientalists search for the origins of the Qur'an in the only place they think they can be found, in the cultural setting. The Muslim position, on the contrary, is that the Qur'an is not borrowed from others: it is a restatement and thus its proclamation, or re-proclamation, is a purification of the expression of the truth already known, however distorted and obscured. The link with the cultural setting is thus absolutely crucial to the Muslim revelation; but that setting reflects, for better or worse, the revealed transcendent truth of God. In implicitly rejecting this view the Orientalists present what seems to me to be a parody of *islam*, a pastiche of sources and gleanings from other traditions. The result is of course offensive to Muslims. An Islam composed of bits and pieces from other cultures serves the Orientalists' purpose; but it is arrant blasphemy.

In sum, the Orientalists have got the matter the wrong way round: Islam did not borrow from other cultures; cultures "borrow," that is reflect, *islam*.

Third, the Orientalists' treatment of Islam as a cultural artifact only lays the foundation for a truly remarkable conclusion, that Islam must reform. Regardless of the program espoused, the Orientalist can think of reforming Islam only after he has established its essence in the manner I have described. But this is gratuitous and insulting. *Islam,* as submission to Allah, *is* "reform," in the sense that it is persistent and profound attempt to live one's life in the face of God, *coram Deo.* In ignoring the transcendent significance and meaning of the Muslim tradition, Orientalists have placed the issue of the survival of a cultural artifact before the more compelling question of transcendent truth. They then urge Muslims to accept this priority and alter their lives accordingly. This is tantamount to a denial of the fundamental nature of the Muslim tradition, to saying that Islam is nothing more than its history, its problems, its contradictions — that it is not aspiration and dedication to the truth. No *muslim* — of any nationality or race — could possibly accept this view.

Bernard Lewis wrote recently that only Orientalists could criticize Orientalism.[137] He intends this conclusion as a summary of his defense of Orientalists. In fact, it is a self-condemnation. If the issues raised here are kept in mind, it seems clear that the Orientalist agenda is irrelevant to the fundamental concerns of *islam*, and in its tone and argumentation degrading, condescending and frankly insulting. I believe that Tibawi is entitled to his sometimes choleric opinion of Orientalism; for it seems to me quite impossible to understand the *muslim* tradition unless it is accepted for what it is, a submission to God. In that light it must be understood, and shared.[138]

NOTES

1. *A recent demonstration of the truth of the observation is Bernard Lewis',* "The Question of Orientalism," *The New York Review of Books,* XXIX:11, pp. 49-56 (June 24, 1982). Summing up a vigorous attack on Edward Said, he writes, "The most rigorous and penetrating critique of Orientalist scholarship has always been and will remain that of the Orientalists themselves."

2. In a treatment this brief I must perforce choose representatives of the Orientalist tradition and thus risk some simplification. However, in drawing largely from the works of Gustave von Grunebaum, H.A.R. Gibb, Maxime Rodinson and Alfred Guillaume I have, I believe, risked little.

3. H.A.R. Gibb, *Mohammedanism: An Historical Survey* (New York: New American Library, 1953, 2nd ed.), n.p.

4. *Ibid.*, p. 84.

5. *Ibid.*, pp. 144-5.

6. *Ibid.*, pp. 43-4.

7. H.A.R. Gibb, *Modern Trends in Islam* (Chicago: The University of Chicago Press, 1947), pp. 46-8.

8. *Ibid.*, pp. 109-110.

9. *Ibid.*, pp. 122, 123.

10. *Ibid.*, pp. 120-121.

11. H.A.R. Gibb, "Religion and Politics in Christianity and Islam," in *Islam and International Religions,* ed. J. Harris Proctor (New York: Frederick A. Praeger, 1965), p. 21, *et passim.*

12. *Cf. Edward W. Said, Orientalism* (New York: Pantheon Books, 1978).

13. Maxime Rodinson, "A Critical Survey of Modern Studies on Muhammad," in *Studies on Islam,* trans. and ed. Merlin L. Swartz (New York: Oxford University Press, 1981) (Orig. *"Bilan des etudes mohammediennes, Revue Historique,* 229 (1963)), pp. 25, 52.

14. *Gustave E. von Grunebaum, "Problems of Muslim Nationalism," in Islam and the West: Proceedings of the Harvard Summer School Conference on the Middle East, July 25-27, 1955,* ed. Richard N. Frye ('S-Gravenhage: Mouton & Co., 1957), p. 13.

15. Gustave E. von Grunebaum, *Medieval Islam: A Study in Cultural Orientation* (Chicago: The University of Chicago Press, 1953), pp. 240-1.

16. Gustave E. Von Grunebaum, *Islam: Essays in the Nature and Growth of a Cultural Tradition* (New York: Barnes and Noble, 1961), p. 6.

17. von Grunebaum, *Medieval Islam,* p. 233.

18. *Ibid.*, p. 230.

19. *Ibid.*, p. 324.

20. *Ibid.*, p. 344.

21. von Grunebaum, *Essays,* p. 159.

22. von Grunebaum, *Medieval Islam,* p. 108, cf. p. 142.

23. von Grunebaum, *Essays,* pp. 66f.

24. *Ibid.*, p. 112.

25. von Grunebaum, *Medieval Islam*, pp. 346-7, cf. pp. 345-6.

26. von Grunebaum, *Essays,* p. 227.

27. *Ibid.*, p. 244.

28. von Grunebaum, *Medieval Islam,* pp. 345-6.

29. *Ibid.,* 320-1.

30. *Ibid.*, pp. 323-4.

31. Fazlur Rahman, *Islam* (Garden City, New York: Doubleday & Co., Inc., 1968; orig. Holt, Rinehart, Winston, 1966), p. 261.

32. *Ibid.*, p. 262.

33. *Ibid.*

34. Gustave E. von Grunebaum, *Modern Islam: The Search for Cultural Identity* (New York: Vintage Books, 1964; orig. University of California Press, 1962), p. v.

35. A. L. Tibawi, "English-Speaking Orientalists: A Critique of Their Approach to Islam and Arab Nationalism," *The Muslim World,* LIII:3 and 4 (July and October, 1963), p. 194; cf. A. L. Tibawi, "Second Critique of English-Speaking Orientalists and Their Approach to Islam and the Arabs," *The Islamic Quarterly,* XXIII:1 (January-March, 1979), pp. 4-8.

36. Tibawi, "Critique" (1963), p. 200.

37. *Ibid.* p. 201.

38. *Ibid.*, p. 202; cf. George Makdisi's discussion of "orthodoxy" in Muslim history, "Hanbalite Islam," in Swartz, *Studies on Islam* (orig. *"L'Islam Hanbalisant,"* Revue des Etudes Islamiques, 42, 43 (1974, 1975).

39. Tibawi, "Critique" (1963), p. 202.

40. Tibawi, "Second Critique," pp. 22-3.

41. Gibb, *Mohammedanism,* pp. 43-4.

42. *Ibid.*, pp. 59-60.

43. von Grunebaum, *Essays,* pp. 13-14.

44. *Ibid.*

45. von Grunebaum, *Medieval Islam,* p. 3.

46. *Ibid.*

47. *Ibid.*, p. 69.

48. *Ibid.*, p. 82.

49. Islam suffered in its profound dependence upon Christianity and Judaism from the fact that it met neither at its best; and yet, writes von Grunebaum, "it may be doubted if

the theory of the Fathers and the ethics of the Rabbis would have proved stronger stimuli to the Prophet than the somewhat vague concoction of a humanitarian monotheism from which he gleaned a variety of concepts, wise sayings, and narrative matter . . . ." *Ibid.*, pp. 322-4.

50. Alfred Guillaume, *Islam* (London: Penguin, 2nd ed. rev., 1956), pp. 60 ff.

51. *Ibid.*

52. *Ibid.*, p. 59.

53. Rodinson, pp. 54, 55.

54. *Ibid.*, p. 25.

55. *Ibid.*, pp. 50-1.

56. *Ibid.*, pp. 57-8.

57. J. Fueck, "The Originality of the Arabian Prophet," in Swartz, *Studies on Islam* (orig. "Die Orginalitat des arabischen Propheten," *Zeitschrift der Deutschen Morgenlandischen Gelellschaft*, 90 (1936) pp. 89-90.

58. *Ibid.*

59. *Ibid.*, p. 92.

60. *Ibid.*, p. 97.

61. Tibawi, "Second Critique," pp. 10, 11.

62. Tibawi, "Critique" (1963), pp. 194-5.

63. Gibb, *Modern Trends*, p. 7.

64. But see also Guillaume, p. 193.

65. Von Grunebaum, *Essays*, pp. 14-15.

66. *Ibid.*, p. 15.

67. Von Grunebaum, *Medieval Islam*, pp. 39-40.

68. *Ibid.*, p. 120.

69. *Ibid.*, pp. 164-5.

70. *Ibid.*, p. 323.

71. *Ibid.*, pp. 3, 323-4.

72. *Ibid.*, pp. 320-321.

73. *Ibid.*

74. V), *Faith and Belief* (Princeton: Princeton University Press, 1979), and *Towards a World Theology* (London: The Macmillan Company, 1981).

I should say also that although, inevitably, I have referred to Orientalists in general, not all of them agree with Lewis or von Grunebaum, among others. This is true obviously of Wilfred Cantwell Smith; but others, too, fall outside the category I have taken as my subject here. For further remarks on this point see Pruett, "The Escape from the Seraglio."

79. *Ibid.*, p. 28.

80. von Grunebaum, *Medieval Islam,* pp. 341-2.

81. von Grunebaum, *Essays,* p. 228.

82. Tibawi, "Critique" (1963), p. 194.

83. Guillaume, p. 59.

84. *Ibid.*, pp. 155-7. See Rodinson, p. 51.

85. Guillaume, p. 158.

86. *Ibid.*, p. 169.

87. *Ibid.*, p. 193.

88. *Ibid.*, p. 155.

89. Gibb, *Modern Trends,* pp. 126-7.

90. *Ibid.*, p. 42, cf. p. 54.

91. *Ibid.*, p. 94.

92. *Ibid.*, pp. 103-4.

93. *Ibid.*, p. 104, cf. pp. 112-3.

94. *Ibid.*, p. 123.

95. Gibb, *Mohammedanism,* pp. 133-4.

96. *Ibid.*

97. Gibb, *Modern Trends,* pp. 120-1.

98. *Ibid.*, p. 123.

99. Gibb, "Religion and Politics," pp. 21-2.

100. *Ibid.*, pp. 16-7.

101. *Ibid.*, pp. 18-9.

102. *Ibid.*, pp. 20-1.

103. Cf. Gibb, *Mohammedanism*, pp. 142ff.

104. von Grunebaum, *Medieval Islam,* pp. 231ff.

105. von Grunebaum, *Essays,* p. 69.

106. We must begin with Napoleon's expedition to Egypt, von Grunebaum concludes, in any history of new enlivenment of Muslim civilization.

107. von Grunebaum, *Essays,* p. 29.

108. *Ibid.*, pp. 72-3.

109. *Ibid.*, p. 75.

110. *Ibid.*, p. 76.

111. *Ibid.*, p. 77.

112. *Ibid.*, p. 185.

113. *Ibid.*

114. *Ibid.*, p. 186.

115. *Ibid.*, p. 127, cf. pp. 198ff.

116. *Ibid.*, p. 229.

117. *Ibid.*

118. *Ibid.*, p. 230, cf. von Grunebaum, *Modern Islam*, p. 71.

119. von Grunebaum, *Essays*, p. 321.

120. *Ibid.*, p. 244.

121. *Ibid.*, pp. 244-5.

122. *Ibid.*, p. 245.

123. von Grunebaum, *Modern Islam*, p. 213.

124. *Ibid.*, pp. 242-3.

125. Rahman, p. 282.

126. *Ibid.*, p. 265.

127. *Ibid.*, p. 264.

128. *Ibid.*

129. *Ibid.*, p. 298.

130. Tibawi, "Critique" (1963), p. 201.

131. *Ibid.*, p. 202.

132. *Ibid.*

133. *Ibid.*, pp. 298-9.

134. In reviewing the work of, among others, Beeston and Serjeant, Tibawi expresses satisfaction with those who stay within the subject of Arab literary survivals and do not stray into the "dangerous realms of religion and politics." It is noteworthy, he says, that, with the exception of Kenneth Cragg, "none of the present generation of Orientalists shows the keen interest of their predecessors [e.g., Anderson, Guillaume] in the call for the 'reform' of Islam." Tibawi, "Second Critique," p. 14.

135. *Ibid.*

136. *Ibid.*, pp. 22-3.

137. Bernard Lewis, "The Question of Orientalism."

138. Readers familiar with the field of comparative religious studies will have noted my indebtednes to Wilfred Cantwell Smith in this essay. I happily acknowledge that debt. See Gordon E. Pruett, "The Escape from the Seraglio: Anti-Orientalist Trends in Modern Religious Studies," *Arab Studies Quarterly*, 2:4 (Fall, 1980), pp. 291-317. For Smith's major contributions to understanding the Muslim tradition, see, for example, *The Meaning and End of Religion* (New York: Mentor, 1964), *Questions of Religious Truth* (New York: Charles

4

THE ARTICULATION OF ORIENTALISM

Aziz Al-Azmeh

The Arabs attain as perfect a facility in writing and reading as the Europeans themselves.[2]

(Volney)

In the Semitic myth of the fall a series of preeminently feminine affects was considered the origin of evil. What distinguishes the Aryan notion is the sublime view of active sin as the characteristically promethean virtue.

(Nietzsche)

Two statements which, but for reference to things Oriental, have nothing in common.[1] Two statements with reference to the Orient, one in its specifically Arab and another in its more generally Semitic mode, but which nevertheless differ utterly in denotative import. Yet both, as we shall see, are constituted by elements from the same province of reality formed into terms of the same semantic universe. We need only look closely at Volney's statement to restitute the significance it loses in the facile triviality which makes it appear altogether absurd. And we must likewise study the meaning of Nietzsche's statement in order to recover the level of significance where it becomes, in a very specific sense, a cognate of Volney's.

What Volney finds particularly arresting is not the Arabs' facility in writing *per se*. This in itself is very unremarkable. What Volney's statement conceals is a proposition to the effect that the relation between Arabs and the skills of literacy is one so entirely lacking in self-evidence as to require special mention. In contrast, and for the opposite reasons, one can safely state that a parallel statement about, say, Frenchmen or Greeks could not be envisaged. It is that utter lack of self-evidence, and hence openness to a hidden vastness of significance, that translates that statement in question from the realm of sheer redundancy to that of determinate relevance. And it is thus that the ordinariness of Volney's statement registers as extraordinariness with the recovery of propositions hidden by this ordinariness and the implicit line of argumentation that runs parallel to them.

Volney thought his observation remarkable because of an implicitly held line of argumentation. Whereas a natural relation does exist between Europeans and the skills of literacy, the connection between literacy and things Arabic is by no means so direct and natural, and is thus occasion for clear reflection and explicit note. That with respect to literacy the Arabs fare as the Europeans is noteworthy precisely because the former are so unlike the latter that instances of concordance must perforce be recorded. Without this absolute difference between Arabs and Europeans, Volney's comparative statement on the quality of their respective literacy would have been absurd for its own author. The Arabs attain one facility which bewildered Volney despite the wretchedness of their culture;[2] and this wretchedness makes their literacy all the more remarkable. In order to be comparable to Europeans and thus be literate the Arabs must be denied one element that should properly belong to their nature, and this denial is the criterion of significance of the trite observation that Arabs can read and write with perfect facility. The disnaturation of the Arabs with respect to literacy is the precondition of affirming the relation that binds them to literacy. By being disnatured, they are robbed of their positive qualities and endowed with the contrasts of those qualities. Hence literacy is apprehended as a betrayal of specificity. Consequently it could not be expressed in terms of itself: the proposition concerning its occurrence had to take the form of a contrasting statement. Its lack of self-evidence is in fact an index of a lack of wholesome integrality. The oddity, the disnature, is of necessity extrinsic to the real substance of things Arabic. Hence it is only comprehensible, indeed, it can only be articulated, in terms of a strict comparison with things European.

The Orient in Volney, specified by the Arabs, is therefore a negative form of the Occident as specified by "The Europeans themselves." Nietzsche's negative is, by comparison, boundless. Nietzsche (not to be blamed for the misinterpretations of posterity) was content with nothing less than Semites and Aryans as representative of the absolute contrast. In the statement quoted, the scourge of Christianity is making a rhetorical digression in the context of unravelling the sublime elements of the Hellenic spirit, to which the Semitic (Biblical, Judaeo-Christian) is explicitly counterposed by way of explication, illustration, and contrastive determination.[3] In the same text, Nietzsche tells his reader that the Semitic myth of the fall is laden with the "pre-eminently feminine affects" of "curiosity, mendacious deception, susceptibility to seduction, lust". Not so the Aryan, one must presume: determinedly impregnatorial rather than susceptible to seduction, manifestly virtuous rather than stealthily perfidious, resolute rather than curious, and totally undefiled, the Aryan myth of Prometheus is a constant and total affirmation. That the circles of connotation in which the terms Christianity and feminity are embedded here intersect is a specifically Nietzschean achievement. But it is an achievement which certainly evinces far more than yet another statement of mysogyny.

In order for Christianity, the religion of sober and manly Prussians, to be made effeminate, it had to be subjected to a lexical expatriation which affected a total alteration in its semantic properties: it had to be metamorphosed into Semitism. A similiar process had to take place in order for Semitism and femininity to stand for one another. The association of Semites and femininity could only be established through the contrast of Semites and Aryans. Semitism not only stands for a determinate sense of the myth of the fall, but has the far more comprehensive function of contrasting the positivity of Greece with a sheer negativity. Semitism is the carrier of a general negativity (in contrast to Aryanism, the carrier of positivity) and negativity for virtually all cultures — not least bourgeois-capitalist society — and Nietzsche certainly did not exclude femininity as a representative type. Hellenes and Christians are therefore contrasted indirectly: their contrast is simulated by terms, Semitic and Aryan, which can readily bear contrast regardless of the content of this contrast and which can thus represent negativity and positivity. The proposition on Greek sublimity is articulated into a statement of determinate positivity of the Promethean myth of sin by means of a contrastive rhetoric whose articulus is the contrast between East and West, an articulus that endows it with determinate sense over and above the particular act of Prometheus, one that integrates the theft of the godly fire into a context that not only underlies the universal significance of Prometheus, but which also serves to reinforce its unique specificity. Hence positivity with respect to all else, and hence the ease with which its sense is transferred onto the term Aryanism, which, in the context of the Aryan/Semitic dyad, is the carrier of an almost universal positivity.

Both Nietzsche's and Volney's statements therefore stem from, and are only made possible by, a contrastive sense that binds the connotative import of Orient and Occident. They are realized within a construct of reality in which things Eastern and things Western are defined by their mutual contrariety, a realm of reality structured by a polar opposition of Orient and Occident (in various avatars: Arab, Semitic, Aryan, European) in which the latter carries normative ascendancy and consequently stands in a paradigmatic position with respect to the former. The former, therefore, is conceived as the mirror image of the paradigmatic Occident and thus a repository of negativity, both as abstract negativity and as particular negativities with respect to things Occidental (literacy, sublimity, etc.). Occident and Orient constitute together a field of reality which generates entities whose reality is prescribed and assured by placement in that field.

It is in the field of the play of negativity and antonymy that the isotopy of Nietzsche's and Volney's statements is displayed. For in both cases we witness the utilization of what was designated as *topos* in that great inventory of the rules of all discourse, antique and medieval rhetoric. We witness in both cases the readiness with which the dyadic *topos* Orient/Occident realizes a proposition and forms it into a meaningful statement.[4] This dyadic *topos*, we have seen, provides semantic force to the propositions realized. This *topos* realizes the propositions by articulating their elements into conceptual units. The normative primacy of Prometheus was conceptualized in terms of this *topos*. And this same *topos* realized the literary facility of the Arabs. In both cases, it was the dyadic relations of the element of this *topos* that engendered the conceptual means of passage between proposition and statement. For had this dyad not been capable of generating discursive units which organize portions of the empirical manifold into thematic units, it would have been incapable of serving as a *topos*.

After all, a *topos* only becomes discursively effective if it acts as a mode of connotative lines of force which draws into itself multifarious thematic units and appropriates them. It is only thus that it can serve as an element in a connected discourse and in the statements that compose the connected elements of this discourse. The means by which a *topos* acquires this modal quality is a metaphorics of discourse in which a semasiological transference of referential elements between one word and another occurs, and hence a transference of the denotative reference of these words between one thematic portion of the empirical manifold and another. In this way a word could denote more than one thing only and could transfer its normative sense to other cognate or contiguous words which in their turn would take on this quality. It is thus that the semantic fields of Orient and Occident are activated in terms of the Orient/Occident dyad. For it is in this way that the material of meaning transferred from 'West' to, say, 'Progress', makes 'progress' Western by endowing it with the positive normative property in the contrastive context. And it is the very same way that the Semites become feminine, and the Arabs, by a positive and explicit comparison with the Europeans themselves (and hence by stealth), require the accoutrements of civilization.

II

In terms of the discrete elements to which they refer, the statements that we have been analyzing are related by pure difference. Yet we have seen that they meet on a common territory which goes beyond their abstact givenness and founds them as semantic and discursive units, endowing them with the reality that is born of the act of constituting them. That territory is Orientalism, which transforms the senseless abstraction of their thematic givenness into determinate thematic and semantic coherence by giving them this territory which constitutes the conditions of possibility of the statements studied, it is the *sine qua non* for articulating propositions about things Oriental into the form of statements. Orientalism it is that designates empirical material, Oriental material, draws it out of the well of inert images and signs that float unstructured in the obscure regions of Western collective representation, and validates it as a distinct and functional *topos,* and then further allows this *topos* to be transformed into determinate conceptual content with a determinate reference to the empirical manifold, i.e. into a unit of discourse, a unit of meaning and logical function. The conceptual contiguity of matters such as those raised by Volney and Nietzsche, amid topical and empirical disparateness, underlies the main theses presented in this article. It is proposed that Orientalism is composed of statements that utilize units of theme and units of discourse which carry an Oriental designation, and that the very use of such a thematic class (and this article is concerned only with Islam and the Arabs) takes on, wherever it may be embedded as a *topos*, or whenever it is directly named (as the Islamic City, as Oriental Voluptuousness) and treated in its own right, a negative normative assignation.[5] This normative property invariably acquires the form of a positive description of the East which is directly derived from the inversion of sense affecting terms by which things Occidental are apprehended (amorphous Islamic city/European municipal communality, casuistic intellect/philosophical free rationalism, etc.) — it is thus that reality in terms of the Orient/Occident dyad is defined. It is the inversion of sense to which the latter is subject that produces units of discourse which organize the empirical manifold on behalf of the former.

The corollary to these propositions is that, thus generated to populate the Oriental world, the units of Orientalist discourse represent a world related to the West by absolute difference in which the entities called Oriental have a specificity which immures them within a nature totally other than that of things Western. This renders their intelligibility a matter acceptable only to a caste formed by the penetration of this disnature. The Orient is the preserve of the expert; it is as expert that the historian of the Middle East is dubbed "rabist" or "Islamist" before he is described as a historian, just as it is the expert on the Middle East who explains Islam to television viewers rather than any other species of commentator; such is required by the weirdness of the Orient. The parallel with "China watching" and "Kremlinology" is very striking, for Communism in the ideology of the cold war carries connotations akin to those of Islam.

The statements of Volney and Nietzsche subsist together in the space where the whole of the Orient resides and from whence it receives its reality. It is the space where everything Oriental is organized in the form of units which makes their identification as segments of the empirical manifold possible, as well as making possible the discourse upon them. It is as Oriental units that they can be seen, apprehended, and discursively organized. And it is this space of fictions which performs the rigorous exercise of what has been described as the "optimum diversity" which defines human societies in relation to one another.[6] Optimum diversity truly reigns within the Orient/Occident dyad: relations between Orient and Occident have been antagonistic ever since the latter became a reflexive cultural category at first episodically in the Carolingian Renaissance and later concertedly and systematically with the Crusades in Spain and in the Levant. And this optimum diversity is very rigorously exercised in the very foundation of the Orient and naturally preserves the historical foundations of academic Orientalism as polemic — from the days of John of Damascus through Peter the Venerable and on to Raymond Lull, Alexander Ross, and the later tenants of teaching positions in Oriental faculties throughout the West.[7]

A polemic is not just a discourse on deficiencies in general, it is the discourse of an essence addressing its privations, the discourse of the truth upon that which lacks its inner determinations in terms of those very determinations. It is therefore little wonder that Orientalism generates its units of discourse, the very facts into which it segments the empirical manifold as well as its concepts, by inverting the inner sense of categories by which things Western are apprehended. This genera- tion by inverse derivation accounts for the very existence of things Oriental as indeed of the Orient itself and it is this which forms the primary operation of Orientalist analytics, the operation which trans- forms a cultural element into a distinct *topos*, and articulates this *topos* by transforming it into a distinct unit of discourse, and which controls this operation throughout by constant reference to the terms of the Western norm whose inversion of sense supplies the operation with its subjects, and thus makes possible the concrete discourse on the Orient.[8]

We shall not take up the *topoi* that form the Orient in its topical capacity. The general forms in which these *topoi* have been apprehended in European literate culture have been very well described in Edward Said's phenomenology of Orientalism, [9] where the units of Orientalist discourse are likened to a harlequinade, for "underlying all the different units of Orientalist discourse by which I mean simply the vocabulary employed whenever the Orient is spoken or written about — is a set of representative figures or tropes."[10] Our purpose here is not a phenom- enology (for this task has in the main been achieved) but the fundamen- tals of an analytics of Orientalism — the generation and the form of units which make Oriental reality and Orientalist discourse possible, the identification of things Oriental and their conceptualization in the form of units of discourse with various functions. The analytics of Oriental- ism is the set of rules by which the Orient is conjured. It describes the operations by means of which Orientalist entities are manufactured and the Orientalist world organized, the means of passage between Occidental and Oriental terms, and the means of connection between Oriental terms themselves and their formation into statements.

First it must be noted that the units ranged under the substance and principle "Orient" (substance and "principle" and employed in the sense of the Greek *arche* or the medieval Arabic *asl*)[11] which are the thematic units carrying the normative properties of the Orient, such as the Islamic city or Islamic law, relate to Orient and Occident in two distinct manners. They relate to the Orient by reproducing it: Islamic law has structures which correspond to those of the Islamic city, and this isomorphy extends to all other things that are defined as Islamic and reproduce the structures of Islamism. In other words, each instance of Islamicism is merely a reconfirmation of this Islamicism. The isomorphy of things Islamic merely confirms each of them in its being-Islamic. The professional Orientalist therefore has as his task the embedding within the Islamic realm of that which Orientalism decrees as appertaining to it. Thus, if he engages in the study of, say, Islamic law, he would be performing two operations. He would describe its structure in terms of that which reverses the sense of law, such as casuistry and abstract rigidity (and hence unreality, and consequently, propensity to corruption). He would now explain this by reducing its details to properties which compose the semantic field of the term 'Islam' whose precise members will emerge in the course of this article. And he would multiply philological and historical information which thematically appertains to the field of jurisprudence in its Western concept and divisions. This mass of detail is organized according to the exigencies of the severe teleology of Islamicism which reduces everything to unity under its name. This organization is undertaken with view to confirming appurtenance to Islamism, to emphasizing its insertion in the ontological fields of being-Islamic.[12].

In this way, the Orientalist therefore describes by adducing and enumerating what he calls 'facts' according to the pedestrian metaphysic of facticity which he cherishes so much. The idolatry of this pedestrianism is practiced under the name of "objectivity." This is well expressed in, say, the structures of Hamilton Gibb against the far superior intellect of Louis Massignon. The latter, Gibb maintained, composed his works in "as it were, two registers" — one at "the ordinary level of objective scholarship" and another containing properly processed "data", i.e. science distinct from sheer learning, which

Gibb reduces to "objective data . . . absorbed and transformed by an individual intuition of spiritual dimensions."[13] For the Orientalist therefore, the particular in its facitity is objective, and any attempt to establish a relation between the particular and the context of its particularity is reduced to arbitrary passion.

A work of synthesis is therefore seen as the sheer summation of its elements, and the factoidal fetishism of the Orientalist integrates his detailed statement of fact with his conceptual structure. This leads to the constant, systematic disassociation of particulars from any discursive context other than the Orientalist and so activates the implicit claim of Orientalism, confirming the exclusive appurtenance of the enumerated particulars to the Orientalist realm. The disassociation of particulars from contexts of history — sociological, cultural, etc. — is a necessary condition for confirming their Islamicism. Such disassociation renders them vulnerable to their conceptual orientation away from that required by the real world into that required by the fiction of the Orient.

This is why Orientalism is (ideally) exhaustively enumerative. Said described it, *mutatis mutandis,* as "absolutely anatomical and enumerative: to use its vocabulary is to engage in the particularizing and dividing of things Oriental into managable parts."[14] It is not, though, the utilitarianism of manageability that is at work in Orientalist taxology. The classificatory placement of units under generic headings serves the grand tautology of Orientalism, by relating all that is Islamic to the syntagmatic class of Islamicism and by confirming Islam as the author of all things Islamic. Orientalism is therefore not at all surprisingly the procedure which identifies thematic units and gathers them under the aegis of thematic classes which never rise beyond what Hegel in his *Phenomenology* termed the "attitude of sensation," the "that there" (*Dies-Da*) stage of consciousness, a naive retrograde sensualism which, outside Orientalism, was never articulated with as much crudity except by some deservedly obscure late German positivists such as Maleschitt.

Orientalism is therefore a mode of apprehension and of perception, and not one of knowledge. It identifies themata of an Islamic nature. Hence the profusion of works of what Croce described as "sumptuous ignorance." The multiplication of detail with little coherence beyond the litany of the Orient — litany joylessly recorded by Oriental philologists profoundly ignorant of the science of language, by historians

profoundly ignorant of historiography, students of literature profoundly ignorant of literature, and even by anthropologists without
much interest in the science of anthropology.[15] Needless to say, this is
reproduced by the structure of studies in Oriental faculties throughout
the Western world, where it is still possible to obtain a doctoral degree
on the basis of editing a text — in effect, such a reading exercise and a
test of basic library skills is testimony of the mastery over things
Oriental.[16] For such is the objective skill transmitted to students by the
primary tissue of Orientalism — university teachers — by constituting
its physical foundation in the form of verbal and written instruction
embedded in academic institutions whose paradigmatic substance is
provided by the implicit categories that permeate all reference to things
Oriental.

The authority of the intellectually neutered scriptor whom Orientalists are wont to regard as exemplary is, as we have seen, based upon the
capacity to multiply facts of a generic appurtenance which fall under a
specific thematic class. Yet there is nothing profligate about the endless
multiplication of detail which the Orientalist proffers. For with the lack
of a conceptual agency capable of setting limits to the necessary, and
clearly identifying the supererogatory and the superfluous, the profusion of particulars takes on an entirely different coloration in the guise
of positive explication. An enumerative discipline such as Orientalism
can only be maintained by the multiplication of numbers, and these
numbers constitute so many subdivisions within the substance of the
thematic class. They repeat it, instantiate it in empirical multiplicity,
but neither analytically elaborate it nor elevate its sensuous materiality
beyond exactly that — sensuous materiality.

The selection of segments from the empirical manifold to serve as
facts, then their assimilation to *topoi*, followed by their designation as
thematic classes and units of discourse, is therefore fundamentally an act
of nomenclature. It is an operation whereby these units are apportioned
to a category and act as members of its litter of denotata. Enumerative
explication by the adduction of discrete illustrations is really the provision of external indices which gesture towards its conclusion. The
arrangement of units of discourse devoid of intrinsic relation between
elements of content or between this and statement can therefore only be
paratactic, an arrangement in which the discrete units of content are
ordered by sheer textual consecution, so that an abecedarian order is

just as acceptable as any other. That is why, incidently, one can argue that the *Encyclopaedia of Islam* and its cognates are the quintessential products of Orientialism. Whatever connected narration there is is not, given the discreteness of the detail, a correlative of the act of cataloguing. It is not the import of statements as much as the result of a superimposed order of consequence.[17]

This superimposed order of consequence is exclusively reductive within the grand tautology of Orientalism — all that is not within ceases to be Orientalist. Orientalist discourse regards the nomenclature of thematic entities, their designation as Islamic as its proper task, and the naming of these units is undertaken in terms of a higher generic reality to which these units are said to appertain and to which they are assimilated, a thematic class, ultimately "the Orient", to which are apportioned, and which appropriates, the visible units falling under its rubric.[18] In this process whereby details are assimilated to a generalized thematic unit which makes the Oriental by calling them so, we do not see the establishment of a necessary logical connection with the higher generic entity which we have designated "thematic class". We see the appendage and attribution of details (not attributes) to a substance.[19] The thematic units appertaining to a thematic class lead, in themselves, an indexal and gestural existence, pointing beyond their singularity to another to which they belong. They confirm this property of theirs by acting as what Barthes termed "informants" which provide the empirical fillings of a topical class and provide it with the mantle of reality by virtue of being discrete units of content without correlative narrative effects.

Reduction to a thematic class — say, "orthodoxy" or "the Islamic city" — goes by the name of "influence." The search for influences and the establishment of lineages of fecundation is the sole structure of any consequence in Orientalist discourse. At the root of each lineage is an origin which is what is taken as a paradigmatic fact or the act establishing a thematic class — the Koran with respect to piety or modesty for instance — and at the root of all origins is a common origin of origins which establishes the integrality of every detail and endows it with special (i.e. Islamic) significance. This Demiurge is Islam. Each member in this system of thematic origins exerts a teleological pull on those units subject to its influence in its capacity as, at once, origin and explanation. In this way, the temporal sequence of units which carry forward an

influence is one of a multiplicatory sequence which traces the linear
insemination of effects and derivative influences from a origin, and
which reconfirms the essence of each influence as the continuation and
repetition of that origin. A consequent therefore adds nothing to a
precedent, neither does it have a specificity definable in terms apart
from this precedent or to the precedent or precedents, which is Islam.
Yet the monotony of this temporal elongation of essence is relaxed by
the quantitative, and therefore essentially inconsequent, force of degeneration.[20] Things Islamic have a history described as the degeneration
from or at best the anchylotic solidification of their origin. The historical trajectory of Islamic civilization is thus customarily described as the
rapid flowering of an origin followed equally rapidly by the coagulation
of its fundamental structures and the maintenance of this state of
ponderous inanity for close to a millenium, during which time the only
change that takes place — apart from dynastic changes and senseless
slaughter — is one of a diminution of equality.

The process of reduction to an origin is a simple operation. In
concrete terms it does not require more than the normal equipment of
Orientalist scholarship, viz, fundamental library skills and an efficient
system of note-taking. It consists of fleecing the manifest content of
texts in question and under investigation in search of parallels: parallel
passages, parallel explicit thoughts, parallel references, parallel terms.
The establishment of an origin by such correspondence amounts to the
Orientalist conception of explanation, a conception to which any
notion of adequacy or inadequacy is totally inappropriate. The amputa-
tion of statements from discursive and historical contexts is standard
practice although it is spotted as a fault in polemical contexts. The
irrelevance of any notion of explanatory adequacy is a reflection of the
lack of any structural coherence in the Orient of the Orientalist beyond
that of repetition. This fact is equally reflected in the epistemology of
Orientalism with its conception of meaning as the mere transcript of the
manifest content of statements —which accounts for the atomistic and
etymological conception of semantics in Orientalist scholarship where
meaning in a statement is the sum of its vocabulary elements. Hence the
scandalously literatist translations of Arabic (mainly) medieval texts
into European languages.[21]

The problematic of teleological origin, articulated by means of this
argumentum ad textum sanctum, applies not only to the relations of particu-

lar texts but, as pointed out, extends to those that tie particular texts, contexts, and thematic classes to a reality, a nature, a fundamental principle, an *asl* to which they all appertain. No particular which falls under the class Islam is self-sufficient in the particularity formed by its own context. Its reality is derived from its Islamicism, and if the Islamic essence that suffuses all that is Islamic is withdrawn from the particular, it ceases to be Islamic. This nature of natures, this explicitly self-defining (but implicitly, defined by the reversal of the West) reality, is the principle of invarigence in Orientalism which ensures the solidity of its thematic material. Being the opposite of the West this nature is really a disnature which in itself has the properties of a nature, a medieval nature where things are natural not in relation to some otherness, but by virtue of their intrinsic properties; just as it is "in the nature" of heavy things to fall, it is in the nature of Islamic things to have the properties that will be detailed further on. It is a nature which, in time, transmits its pristine properties, its Islamicism, by temporal contiguity (influence) which transmits the Islamic designation from particular to particular. The particulars lack substance and, therefore, justification and explanation without reference to this nature; they lack narrative properties except insofar as the narrative whose discrete elements they constitute is oriented towards the Orient, which is the node of the order of consequence superimposed upon the paratactic staccato of factual enumeration.

This description of Islam as principle and nature is that which trans-mutes a stray particular into a fact of the Islamic order. Islam, that phlogiston of the social sciences, activates torpid fact and transforms it into Islamicism, into appurtenance to principle. Such is Islam for a sophisticated modern scholar.[22]

> Islam must be seen from the perspective of history as an always changing evolving and developing response of successive generations of *Muslims* to their deepest vision of reality . . . *The link* among this diversity of responses is their common origin in the prophetic experience and their common agent, the Islamic community.

It is very easy for the author of this quotation, C. Adams, to demon-strate that by change he means change and thus refutes any suspicions of ahistoricism. All that has to be done to show this is to present a diachronic enumeration of various "responses" to fulfill the require-ments of Orientalist scholarship. But, over and above these "responses"

— and they are the responses of a temporal string of *Muslims* to *their* "vision of reality" — the origin which they have in the Islamic community and in prophecy is that which accounts for the integrity of Islam and for its historical continuity as Islam. Islam is therefore the self-explanatory, self-sufficient, and utterly *sui generis* nature and reality whose historical vicissitudes are internally propelled by "the community" in its successive generations, responding to "their vision" under different external circumstances. But these circumstances are sheer accidentals in connection with the solidity of trans-historicity. For these circumstances alter nothing essential within the sense of Islam: and changes undergone by Islam are changes for Muslims in response to themselves. Theirs is the triumph of absolute specificity (and hence of teleology), of changeless specificity, inscribed in the behavior of the *homo islamicus*, a creature fully and wholly apart, endowed with a specificity which although real, is detached from history, and validated as transhistorical substance.[23] One wonders whether it is possible for any scholar apart from some provincial pastors with a bookish bent to conceive of a *homo christianus* who traverses twenty centuries and five continents and whose constancy expains the Flagellants of fourteenth century Thuringia no less than neo-Thomism and the course of Chilean history, all by virtue of his possession of the Gospels.

But of things Islamic, such a view is eminently possible, indeed necessary. Without Islam as an immutable nature there can be no Orientalism. So essential is this conception that even the almost omnipotently urbane ironics of Albert Hourani's Orientalism cannot do without it. After explicitly rejecting the idea of an "essence" determining all aspects of a culture, Hourani refers approvingly to the work of Clifford Geertz and states that

> . . . even when we can use the concept of "Islam" to explain something in a culture or society, we must use it subtly and in conjunction with other principles of explanation . . . there is no such thing as "Islamic society," there are societies partly moulded by Islam, but formed also by their position in the physical world, their inherited language and culture, their economic possibilities and the accidents of their political history.[24]

Hourani takes explicit cognizance of sociological, ecological, and other realities that enter into the making of "concrete history." "Islam," he states, is not and cannot be an explanatory principle by itself. It is merely one in an aggregate of explanatory principles whose precise register or conformation does not appear to have much importance for the author. Islam for Hourani is a single factor active in societies "partly moulded by Islam." But its intrinsic properties are not altered by this defenestration of omnipresence, they are simply subject to a relative devaluation. From being a totalitarian principle, Islam becomes a component in a pluralism of determinants. It is also shifted back firmly onto the religous sphere — it is "a statement about what God is and how He acts in the world, embodied in a book which Muslims believe to be the Word of God, and articulated in a system of law and worship by which millions of men and women have lived for many centuries."[25] Thus thrust down from transhistorical omnipotence to the low common denominator of basic beliefs, rituals, devotions, and precepts, it should be really regarded as either too trivial a factor to rise beyond the level of individual consciousness, or as Islam should be properly treated like all religions, as a severely nominalistic entity which functions in a purely designatory capacity in the sphere of Islamic societies, histories, and geographical units, without this Islamism having further[26] consequences as to the internal determination of these units beyond the same. Yet Islam remains as one among other equally determinant factors in the history of certain societies, but this does not make its own specific effectivity any less real — only limited in the context of determinants in ontological parity, yet simultaneously not bereft of its essence as Islam. Millions of men and women have been guided by it in their lives and the scope of this guidance is almost infinitely flexible in dimensions, especially as Islam is articulated in that hazy term "a system of law" of unspecified extent. Islamic law for Orientalists, however, is the sole surface of contiguity between things Islamic and worldliness. Its scope and extent is therefore almost integrally coterminous with Islamic societies insofar as they are Islamic, to which "Islamic law" stands in a fully metonymic relationship. Without this system of guidance, Muslims would not have been defined as Muslims and would therefore not have been the objects of Islamistic investigations. Without Islam as essence, even if it has to shift ground, there is no Islamic history, no Islamic subject matter, and there are no Islamic Studies institutions. Without it the Muslims, as social beings, "act like other men caught in the web of traditions and present needs."[27] Except that "traditions" here can be none else than the Islamic traditions that define Islamic societies.

Not strictly the *homo islamicus* in all his glory then, but only partly *homo islamicus* and partly Man. Only part Islam, only part nature particularized into a Book and a Law, but still Islam, not merely as Book and Law, but as transhistorical paradigm. Otherwise, there will be no criteria by which "Islamic and Middle Eastern History" can exist; without the Islam that becomes an historical and geographical location, among many other things, and without the totemic geography which concretizes the subdivisions of Orientalism, there can be no Islamic studies.[28] The conservation of the category Islam in Orientalism is therefore, ultimately, a sociological conservation of the institution whose stock in trade is constituted by the category.

No Islamic subject matter can therefore exist without Islam in its full tautological power, in which things are Islamic because they are constituted (partly or wholly) by Islam, because it is their nature to be Islamic. This is true of both archaizing Orientalists and of the limiting cases of Orientalism set by subtle and accommodating Orientalists who evince explicit doubt about the relevance of Islamism while being paradigmatically incapacitated from realizing its irrelevance. Whether or not *homo Islamicus* bears full or only partial (or diminished) responsibility for the formation of the Islamic subject matter, he can never be denied the decisive act of nomenclature. He is infused with an almost pneumatic force which runs its natural course without regard to anything intrinsic, including time, and is a force which permeates, with its characteristic nature, all that is apportioned to it.

III

Having unravelled the structures of Islamicizing Orientalism, we shall now turn to the descriptive content with which these structures are stuffed and then progress to a more integrated description of the structure of Orientalist units of discourse. The detailed content of Islam relates to its origin according to the structures of generality we have discussed and which, for the purpose of the present analysis, can be expressed by saying that Islam is the generalizing synecdoche of things Islamic, just as Islamic details, be they general like the thematic classes or specific like the thematic units, are particularizing synecdoches of Islam. Islam is the fount of influence transmitted by time through its thematic classes which, we have seen, spend their phenomenal existence in the form of discrete units of content (be they texts, statements, or reported events) to which reductive reference is made in the process of confirming their Islamicism.[29]

We have also seen that in this reductive process we do not witness a deduction as much as an appendication, for the connection of statements established in Orientalist discourse is not one which bears conceptual or logical necessity but is activated by the contingency of an act of naming based on convention. This convention is that of the Orientalist physiognomy of the Orient, the stylization of things Oriental which produces the Orient of Orientalism. It consists of a conformation of *topoi* which subsist in the folds of European literacy and folk cultures and which interpolate one another. This topical system of Islam constitutes what we have just referred to as a "convention." As units of collective representation, these units are *topoi*. As narrative components, thematic units. As propositional elements, categories.

It is these which make up the "convention" according to a simple rule of manufacture which we have stated and which we will presently elucidate. But we must first make explicit note of this thematic repertory of which we have so far encountered instances which remained without integral confirmation. And what better way is there to look at a comprehensive statement of the very familiar cultural vulgate than to sketch and scrutinize the account of "Mahometanism"[30] in that all-inclusive manual of historical topics relevant to the bourgeois-capitalist epoch, Hegel's *Philosophy of History*.[31]

The fundamental of Islam for Hegel is the exclusive worship of the One, as a counterpart of which exists "the design to subjugate secular existence to the One". Secular life, real life, then, is regarded as a sphere of negativity, totally lacking in structure, to such an extent that Muslims as a whole can only be united by the vertical bond which ties them exclusively to the One. Apart from this rigorous and exclusive bond in the One, Islam displays nothing but amorphousness in "the boundless amplitude of the world". Indifferent to social fabric, the Muslim "rushes on in the ceaseless whirl of fortune", erecting dynasties "destitute of the bond of organic firmness" — which therefore, as other Oriental empires are described, belong "to mere space, as it were"[32] and which, bearing such a formless relation to the concrete, did nothing but degenerate. The natural corollary of this exclusive principle of relevance is that action in the unstructured world of concreteness can only be action heedless of everything concrete: fanaticism. Fanaticism is a perfectly opposite type of motivation, as it is enthusiasm for something "abstract," an enthusiasm "abstract and therefore all-comprehensive . . . restrained by nothing finding its limits nowhere, and absolutely indifferent to all beside." Yet when fanaticism for the One cooled, and with the absence of all but individual passions alongside it, "the East itself . . . sank into the grossest vice . . . and as sensual enjoyment was sanctioned in the first form which Mahometan doctrine assured, and was exhibited as a reward of the faithful in Paradise it took the place of fanaticism. At present, driven back . . . Islam has long vanished from the stage of history at large, and has retreated into Oriental ease and repose."

A close look will reveal both specific *topoi* and the fact that they are related by linear presupposition and the reproductive hierarchy of synecdoches. The origin of Islam and its fundamental principle is its conception of Deity. This is the unadulterated abstract One which reduces all that does not belong to it to utter formlessness, senselessness, and chaos. We thus have two fundamental classes of topics with very well-defined contours: all inclusive Islamic religiosity, and its logical and phenomenal counterpart. The first is the impress of the idea of a divinity so severely structured as to be reduced to a mere point which immures all else within its unicity and the second is the Chaos of which the worldly residue of divinity consists, for that which does not directly relate to divinity can be subject to no laws or principles of structuration. The unicity of the Islamic God is one which not only derives its demonstration in theology, but performs a constant practical demonstration in being the exclusive repository of power in a power relationship where it is the sole criterion of reference.

From these simple fundamentals we can derive other elements of the vulgate. The exclusivity of reference makes not only for a stultifying theoretical inflexibility, but given the abstraction of the all-structuring unit of deity, for an inflexibility in those aspects of life which bear a relation to religiosity; fundamental among which is Islamic Law. The spheres of jurisprudence therefore copy the structure of religiosity of the One, and their function ceases to be one of regulating real life and becomes, for the Orientalist, merely a concrete manner of upholding the idea of unity. It becomes, exclusively, piety, which may exist in the selves of legislators, but this is irrelevant to law. Law is comprehended by religiosity; that which is not cannot have any relation to religiosity.

We see how the progression by ramification and multiplication and the duplication of structures from the idea of the Islamic deity as absolutely exclusive and absolutely one leads to more particular, lower order *topoi*; an obsessional theology and a paradigmatically indistinct ritual jurisprudence which does not in substance or in essential form differ from devotion. Islamic sciences are equally indistinct. They are certainly distinct as to their thematic detail, but do not differ in the fundamentally ritual property which marks them; they are almost exclusively affirmative of the religious idea, to which all else is incidental. The purpose of all sciences — be they Koranic exegesis or its numerous ancillary linguistic and other sciences, the science of traditional narrative, the science of jurisprudential logic, the science of theology, and others — is almost exclusively scripturalist, aiming at constant confirmation and restatement of basic devotional positions. They are therefore seen by Orientalists as forming a homogeneous mass of 'Islamic learning' indistinct in substance and aim from other functions of religion. Their constant reconfirmation of their origin is unadulterated by paradigmatic distinctions and their concomitant sociological and cultural specificities, by historical factors, or by politics (except insofar as the last allows or disallows). Hence we can explain the remarkable fact that Orientalist literature insists that Islamic culture is the work of that amorphous indistinct mass they call *fuqaha* without any further qualification, who traverse centuries as the guardians of 'learning' and who are as indistinct and undifferentiated as the essentially identical sciences whose purity they police. It is also thus that we can explain the fact that the study of Islamic law in the West is confined to sketching particular legislation concerning matters that occur in thematic categories of Roman inspired jurisprudence, while the fundamental principles specific to Islamic law as elaborated in the synthesis of linguistic, semantic, historical, and logical investigations in the science of the Principles of Jurisprudence are almost totally ignored.[33]

Religiosity as pure religiosity, and as that worldly religiosity that is expressed in sciences, is further duplicated in the real world. Immersion in the whirlpool of fortune occurs because the total system of Islamicism is devoid of any structural idea which can articulate anything that escapes the purview of the One. In the concrete world, this One is duplicated in Islamic polity. There reigns in this context a condition of absolute sociological indeterminacy whereby history becomes political history, in the most superficial sense of the term — in which content consists of the arbitrary struggle for arbitrary power between forces defined by nothing else than their being parties in a power struggle. This is the sense of "factions" in Islamic history as well as in contemporary news reporting. Duplicating the relation of God to the world, the Islamic state can only relate to its subjects by arbitrarily appropriating them into its system of exclusivity. The abstract spoilation of the world by Islamic sovereigns is in their nature as well as in that of their world: in their nature, as they are abstract autocrats, and in that of their world insofar as it is formless, and hence absolutely open and unresistant to arbitrary rule. The counterpart of the absolute ruler is the famous Muslim fatalist. Further particularized, this conception will produce a wealth of topics that Orientalist scholarship could only conjure, such as the fissiparous nature of 'Islamic cities.'[34] It goes without saying that it is the nature of this amorphous city, not the sociology of amorphousness which is of interest to the Orientalist. This is because no such thing as an amorphous social collectivity can exist, let alone something whose formlessness is its criterion of definition. The Orientalist is interested in the Islamic city precisely because of the fact of formlessness entailed by the absolutism of its fundamental idea, and hence of the fundamental unreality and disnature of this idea and the order it engenders.[35] The senseless eruption of Islam, moreover its eruption from the desert and its irrational conquest of the world, can only have its counterpoint and meet its Pyrrhic fate in instant decline. But only so much can be inferred from the irrationalism that binds Islam to the world.[36] For the rest the idea of decline is separately guaranteed by the simple fact of the power relation that exists between East and West following the Crusades in Spain and the capitalist expansion of Europe — prior to this, it was not decline of world order that was the fate of Islam, but moral degeneration.

The specificity of the West and its difference from the East is the main constituent of the East itself and of the topical material out of which it is generated. Such provincialism is the perogative of all cultures. But, dizzy with universal power and expansion, the West affected the intellectual assimilation of other cultures and would not admit pure otherness. The West fixed the specificity of other cultures and specified their distance by the means proper to the triumph of this provincialism: it measured them upon itself, not only in absolute terms but also in terms of the categories it uses to apprehend self.

For Hegel, the Divinity of Islam is defective precisely in comparison to that of Christianity, where self-consciousness is superimposed upon substantiality and thus achieves the complete and mature form of all godhood. This allows for the development of free reflexive — and therefore rational — morality (*Sittlichkeit*) in place of the moralizing absolutist conformism (*Moralitat*) of the Orient and therefore permits the unfolding of the concatenated and ordered world of individuals which is civil society — the 'system of needs' as it is termed in the *Philosophy of Right* (p. 189ff.). Islamic religiosity and its concomitant social disorder are conceived as incomplete forms of the Christian-Germanic order. They are to the latter as defective versions, an identity subject to privation: an incomplete holiness, a sheer external morality, and the mere proliferation of needs and passions without the benefit of a system. Hence we see an abstract divinity devoid of the substance of subjectivity, and an abstract temporal power devoid of the discipline of rationality, and its corollaries in the realm of passions and individual needs.

In logical terms, we see in Hegel's Islam the play of two elements: the positing of the spirit of the Christian-Germanic world as *telos* and therefore integral normalcy, and the establishment of a difference, first between the original principles of the two religions, and then between derivative manifestations thereof. This process is reproduced throughout Orientalism. But while Hegel establishes differences based upon criteria of historical unfolding, his historical and cultural contemporaries understood by teleolgy and determinism only the product, and severed this from process in all but a nominal sense. Their establishment of differences between West and East was far more radical and provincial. Difference became antonymy.[37] Renan expressed this very forthrightly a very long time ago: "*ainsi la race semitique se reconnait presque uniquement a des caractires negatifs . . . en tout, absence de complexite, de nuances, sentiment exclusif de l'unite.*"[38] East is determined as not West, not as sheer difference, but as determinate difference, just as the difference is established in the Hegelian account we have discussed.

Orientalist discourse generates its thematic classes by reversing the sense of the terms in which the culture of the West customarily describes its values and institutions (rationality, polity, society, science, cities, etc.), and thus politics, religion and folk prejudice are turned into scholarship. Islamic determinations reverse Western ones: whereas the order of the West and of its sciences for its liberal spokesman is conceived as one of rationality (in politics, in ethics, in economics) —what Hegel termed self-conscious subjectivity and what Weberians call instrumental rationality — and of scientificity, the East is character-ized in its same manifestations by the irrationality of abstract despotism in politics, arbitrary passion in ethics, rapaciousness or autarchy in economics, and ritualistic scripturalism in learning. These reversals of sense affect both the determination of units composing the Orient and the units themselves. When the irrationality of despotism is generated by the rationality of democracy, it is both the inner determination of the term 'despotic' that is generated as well as the thematic classes 'despotic system,' 'despotic ruler,' etc. Similarly, when belief is generated by reason it is not simply the inner structures of the obscurantist belief of Oriental religiosity that is countered to the crypto-deistic religiosity of the West; nor is it simply the counterposition of a system of exegetical sciences, whose method is recursive and whose sole purpose is to reconfirm their origin (Koran, etc.) to one of noble, rational freedom and 'problem-solving,' and open enquiry generation of belief by reason. It is the creation of a fictional system of sciences dubbed Islamic (in counterposition to European social and natural sciences), sciences whose recursive structure is their exclusive structure — sciences which in reality do not exist in this recursive form (although recursive pur-poses are never absent) unless their essential structures are stripped and defenestrated — as we have remarked earlier with respect to Islamic law, where it is not only the logical structure of the science that is ignored, but its very legislative action. This can readily be seen in the works of Gibb and F. Rosenthal on Mawardi's writings on the caliphate, which is not seen as an act of legislation but one of 'reconciling' reality and the belief-bound, moribund caliphate. It is similarly that God is generated by Man (or by Hegel's Christianity, which carries many of the structures of Enlightenment Man), the amorphous city by the commune, fatalism by technologism and democracy, and the East in general by the West under so many denominations that constitute the units of Enlightenment anthropology.

If we therefore represent the East by E and its specific thematic classes

/categories by E^1, E^2, etc., and the West and its thematic classes/categories by W, W^1, W^2, etc., we can arrive at the following generative paradigm:

$$W \ — \ — \ — \ W^1 \ — \ W^2 \quad \ldots \ldots$$
$$E \ — \ — \ — \ E^1 \ — \ E^2 \quad \ldots \ldots$$

We have already seen that the relationship between the elements of the syntagmatic chains E, E^1, E^2, . . . and W, W^1, W^2, . . . is one of particularizing synecdoche and its reverse.[39] After all, when performing an exercise in nomenclature, Orientalism assimilates to the general denomination of the Western particular, out of which Eastern particulars are generated by a reversal of sense. The relationship between elements of W or of E is generic. But since in the provinces of the East the task is one of appellation, and since these provinces subsist in a continent of profuse Eastern determinations which interpolate one another as images interpolate one another in the context of representative figures, E^1, E^2 . . . , could well be interchangeable within the limits of contiguous thematic classes, and within these classes themselves, for all perform the same function of proving Islamism. After all, in terms of abstract structure, the movement from E to its elements is one of the transference of value with respect to the relationship between W and E. No such interchangeability exists, however, between elements of W, for they are the determinate means of naming rather than elements named for the sake of nomenclature. Thus:

$$+W \quad W^1 \quad W^2 \quad W^3 \quad \ldots$$
$$-E \quad E^1 \quad E^2 \quad E^3 \quad \ldots$$

Within both the realms of E and of W, there are also relations of thematic, generic hierarchy which we have illustrated during the discussion of Hegel's account of Islam and elsewhere in the foregoing, and which reproduce within the thematic units that appertain to E and to W the same relations that exist between the thematic classes that belong to E and W. Thus:

$$+W \quad W^1 \quad w^1 \quad w^{12} \quad w^{13} \quad \ldots \quad W^2 \quad w^{21} \quad w^{22} \quad w^2 \quad \ldots$$
$$-E \quad E^1 \quad e^1 \quad e^{12} \quad e^{13} \quad \ldots \quad E^2 \quad e^{21} \quad e^{22} \quad e \quad \ldots$$

where capital letters stand for thematic classes/categories and where lower case stands for individual units of content which aggregate in the classes. Units of both orders are almost indefinitely extensible under the sole constraint of the negativism of E with respect to W, or the one more contingent generator of Islamic specificities, the exotic ephemera of a *Zeitgeist*,[40] which do not always have a position in the structure under discussion. This infinite thematic elasticity is, needless to say, occasioned by the recovery of increasingly extensive sections of the empirical manifold by Orientalist discourse. But this elasticity does not permit or imply an elasticity with respect to the generative node of the structure. The series E and W are by no means completely open. Their thematic liberality has its counterpart in the closedness of origin. W, which can be extended but cannot comprehend all, is the base value of this circle to which E stands as a sort of inverse metonym.

It will be possible but pointless to make an inventory of those thematic classes realized by the paradigmatic structure that has been indicated. To do this, all one has to do is to undertake the tedious task of combing that *Summa Islamica*, the *Encyclopaedia of Islam*, with a view toward making a thematic classification of its material. Such a taxonomy could be organized in terms of categories which organize the Western order — economy, society, polity, religion, culture — or in terms of Enlightenment anthropology — reason, freedom and their cognates. The two intersect in the specific instance of discourse on the Orient. Such an inventory will contain as fundamental elements of opposition (W^1/E^1, W^2/E^2, etc.): Men/God; Here/Beyond; democracy-/tyranny; individuality/conformity; progress/stagnation; evolution/degeneration; science/theology; politics of interest/politics of fanatical passion; nationality/ethnicity-Sectarianism; inwardness/extraneousness; rationalism/traditionalism; and, ultimately, culture/nature as the equivalent of nature/disnature. The list can be extended.

In such a perspective, the omission from scholarly scrutiny of real things existing in the real Orient and their relegation beyond the pale of things Oriental finds its explanation. Why do we not find an entry for the vast topic *tabi'a* (nature) in the *Encyclopaedia of Islam?* Why do we not find studies of the relation between Al-Farabi and Avicenna on the one hand, and the Islamic sciences on the other? Why do we not find even studies of the activities and controversies of the extensively studied Averroes with the Zahiri and other legal schools?[41] And why is it that Arab-Islamic medicine and natural science is disproportionately left to historians of science and medicine by the same Oriental philologists who consider history to be no less than literature and political and religious institutions as comprehended by their field of study?

The answer to all these and innumerable other similar questions is that, for the Orientalist, those palpable facts that cannot be ignored but which do not fully conform to the physiognomy of things Islamic constitute those things which E. Said has termed 'dis-Orientals.' They are Oriental and Islamic simply by virtue of geographical and temporal location. Hence they are only nominally Oriental, for they are decidedly Occidental, conforming to the determinations of the Occident. Philosophy is certainly one of these dis-Orientals. It is the patrimony of the West, being an expression of the free inquiry of the Greeks. That is why an Aristotelian commentator such as Averroes becomes subsumed under the category 'philosopher' — which, in Orientalist writing, is a human type opposed to that of *faqih*. What relevance can there be then in his juristic activities? And even when Averroes' activities in the Islamic sciences is the topic of scrutiny — or of Ibn Khaldun, for a scholar such as Mahdi — the philosopher and the jurist are kept apart, as if they were two substances that repulse one another and can never achieve any measure of contiguity except the accidental fact of residing in the same individual. Likewise, no relevance is attached by Orientalism to the connections of Avicenna to Islamic sciences — not even his interesting polemics against the logic of the theologians. For we have two irreconcilable substances, and Averroes is seen as 'reconciling' them in the interest of philosophy when in fact the supposed 'reconciliation' is neither a reconciliation nor undertaken in the name of philosophy, as I have shown elsewhere.[42] The important thing for the Orientalist is to demonstrate the disnature of each with the respect to the other; hence their connection can only be external and tenuous and touches the nature of neither: it is a 'reconciliation', a conception that we come across very often in Orientalism as for instance in the 'reconciliation' of the law and reality in the theory of the caliphate.

Other intransitive substances are the rational enquiries of the esotericist schools and of varieties of mysticism. The former is seen as hidden among groups of faithful savants whose esoteric writings are forms of subterfuge which are the only way of preserving dis-Islamic precepts within Islam; the history of the latter is seen as the faith of groups opposed to the Islamic political and devotional order and thus as dis-Islamic manifestations which had to be fought in the beginning and then grudgingly accepted as representing the majority — forgetting that revolutionaries in Baghdad and Damascus and elsewhere were in fact often the members of Hanbali families who belong to what are commonly regarded as the most literalist and obscurantist school of Islamic law, one which is bitterly opposed to the gnostic 'free spirituality' of the mystical orders. It is no surprise therefore that, even the externalists to Islam of philosophy, mysticism, and their cognates, attributable to intellectual and spiritual boldness and freedom, these have to be given not only a dis-Islamic essence, but a concrete origin and reality outside Islam as well. Islamic philosophy is therefore generally studied not in terms of its inner structures, its external conditions within Arab-Islamic culture, its connections with other paradigmatic formations within that culture, but rather insofar as it is derivative from Greece and a vehicle of the unerring movement from Greece to later European thought.

Indeed, the history of translation from Greek and Syriac into Arabic which brought Aristotle and others into the Arabic cultural field is construed as a haphazard process in which translators who first rendered medical and other texts of useful values into Arabic stumbled upon philosophical texts (and especially, in the beginning, logical texts of use to grammarians and dialectical theologians) which they could not but translate — and one wonders whether this necessity for translating the texts of the philosophers derived from anything but their ulterior use in Arab-Islamic culture, thus denying any immanent criteria for the necessity of their translation derivable from the very age in which they were translated.

The truth of Arab-Islamic philosophy is fully contained in its antecedents.[43] Hence we see that acknowledged authority on Arab-Islamic philosophy, the late R. Walzer for instance, was almost exclusively concerned with the transmission of Greek philosophy to the Arabs. Hence too, we witness the Persianate romanticism of H. Corbin and S. H. Nasr, attributing gnostic metaphysics (and much else that has the external stamp of freedom) to Persia — in terms almost fully reminiscent of the determinations of Aryan thought in the last century, determinations which have been transferred to other fields of enquiry — as to architecture, for instance, in the work of N. Ardalan. The case of Ibn Khaldun is analogous: the supposed sociology he founded is normally seen as an anticipation of ideas that were formulated in later times by Montesquieu, Tarde, Feuerbach, Vico, Marx and a great many others, thus reducing his 'truth' to the teleological end of a process in which he certainly did not participate, but to which his attachment is made imperative because of the apparently dis-Islamic character of his thought.[44] And finally, one could well mention the Arab nationalism of the Orientalists. It benefits from both forward and backward reductions as either a clock for a really Islamic essence or, more appropriately to our content, as a betrayal of things Islamic in the form of liberal democracy. The dis-Islamic is always explained by reference to the West. Just as the dis-Arabity of the arts of literacy for Volney could not bear sheer expression in its own terms but had to be stated in terms of a comparison with the European ability to read and write.

*   *   *   *   *

But we have not opened for ourselves any vistas since we took up Volney and Nietzsche, we have, so far, described a circle whose locus is set by its cardinal progenitor, the parochialism of a culture. Orientalism itself as a scholarly discipline (or as fold representation) has not traversed much of a distance since Volney, and has not substantially advanced the conception of the East that we found in Nietzsche.

Only in 1980 did London publishers see fit to exhume and reprint books by Brockelman and O'Leary on Islamic history and Arab-Islamic philosophy which stand well below the average that the nineteenth century could offer in terms of both factual accuracy and conceptual content. Orientalist scholarship has produced much writing of which by far the greatest amount is conceptually so systematically misleading and misdirected as to be worthless. The contribution of Orientalist scholarship to learning is very small and can virtually be reduced to editions (some of outstanding merit) of Arabic and other texts, to cataloguing manuscript sources, to the compilation of bibliographies, the preparation of textual concordances, the compilation of some dictionaries, and cognate acts of scholarship. Orientalist discourse, we have seen, is a repetition of motifs and their constant discovery through the simple techniques of Oriental scholarship, so that this scholarship consists fundamentally of so many transferences of value judgements, as Laroui has pointed out.[45] Why is it that, after almost two centuries of continuous research, nothing better exists in Arab-Islamic historiography than an encyclopedia article by H.A.R. Gibb and an unperceptive and super-ficial book by F. Rosenthal (which has run into two editions)? And is it not baffling that of the scores of hundreds of books and articles on Ibn Khaldun all but a score are worthless?

Indeed, anyone who reads extensively in Orientalist writing cannot but be struck by the fact that the scholarly vulgate of Orientalism was established very early on — the latter part of the nineteenth century at the latest — and has been virtually unchanged in its main conceptions ever since. We do not find changes and transformations, only improve-ments of detail, on the seminal works of Goldziher, of Macdonald, of De Boer (a very perceptive Orientalist), of Gibb's conception of Arabic historiography, of Wellhausen (despite serious challenges which, in fields other than Oriental history, would have rendered his work obsolete). We have here more than the sheer dead weight of tradition: we have that steeled by general culture. This perhaps accounts for one reason why Islamic scholarship has played such a very minor role in the history of religions.[46]

Orientalism is congenitally incapable of truly synthetic studies which go beyond the enumeration of Islamic things. Work such as that of the late Marshall Hodgson commands respect for its open and bold spirit but no conviction except in some points of detail. In an age such as this, the computer can slog through the technical tasks demanded of an Oriental-ist, the work of concordance, correlation, indexing, and referencing, and a good but small start is taking place in France in this direction under the auspices of the Institute for the History of Texts. This does not, of course, exhaust philology. The Orientalist can still inspire in himself the spirit that inspires the superior philologies undertaken in other fields which he can set for himself as examples. The superior philology of Auerbach and Curtius in the field of Romance languages (and much more), the work of Trier, for instance, and his numerous followers in Germanic philology, even the great nineteenth century classical philologists such as Wilamowitz Millendorf, Mommsen, and Rohde (not to speak of his sometime friend Friedrich Nietzsche) and later Greek scholars as Jaegar and Cornford and, today, J. P. Vernant, are no less an example of philological possibilities than the work of numerous Biblical scholars since Spinoza, Strauss and Schleiermacher, of comparative Indo-European mythology such as that of Dumezil and, in a more polymatic vein, the investigations of Frances Yates and of A.

Lovejoy into the general history of ideas, of other scholars attached to the Warburg Institute, which should not be excluded from the province of philology. A very small number of scholars with Orientalist training have in fact eschewed the problematics and thematics set by Orientalism and ventured into territories previously untrodden by this science: one could mention in this vein the work of R. Arnaldez, A. Miquel, and perhaps in a slightly more old fashioned manner, J. Van Ess.

Yet one cannot say that these instances represent the instauration of a new order within Orientalism. The texture of Orientalism is composed of its institutions with their oral delivery of the vulgate and narrow philological training, not of enlightened and cultured scholars; even superior philology cannot thrive in the debilitating warmth of that bovine tranquility induced by the implicit paradigmatic understanding prevalent in Orientalist institutions. Even superior philology in its traditional acceptation has determinate limits,[47] although some of its products, E. Auerbach for instance, have unreflexively crossed these limits. And it must not be forgotten that the works of Trier and Vernant, for example, were written and conceived with explicit reference to social sciences (Saussurian linguistics and Levi-Strauss's anthropology) beyond the pale of philology. Similarly, it must be pointed out that Miquel's study of a tale from the *Arabian Nights* and Izutsu's studies of the Koran[48] are also undertaken with particular reference to linguistics. And beyond linguistics proper we now have the science of narrative and of culture as developed by Barthes and Foucault, among others.

The perspectives open to Oriental philology are therefore by no means closed, except by the existence of Orientalist institutions. In the context of the study of the Orient, improvement would only be possible if Arabic and Islamic studies were to cease to be Arabic and Islamic studies as such, and if its components were placed in their respective social science contexts while Arabic philology became, once again, strictly Arabic philology, or Persian philology strictly Persian, etc. It is far worse to have 'multidisciplinariness' in conjunction with the dead lumber of Orientalism (for it will attach to no discipline) than to have what is called departmental specialization. It is only by removing the disnature of Arabs and Muslims and naturalizing them that one can put into effect E. Said's worthy advocacy of a deabstractionist humanism.[49] But to do so one requires rather more than E. Said's hermeneutics, and more than his conception of intellectual history as a form of *Geistesge-*

schichte in the best central European humanistic tradition.[50] And, for this same purpose, one also requires more than just the purified Marxism advocated by B. Turner on the grounds of its being 'fully equipped' to destroy Orientalism in the process of purging itself of the nineteenth century.[51] Both are commendable, in conjunction with much else, on the condition that there is no question of grafting onto the existing structure of Orientalist learning as the means of reforming Orientalism. The sheer intromission of knowledge into the Orientalist institution is, with few exceptions, likely only to produce scholars about whom we may comment (with Nietzsche when, in the eighth paragraph of his *Beyond Good and Evil*, he quotes an ancient mystery):

> *Adventatit Asinus*
> *Pulcher et fortissimus*

NOTES

1. There is, of course, an historical hierarchy of things Oriental falling under semitism: Judaism, Islam and Arabism. But this hierarchy is neither historically strict nor is it valorized as such in Orientalist scholarship except episodically. The relationship between those who share Semitism is the same between them and other members of the Orient: India, China, Persia and others. The relationship is one of duplicative conceptual homology in which they figure as so many topics with an identical conceptual physiognomy. A comparative study of Orientalism in its Arabistic, Islamistic, Indic, Chinese, Turkish and Persian topics would certainly be illuminating, as well as a study of the homologies between studies of the Orient and of Africa. Comparative notions of primitivism and, indeed of aspects of premodern Europe, should be included in such a study. One could, for a start, usefully read Victor Kiernan, *The Lords of Human Kind: Black Man, Yellow Man, and White Man in an Age of Empire* (Boston: Little Brown, 1969).

2. Constantin Francois Volney, *Travels in Syria and Egypt in the Years 1783*, 2 volumes (New York: J. Tiebout, 1798).

3. The relation of the Semitic Jews to the East is difficult and ambiguous, to say the least, and is far more complex than that of Arabs, Islam or the Indians. For instance, Jewish conception is not the conception of things made eastern by being semitic. The Jews formed, for many, a part of Christianity, and hence of the West, albeit in a remote manner. In the past century, they have taken on decidedly modern European features with Zionism. Indeed, one of the earliest Zionists, Moses Hess, took offense at Bruno Bauer's contention that the Jews were Orientals. In this regard see Julius Carlebach, *Karl Marx and the Radical Critique of Judaism* (London: Routledge and Kegan Paul, 1978).

4. This contrasting *topos* has constantly been afloat in the symbolic and topical repertory of the West since the time of the Greeks, and merits a special study in this special capacity. Such a study could perhaps first take the form of an historical inventory and typology of the cultural locations within which its forms subsist and of the thematic associations which it interpolates. This could form the starting point of the mythologies of Western culture advocated by Claude Levi-Strauss, *Structural Anthropology*, two volumes, trans. from French by M. Layton (New York: Basic Books, 1976).

5. Edward Said, *Orientalism* (New York: Vintage Books, 1978) devotes an entire chapter to the scope of Orientalism which he saw as the forms in which the Orient is constituted and apprehended. And although his analysis points to the extension of Orientalism discourse on the Orient, whether that discourse be scholarly, colonial or literary, he does state that the Orient is "Less a place than a *topos*," but he does not analyze the Orientalist *topos* as a *topos* with a cultural patrimony attached to the literary culture. It is due to this embeddedness in the cultural repertory of Europe, to its living in the matrix of European scholarship and culture, that Orientalism could become the enormously systematic discipline by which Europeans produce and manage the Orient politically, sociologically, militarily, scientifically and imaginatively during the post Enlightenment period (Said, p. 45). On the Islamic Orient in medieval polemic, one has the choice between the dense detail of Norman Daniel, *Islam and the West: The Making of an Image* (Edinburgh: University Press, 1960) or the short perceptive essay of R. W. Southern, *Western Views of Islam in the Middle Ages* (Cambridge: Harvard University Press, 1962). The reader should in all cases read Maxime Rodinson, "The Western Image and Western Studies of Islam," in *The Legacy of Islam*, 2nd edition, eds., C.E. Bosworth and Joseph

Schacht (Oxford: Clarendon Press, 1974), pp. 9-62. On individual Orientalists and their scholarship until the beginning of the present century, one should also read Johann Fück, *Die Arabischen Studien in Europa bis in den Anfang des 20. Jahrhunderts* (Leipzig: Otto Harrossowitz, 1955). The ideological and political ramifications of Orientalism have been amply indicated by Anouar Abdel-Malek, "L'Orientalisme en crise," *Diogenes*, 44 (1964), pp. 130-140; and Abdul L. Tibawi, "English Speaking Orientalists," *The Muslim World*, 53:3 (1963), pp. 185-204 and 53:4, pp. 298-313. The same article is also printed in *The Islamic Quarterly*, 8:3 (1964), pp. 23-45 and 8:4, pp. 73-88. It has also been published in bound form by Luzac & Co. Ltd., for the Islamic Cultural Center (London: 1964).

6. Levi-Strauss, p. 327. In a reply to Abdel-Malek's article mentioned above, an eminent Orientalist, Francisco Gabrieli, "Apologie de l'orientalisme," *Diogenes*, 50 (1965), pp. 128-136, sees Abdel-Malek's advocacy of writing Oriental history from an Oriental viewpoint as a call for unjustified fair play, as "*il est evident que ... l'Occident ne pourrait jamais accepter cette exigence sans se renier lui-meme et son autoconscience, sa raison de vivre.*"

7. Witness the articulation of optimum diversity in contemporary Western eschatological myth-making in which the unit 'West' is opposed to forces whose description is identical in substance and exhausted as hostility, but which differs in name — Arabism, Communism, Islam — to an extent which cannot but emphasize their essential identity as demonic manifestations of doomsday agents, be they Muammar Qaddafi or the Soviet Union or the forces opposed to the Crusades. On this topic see in particular Jean Charles Fontebrune, *Nosterdamus Historien et prophete: les prophetes de 1500 a l'an 2000* (Monaco: Editions du Rocher, 1981), pp. 361 ff. and 399 ff.

8. The contribution of Oriental thematic units by direct inversion of sense of Western conceptions was elaborated in specific contexts in my "What is the Islamic City?" in *Review of Middle Eastern Studies*, 2 (1976) and Abdallah Laroui, "The Arabs and Cultural Anthropology: Notes on the Method of Gustave von Grunebaum," in *The Crisis of the Arab Intellectual*, trans. from French by Diarmid Cammell (Berkley: University of California Press, 1976). Some of these same themes are developed further in my *Ibn Khaldun in Modern Scholarship: A Study in Orientalism* (London: Third World Center for Research & Publication, 1981); Edward Said, *Orientalism*, p. 141 expresses the same conception in relation to semantic philology. Bryan Turner, *Marx and the End of Orientalism* (London: Allen & Unwin, 1978) has made extensive use of this idea. I am indebted to Bryan Turner for the kind mention in his Preface.

9. Said, *Orientalism*.

10. *Ibid.*, p. 71.

11. A fecund duality of sense reigned in the context of this conception until Kant, before whom the physical and the conceptual acceptations of the term were embroiled together, as has been shown by the analysis of Arthur Schopenhauer, *The Fourfold Root of the Principle of Sufficient Reason*, trans. from German by Karl Hillebrand (London: George Bell and Sons, 1907), pp. 9 ff.

12. Laroui has shown how the dictation of an entire culture by a central idea in the work of Gustav von Grunebaum results in a totality where no concrete element predominates and in which the layers of the culture-society, state, morality, literary expression, etc. — are completely isomorphic.

13. Quoted from Albert Hourani, *Europe and the Middle East* (Berkeley: University of

California Press, 1980), p. 113.

14. Said, p. 72.

15. Richard Antoun, "Anthropology," in Leonard Binder, *The Study of the Middle East* (New York: John Wiley & Sons, 1976), p. 169. The comments of Claude Cahen, "L'Histoire economique et sociale de l'orient musulman medieval," *Studia Islamica,* 3 (1955), pp. 93-115 are still valid today. On Oriental philology today, see Said and the philology and translations of a specific Arabic author see my *Ibn Khaldun*, especially chapter 2.

16. The sole respite in a feeble apology for reactionary Orientalism is Bernard Lewis, "The State of Middle Eastern Studies," *The American Scholar,* 48:3 (Summer 1979), pp. 365-381 where the author likened Orientalists to Germanic philologists whose studies are limited to the *Neibelungenlied* and "who insist that such a study is not only a necessary but also a sufficient preparation for work on modern Germany and, on the other hand, a group of social scientists specializing in modern Germany, who have no knowledge of German beyond elementary hotel and restaurant requirements." Lewis insists that, even if this were to happen, the results would be rather better than those of modern Middle East studies. One of the most eminent Orientalists of this century, armed with knowledge of Arabic, derived out of Ibn Khaldun's theory of *asabiya* his own sociological theory which included maxims for the treatment of domestic servants. See Helmut Ritter, "Irrational Solidarity Groups. A Socio-physochological Study in Connection with Ibn Khaldun," *Oriens* (Leiden), 1 (1948), pp. 1-44.

17. As for this superimposed order of consequence, one could surmise that it only became implicit or incidental after the end of the 1930s, when it was no longer scientifically respectable to organize discrete detail by attributing its essence to racial characteristics.

18. On the imaginative geography of Orientalism see Said, pp. 54 ff.

19. I must agree with Said, p. 72, that Orientalism is a form of radical realism.

20. Degeneration is a *topos* constantly interpolated by things Arabic and Islamic and which merits study.

21. On the whole question of such influence see my *Ibn Khaldun*, especially chapter three and on translations from Arabic, pp. 49 ff.

22. Charles Adams, "Islamic Religious Tradition," in Leonard Binder, *The Study of the Middle East,* p. 31.

23. On *homo islamicus, homo arabicus, homo sinicus,* etc. see Abdel-Malek, p. 113; Rodinson, 47; and Said.

24. Hourani, *Europe and the Middle East,* pp. 14-15.

25. *Ibid.*

26. I have argued the case for such a nominalism in terms of the sociology of religion. I stated that, like other religions, Islam is the articulation in specific instances of a specific historical formation of signs which relate to that opposition between sanctity and profanity which history and accident has specified as being Islamic. The specificity of Islam is affirmed in a number of historical forms which do not express an Islamic essence as much as perform specific valorizations of elements which form the bare features of this

specificity: elementary dogmatic items, fundamental devotions and a system of basic prescriptions and prohibition. There is as such no 'Islamic revolution', for instance, but a revolution in Islam. Especially in this regard see, "Muqaddimat asasiya lil-Islam al mu'asir," *Dirasat Arabiya,* 17:6 (1981). A similar basic idea informs the fundamental prefatory points made by Jean Charles Charnay, *Sociologie religieuse de l'Islam, preliminaires* (Paris: Sindbad, 1977), but it is unfortunately not deployed throughout the book.

27. Hourani, p. 15.

28. See Albert Hourani, "History," in Leonard Binder, *The Study of the Middle East,* pp. 97-135.

29. In a recent book on Ibn Khaldun, for example, A. Oumlil, *L'Histoire et son discours* (Rabat: 1979), pp. 198 ff. seeks to prove that Ibn Khaldun's conception of the political order is dictated by the Koranic conception of *istikhlaf,* briefly, that God mandated Man to ennoble the world of creation with this image. In order to demonstrate this, he has recourse to quoting the Koranic exegesis of Baidawi and asserting that his conception and that of Ibn Khaldun were identical. Although Ibn Khaldun does use the term *istikhlaf,* there are no grounds for assuming that the origin of his conception is the Koran or Baidawi's commentary. But Oumlil saw fit to quote an analysis of this conception virtually at random; one assumes that the exegesis he quotes was simply physically handier than others. The matter for Oumlil obviously did not bear any further investigation — for his sole purpose was evidently to insert Ibn Khaldun in that generality which is his culture in order to name his conception 'Islamic.'

30. More than the misbegottenness of this term requires comment. Its barbarousness underlines two things: that Islam is thinkable in terms of Christianity, being analogously the work and the worship of its prophet, a notion which is heretical to Muslims; and that despite this fact, which might not have been known to the medieval authors of this term but was certainly clear to H.A.R. Gibb, the learned author of *Mohammedanism: An Historical Survey* (New York: Oxford University Press, 1962), Muslims are to be called what the West wishes to call them — the West which is, after all, the sole and autonomous fount of real knowledge about Mohametanism. It is a term which bespeaks a power relationship.

31. Georg W.F. Hegel, *The Philosophy of History,* trans. from German by J. Sibree (New York: Dover Publications, 1956). The ambiguity of the position of Islam in the temporal march of history — it is treated as part of the Germanic, not the Oriental world — does not effect the topical content it is given.

32. *Ibid.,* p. 105. It is impossible to say whether this description is borrowed from Montesquieu or simply runs parallel to it. Oriental empires are viewed as structureless, devoid of laws, reduced to passion and rule over vast undifferentiated spaces devoid of social space and consisting of empty uniformity. On this topic see the excellent account of Louis Althusser, *Politics and History: Montesquieu, Rousseau, Hegel and Marx,* trans. from French by Ben Brewster (London, NLB: 1972), pp. 75 ff. I could not, unfortunately, profit from the penetrating insights of Alain Grosrichard, *Structure au serail la fiction du despostisme asiatique dans l'Occident classique* (Paris: Seuil, 1979) which I only had occasion to read after this article had been completed. This monotony of history, this indistinctness of space and of time has been noted by many, of which Ernest Renan, *Historie generale et systeme compare des langues semitiques* 5th edition (Paris: Clicy, 1878), p. 11, is perhaps the most classic. This point is expressed particularly pungently by Emile Felix Gautier, "Un passage d'Ibn Khaldoun et du Bayan," *Hesperis,* 41 (1924), p. 311, *"si on ecrivait l'histoire du Maghreb . . .*

l'interest serait necessairement l'analys et, s'il se peut, l'explication des grands épisodes sans lien les uns avec les autres."

33. One must mention the notable exception of Jacques Berque, *Essai sur le methode juridique maghrebine* (Rabat: 1944) and in a more traditional vein the work of Robert Brunschvig, "Averroes juriste," *Etudes d'orientalisme dediees a la memoire de Levi-Provencal,* two volumes (Paris: Maissonneuve et larose, 1962).

34. On this topic see my, "What is an Islamic City?"

35. The voluptuousness of Islam is an idea of obscure origins which has titillated the collective libido of Europe for more than a millennium, for example, Giovanni Battista Vico, *The New Science of Giambattista Vico,* trans. from Italian by Thomas G. Bergin and Max H. Fisch (Ithaca, New York: Cornell University Press, 1948) equally but without exoticism, finds nothing else to say about Islam other than its belief in God, an infinite free mind "and an infinite free body, for they [the Muslims] look forward to the pleasures of the senses as rewards in the other life" in the context of his characterization of nations that believe in a provident divinity.

36. This stylization of history has been well described by an Orientalist unsympathetic to the Arabs. See Elie Kedourie, *Arabic Political Memoires and other Studies* (London: Frank Cass, 1974), p. 162.

37. It is thus clear that, while agreeing with the invaluable analysis of Laroui, p. 53 on the play of contrasts in Orientalism, I differ from him on the aetiology of this play: he sees it as a methodological exigency of almost toally heuristic import rather than a fundamental structure.

38. Renan, *Historie generale,* p. 16.

39. This pair of opposites has been discussed by me in *Ibn Khaldun,* chapter 3.

40. Note, for instance, the fact adduced by Antoun, "Anthropology," p. 161, that in spite of the low statistical incidence of 10 to 15% of marriage with the father's brother's daughter in Middle Eastern communities, a vastly disproportionate interest is generated by this institution. Exoticism is naturally one aspect of this interest, but one could also safely surmise that this institution is considered more appropriate to the nature of Middle Easterners because of the opposite restrictiveness it displays.

41. Brunschvig's study of Averroes is one of the few studies we have on this important topic. We also now have the brilliant study of George Makdisi, *The Rise of Colleges: Institutions of Learning in Islam and the West* (Edinburgh: Edinburgh University Press, 1981).

42. See my *Ibn Khaldun,* chapter 3.

43. The statement of Ernest Renan that there is no such thing as Arabic philosophy, but only philosophy written in Arabic, is classic. Renan stated 'philosophy written in Arabic' was "*la reaction de la genie indo'europeen de la Perse contre l'Islamisme.*" It is only recently that Arab-Islamic philosophy has started recovering its autochthonous structures. In this regard see especially the recent work of M.A. Al Jabiri, *Nahnu wat-turath* (Beirut: 1980), which includes studies of Al-Farabi, Avicenna and Averroes.

44. See my *Ibn Khaldun,* chapter 5.

45. Laroui, *The Crisis of the Arab Intellectual,* p. 53.

46. Mircea Eliade, *La nostalgie des Origines; methodologie et histoiree des religions* (Paris: Gallimard, 1971).

47. I discuss these matters in a forthcoming epistemological essay on philology.

48. T. Izutsu, *The Structure of the Ethical Terms in the Koran* (Tokyo: 1959). This book was also published under the title, *Ethico-religious Concepts in the Qur'an* (Montreal: McGill University Press, 1966); Andre Miquel, *Un conte des mille et une nuits* (Paris: Flammarion, 1977).

49. This seems to be the positive impulse of Said's work.

50. It is surprising for an evocator of Foucault, as Edward Said is, to thrust his argument for humanization in the direction of an almost empiricist concern with particularization and *sui generis,* specification of subjects of various descriptions, including the Orient.

51. Turner, p. 95.

5

DUNCAN BLACK MACDONALD: CHRISTIAN ISLAMICIST

Gordon E. Pruett

D uncan Black Macdonald devoted half a century to the study of the Islamic, the Hebrew and the Christian traditions.[1] Each had its roots in the Semitic prophecy. Christianity was rooted and grounded in the peculiar strengths of the great Hebrew prophetic tradition. The truths of Christian doctrine grew from the prophets' experience of Jehovah. As for Islam, its prophecy failed. It never advanced beyond the overwhelming experience of the supernatural, the reality of the unseen, to a fully-fledged idea of the holy. Where Christianity, with its Old Testament roots, brought the unseen into the realm of history and reason and thus santified human life, Islam was simply overpowered and rendered unintelligible by the uncanny.

Macdonald's understanding of Islam amounts to a perception of its failure as a theology, and his analysis of Islam consists in the exploration of the ramifications of this theological failure. He sought to explain Islam as one would explain and solve a problem. Christianity, on the other hand, required not explanation but hermeneutics; and Islam served as his foil. Further, the enterprise to which Macdonald committed himself was no mere intellectual exercise. The failure of Islamic prophecy required a Christian response, the missionary effort. This effort was not to be merely humanitarian — though it certainly was to be that — but also theological and evangelical. Macdonald believed that Muslims are imperiled in the modern world (a situation not solely of their own making); Christianity — and Christian civilization sweetened by the Gospel — could save them. The missionary effort was the effective arm of Christian theology and the proper response of Christians to the failure of Islam.

Explaining Islam

Macdonald set out to explain Islam. The need to explain implies the failure to understand and to participate. Unlike the process of under-

standing and participation the process of explanation is applicable only
to that which is foreign — distant, incomprehensible on the face of it,
irrational, separated from the personal commitments of the observer
and explainer. Macdonald's attitude toward Islam is dominated by these
assumptions from the beginning. Muslims may be saved (it should be
noted that Macdonald's conception of what this means is generous,
sympathetic, tolerant and even understanding); but Islam must be
explained — and finally explained away. The task of explaining Islam
occupied Macdonald throughout his scholarly life. I want to depict this
task and its effects by describing his treatment of the major elements of
Islam. I shall begin with Islam itself.

Islam

Islam is a monolithic unity, writes Macdonald, indivisible and
unchanging. Speaking to an audience of Christians involved in the
missionary work among Muslims he suggests that the nearest parallel in
Western terminology to "Islam" is "Christendom":

> It is a unity for them, a unity more absolute than the term Christendom
> covers for us; but it is a unity of the same nature; and only as you look at it
> in this way — as a unity and not as a multitude of details — can you
> possibly get any idea of its real essential nature.[2]

This characteristic of absolute unity is one of the major sources of
difficulty, even ineptitude, for Islam in the modern world. This Islam,
further, is almost precisely what sprang from the "brain of Muhammad"
(the phrase is significant). It was passed on to his "Church," fostered
there as an idea in the minds and lives of the theologian-statesmen of
Medina, and spread through the followers to this day.[3] But it is in essence
what Muhammad said it was. He said that it was, as its name means,
complete and utter submission. Thus Islam has always been unable to
distinguish between church and state.[4] Such a monolith enjoys no possibility of survival in a world in which its political fortunes fail.

Islam "itself" must be distinguished from Muslim culture. That is,
one must distinguish between the Islam of Muhammad on the one hand
and the attempts to establish it in self-sustaining cultural forms on the
other. Theology, philosophy, education, art, science (political and natural) all arose and decayed in the course of Muslim history. But this
Muslim culture is not the same thing as Islam. In a speech given in 1904

to the International Congress of Arts and Sciences in St. Louis (USA), Macdonald argued that Islam and Muslim civilization have always been separable (the relationship between Christianity and Christendom is markedly different):

> The Muslim civilization may be said to have flourished in spite of Islam. The great thinkers of Islam, apart from some professed theologians, drew no stimulus or guidance from it; often they were hopelessly at odds with it. In the case, even, of the more original theologians, it would be possible to knock away the Muhammadan scaffolding and to let the religious edifice, which they had reared, stand by itself. Their necessary conceptions are purely general, compounded of mysticism and theism. The pecularities of Islam, the bizarre concreteness, sprung from the brain of Muhammad and his immediate constructive followers, drop easily away from them.[5]

It was Islam that survived, not Muslim civilization. Indeed Macdonald holds that Islam is anything but conducive to the construction of civilization. A major cause for this lies in the irrational nature and enormous influence of Muhammad's religious experience. From the start it actively precluded the construction of a self-sustaining culture.

Muhammad

Macdonald's explanation of Islam could be said to be in effect an explanation of Muhammad. For the Arabs, says Macdonald, Muhammad is the greatest of these literary artists;[6] in so saying he passes over in a revealing manner the fundamental claim of Islam to the divine authorship of the Qur'an, that Muhammad could not have written it himself. Macdonald set himself the task of explaining how the revelation of Allah came to be associated with this remarkable man.

Muhammad was a prophet. What kind of prophet Macdonald thought he was is indicated in his concern for explaining the psychological states, the trances, in which tradition says Muhammad received the Qur'an. The manner of explanation is drawn in part from the world and studies of parapsychology:

> . . . there is another source which is open to us and which, with one exception [the individual is not named, although it is probably either Ibn Khaldun or al-Ghazzali] has been entirely neglected by Muslims. It is the study of the parallels which appear in the case of what we call now-a-days trance-mediums; the phenomena exhibited by those mediums who

enter a trance, speak in that trance, and give signs in one way or another while in a hypnotic state. In such cases, I have no question, is really to be found the clue to Muhammad.[7]

Moreover, whatever else we may say about Muhammad, Macdonald concludes, "he was essentially a pathological case."[8] It is, then, to Muhammad's psyche, an unbalanced psyche, that he turns for explanation of Muhammad's prophecy. Muhammad was oppressed by a sense of overwhelming evil. This evil lay behind the visible world as an unseen reality, but dreadfully near. "At every turn he felt . . . a sense of the wrath to come."

Now the oppressive evil of the world and its impending doom was a message he had gleaned, in erratic and disjointed fashion, from Christian hermits living in the desert whom he met in his travels, and from Christian groups observed in worship.[9] The teaching which emerged was a jumbled recollection of Christian tradition proclaimed by a trance-medium (in fact, a *kahin*, a soothsayer, on which see below). He did not have any very clear idea of what being a prophet meant. He was aware of the sacred books of the Jews and Christians. He knew that they had a series of prophets. What his mind did was this:

> These scattered fragments that he had picked up of the history of the Old Testament he proceeded to weave together into a whole. To these, too, he made additions. It is evident that in his time there were additions of prophets who had come to the Arabs themselves. These he wove together from the stories of the Old Testament in strange, broken fragments and confused, anachronistic order, and made them into what has since become to the Muslim Church its canonical history of revelation.[10]

His memory of them was fallible in the extreme. These stories had been stored up in Muhammad's brain with the "most singular, most unparalleled inaccuracy," and made over with the "utmost freedom of imagination."[11] This explanation allows no acknowledgement that Muhammad had received the Qur'an in the manner in which Muslims believe he did. Islam is in fact a kind of Christian heresy proclaimed by "a pathological case."[12]

In the West it has long been held that Muhammad was an imposter. Nothing could be further from the truth, Macdonald argues. "The mere fact of what he did; the witness of the men whom he gathered about him; the impression that he made upon his people; . . . all these things show that the man was real. . . ."[13] Muhammad was absolutely sincere

— at least in the first part of his career as prophet. It is true, Macdonald insists, that Muhammad was a failure as a politician. He was neither politic nor a schemer. He was anything but clear-headed. But he possessed what Max Weber called charisma. He attracted powerful loyalty; and he was a superb judge of character. This personal influence, all unconscious, is the key to understanding the power of Muhammad among his Arab followers.[14]

But there can be no question, says Macdonald, of the fact that Muhammad abused his prophetic role and his power in the last years of his life, the years between the Hijrah and his death. He forged "the awful machinery of divine inspiration to serve his own ignoble and selfish purpose. How he passed over, at least, into that turpitude is a problem again for those who have made a study of how the most honest trance-mediums may at any time begin to cheat."[15] The moral declension of that period, Macdonald asserts, is undeniable and can never be explained away.

As for the crucial issue of the theology of Muhammad, it is one of confusion and contradiction. From it Islam was never to escape. On the one hand, for example, Allah is the sole reality. On the other, the world cannot participate in any manner in the divine reality. This is a dualistic view, drawing the line between the world and Allah. Yet at other times Muhammad speaks like the monist: " 'Allah's are the East and West; wherever ye turn, there is the Visage of Allah.' "[16] The truth is that Muhammad "could never have framed a rounded system or held to it."[17] One could expect nothing else from a "diseased genius," "ever greedy of the strange," caught in "his trances and the visions and the voices that came to him in those trances,"[18] susceptible to "Syriac, Greek, Ethiopic and Persian words and ideas."[19]

Muslims came to see Muhammad as the first created being, the light of light, for whose sake the worlds were created and who possessed a perfect, sinless moral nature. This last, notes Macdonald, is in the teeth of Qur'anic teaching (e.g. 48:1, 2) on Muhammad; but "the logic that is derived from the aspirations of religion does not care anything for such contradictions. . . ."[20] As a moral model Muhammad is a dubious proposition; and consistent with its skewed nature Islam often chose to imitate him at his worst. The doctrine of the imitation of Muhammad distinguishes between imitation with respect to his internal character and his external behavior. It is of course the latter in which imitation is obligatory. But in the case of Muhammad's treatment of women, for example, the effects have been disastrous for Islam, for Muslim civilization and especially for women. The position of women in Islam, says Macdonald "is practically due to the attitude of Muhammad himself," despite modern reforming attempts to show that in this particular respect Muhammad cannot be imitated because of his singular role as prophet. Polygamy and purdah are Muhammad's doing. The women of the pre-Islamic Arabian culture were free and equal in their relations with men. It was, frankly, "the insane jealousy of Muhammad" which brought that happier situation to an end and condemned the Muslim woman to her present servile state.[21] In truth, observes Macdonald, Muhammad is an enormous liability for modern Islam. So long as his figure was obscured by belief in his mystical powers, his sinless nature, his status as the Seal of the Prophets, as the earthly source of Allah's truth, he served as a refuge to which all Islam might repair in the face of confusion and opposition. But the fact is that the literary and historical science of the present reveal a figure with obvious feet of clay. When viewed critically as a moral paradigm he constitutes a peril to the unity of Islam. "As the moral standard of the masses of Islam is raised and the facts of the life of Muhammad become more widely known," writes Macdonald, "a tremendous overturning will be inevitable."[22]

Finally, Macdonald notes that since we cannot take the teachings of Muhammad nor the content of his message to be explanatory of his greatness we must look to his character, his command:

> It was not the content of his teaching that was the principal thing; it was the fact that he was there to teach. From this point of view his position was: Accept me and obey me; not, Hear the word of Allah which he has spoken to me. The result of his mission was to provide an autocratic chief, acting as representative of Allah in a theocratic state.[23]

His conviction that he was no mere mouthpiece of Allah, but a ruler, was absolute. "How the streams of deception and self-deception crossed and tangled in his brain we cannot determine." But Muhammad proclaimed himself above all.[24] It was his right to demand the obedience of all, and to proceed against any if they rejected him. Islam may have the message for all mankind; but Muhammad meant to rule as the divinely-chosen head. Against this conviction of his teaching, the Qur'an, and all subsequent constructions pale into relative insignificance.

Qur'an

From the viewpoint of explanation the place of the Qur'an is a relatively simple matter to grasp. The Qur'an is "trustworthy throughout, and . . . gives us access to the central face of Islam, the personality and religious experience of the Prophet."[25] That experience is faithfully expressed, Macdonald concludes, in the "contradictions and assumptions of the Qur'an — knotted and twisting as Muhammad's own brain."[26] The Qur'an is "simply a collection of fragments gathered up from those trance utterances of Muhammad."[27] It is an "absolute chaos," yet a chaos with a curiously mechanical arrangement, rather like that of the book of Amos in the Old Testament. The traditional organization of the Qur'an has two corresponding characteristics: (1) the shorter sentences, and thus the shorter surahs, occur at the end of the text, and the longer at the beginning; (2) the shorter sections belong to Muhammad's earlier period, and the longer to the latter. At first glance this seems a highly mechanical and arbitrary arrangement. But, says, Macdonald, external as this critical arrangement was, it is entirely sound.[28]

The distinction drawn by this arrangement is between the genuine ecstatic prophetic utterances emanating from the trances and experiences of the unseen — i.e. the shorter, jerkier ones — the longer, contrived and fabricated sentences of a Muhammad who had lost the gift but desired the power that attended it. There can be no doubt, Macdonald observes, that in his earlier period Muhammad fell into trances, heard voices and saw visions. These he reported as faithfully as his unconscious demanded. They "were pressed out of him, as it were — out of his sub-conscious self, or whatever you choose to call it — and naturally they were short and broken; they were scattered; they came in jerks." But the later, rolling paragraphs tell a different story, "when he came consciously to manipulate these utterances."[29] Here the imitation is obvious, and obviously a failure. For Muhammad's later pronouncements on inheritance, marriage, the position and dignity of the Prophet emerged not from trances but from his desire to achieve "his own distinct objects."[30] Of this later period, concludes Macdonald, the less said the better.

As for the genuine article, those early, jerky, powerful pronouncements, they (and Muhammad with them) stood in the line of the particular prophetic and ecstatic tradition of the *kahin*, the soothsayer, of pre-Islamic Arabia. It is perfectly understandable, Macdonald argues, that the heathen Meccans should have accused Muhammad of being nothing more than yet another old soothsayer, for he spoke their language, their rhyme and their rhythm. "In every respect his external appearance was that of the soothsayer."[31]

The Muslim world will not and cannot concur in this view of the Qur'an. Thus, says Macdonald, it is the task of the Western scholar to improve on the vast but incomplete Islamic work of interpreting the Qur'an; for those of the Western world "come with, I think, on the whole, clearer eyes, fewer prejudices and a really wider knowledge of the external surroundings of Muhammad."[32]

It has been said frequently that the real analogy between Christianity and Islam is between Christ as Logos and the Qur'an as the Uncreated Word of God; both are self-revelations of God. Macdonald accepts this analogy, for the notion of the Uncreated Qur'an is simply a borrowed, altered and misunderstood version of the Logos doctrine of Christ. Islam has replaced Christ with the Qur'an; it has replaced the ideal of divine paternity and the sonship of Christ and men with the doctrine of a fixed and unchanging Book.

> Here again, the tendency of Islam to assimilate doctrines from without early asserted itself, and there can be no question that the development of the doctrine of the Qur'an was very early affected by the doctrine of the Word of God that became flesh and dwelt among man, especially as that was formulated by the Greek Church. The view which we find crystallizing may be put thus: The Qur'an is to be regarded as uncreated.[33]

This Eastern Christian doctrine had removed virtually every human element from its concept of Christ's nature. Such is true also of the Qur'an. Its actual phrasing, Macdonald points out, is attributed to the movement of the Pen upon the Preserved Tablet in response to — and only in response to — the Will of Allah. It contains no human element whatsoever; and although the theologians attempted to be more "precise than they logically could" on this point,[34] the issue was settled. Macdonald laments for Islam; for if there had been a secure footing established for the human element in the Qur'an, the awful gap between man and Allah might have been narrowed. The fact remained that the Logos doctrine of Christology was imported, applied to the Qur'an, and interpreted in a distorted and literalist manner which, in Macdonald's view, came to be characteristic of Islam.[35] The modern Muslim, beset with doubts, has recourse to the Qur'an. But this Qur'an is the product of the "wild statements" of Muhammad and the attitude inculcated in his followers. It offers no solace.[36]

The Oriental/Muslim Mind

Essential to Macdonald's explanation of Islam is his view of the Oriental mind. It is for him foreign and uncanny. Islam is simply the best expression of the Orient. It is essential, he urges, that the West understand this mind; for its success in dealing with the Orient will otherwise be greatly endangered. I have elected to present two major characteristics of the Oriental mind as Macdonald describes it. First, he says, it cared little for fact and allowed fantasy free reign. It was not bothered by contradiction. Second, the Oriental mind was committed to an unqualified pragmatic utilitarianism and was therefore distrustful of research, pure thought and free intellectual endeavor pursued for its own sake.

Fact, Fantasy and Reason

In his address to the St. Louis Congress in 1904, Macdonald stressed the fact of a fundamental difference between Islamic and Western modes of thought. One must learn, he said, "a whole habit of attitude of mind, foreign to us at every turn."[37] Muslim philosophy, he noted, was contradictory, inadequate, irrational, and doomed from the start by the model of Muhammad and the inability of the Oriental mind to think clearly. Of Ibn Arabi, for example, he writes:

> He had no need for analogy [*qiyas*] or opinion [*ra'y*] for any kind of the workings of the vain human intelligence so long as the divine light was flooding his soul and he saw the things of the heavens with plain vision. So his books are a strange jumble of theosophy and metaphysical paradoxes . . . To what extent he was sincere in his claim of heavenly illuminings and mysterious powers it would be hard to say. The oriental mystic has little difficulty in deceiving himself.[38]

Ibn Arabi's problems with logic and structure were hardly unique. In his extended essay, *The Religious Attitude and Life of Islam*, Macdonald summarizes the "acknowledged difference" between East and West:

> It is not the attitude to God, but the attitude to law. The essential difference in the oriental mind is not credulity as to unseen things, but inability to construct a system as to seen things.[39]
>
> It has been well said, that the oriental has the most astonishing keenness in viewing, grasping, analyzing a single point, and, when he has finished with that point, can take up a series of others in the same way.

> They may be contradictory; that does not trouble him. When he con-
> structs systems — as he often does — it is by taking a single point, and
> spinning everything out of it; not by taking many points and building
> them up together.[40]

In other words, the Oriental has no sense of law and order. "There is
no necessity in themselves why the things that have been should be the
things that will be."[41] The consequences for the possibility of science (in
the Western sense) among Muslims are great and clear; but they are
there for all possible forms of systematic thought, philosophy and
indeed culture as a whole. The Oriental needs but one point, an atom of
thought, and he will develop an entire cosmology from it — but
without reference to any other thing, idea, or event. Start, for example,
"the idea that [Muhammad] is a messenger from God and that his words
are the words of God, and the oriental mind would carry it out to its
utmost limits. A theory of all things in heaven and earth would be
developed from this single idea." Incompatibility with other ideas is
simply ignored.[42] It is important, Macdonald argues, that the Western
student understand two summary points about the religious life of
Islam: (1) "*Inability* to see life steadily, and see it whole, to understand
that a theory of life must cover all the facts;" (2) "*liability* to be
stampeded by a single idea and blinded to everything else — therein, I
believe, is the difference between the East and the West."[43]

This fundamental lack of integration of thought with thought is
compounded by the inability to distinguish between thought and deed,
between fantasy and reality. The East, Macdonald notes, has "suffered
for centuries from creeds without relation to conduct and mystical
religion without contact with realities."[44] How may we explain this?
Macdonald looked to the popular literature of the Muslim world for the
answer. He found it in what he believed to be the essentially romantic
nature of the Oriental mind. And he was sympathetic; for the romance
of fantasy has its own power for him, deceptive though it be. He notes
that he has

> a weakness for saints. They make the romance of the religious life, and
> their biographies — try, for example, *The Golden Legend* — move in the
> air as remote from our treadmill existence as *The Arabian Nights*, and yet
> are instinct with [*sic*] spiritual realities and vitalizing energies. For them
> the ancient world is ever fresh and young, and the Spirit of God still
> broods visible over it. The milk of Paradise is on their lips and they hear

the footsteps of the Almighty. There is nothing too wonderful to happen to them, and through everything that happens they look straight back to God.[45]

Sympathetic as one must be for the romance of religion one must also realize that in the East it annihilates any appreciation of facts. Macdonald's travels in the East provided many examples of what he referred to as a "conspiracy of misinformation" joined with a readiness to construct fables on the spot. On some points, he says in exasperation, "I was driven, at last, to absolute agnosticism when it came to getting information about questions of fact — not of theology or anything of that kind but of historical events in the past and situations and attitudes in the present."[46]

There is, then, no ethical sense of fact in the East. This is not, Macdonald thinks, a deliberate attempt to mislead others or even oneself. Rather it arises out of the supremacy of imagination and the stunted growth of empirical thought. The Oriental "has the creative imagination of a child. . . . " He will make something up for you, dress it as an answer to your earnest question, and give it to you. ". . . [A]nd he is so well pleased with his creation that it becomes solid and real in his eyes." He does this, moreover, with a good conscience![47]

Given the power of imagination in the Oriental mind, one should not expect much from their historians. And indeed, concludes Macdonald, with one or two exceptions there is no historical sense among the intellectuals or the masses of Islam.[48] The central place of the chain of tradition (isnad), of Hadith, proclaims the absence of any good historical consciousness. The chains, he notes, were for the most part forged in both senses of the term; yet the Muslim historian goes to work with them as his source. "If our methods," observes Macdonald, "tend to subjectivity run wild, theirs tend to objectivity without basis."[49] The situation is no better among those reformers who have attempted to bypass the problems of Hadith and return to the Qur'an itself, or even among those who have attempted to modernize Islam by explaining away everything which they cannot rationally accept. In each case the lack of an historical sense, the sense that it is important to know as much as one can about what did in fact happen, hinders and hobbles every step. Muslim history is as much a failure as any of the other cultural artifacts of Islam.[50]

This failure is related to the strangely mechanical and arbitrary nature of Muslim argumentation. "The Muslim reasoner deals with ideas as if they were blocks of wood, solid things in your possession, as to which there was no question what they were; you could handle them as you pleased and move them this way and that."[51] So in the vital area of the Muslim attitude toward revelation and scripture there is simply a confused jumble of ideas derived in a myriad of different and unconnected ways. No attempt is made to think things through with unwavering attention to logical connection and historical evidence.[52] There is, indeed, no moral sense of correctness. Al-Ghazzali himself, for whom Macdonald has great respect, was culpable.

> We find him saying very gravely, "Moses [sic] says in the Law, 'Rend your hearts and not your garments.' " Had the whole moral sense, all feeling for fact, been rotted away by lightness of belief? This man was a great theologian and yet he could play fast and loose in this fashion.[53]

An explanation for this extraordinary behavior may lie, Macdonald suggests, in the Muslim fear of verifying references. They were afraid to "risk their faith" by reading the scriptures themselves, instead accepting the scraps which various proselytes had brought them.[54] Islam managed to exist without ever conducting a systematic comparative examination of the scriptures of the Jews and Christians and the Muslim versions of their content. Moreover, even the great histories of the golden age set down the strangest fabulae alongside the results of their sporadic researches into the actual facts. Edifying tales and historical record appear side by side as though they were equally true and accurate.[55] Of historical imagination, further, we find very little in Muslim literature; but there is an "indefinite amount of mythologizing fancy."[56]

Troublesome as all this failed historiography is to Macdonald he recognizes that it is not a cause for concern among Muslims. The Muslim knows the old stories and romances, and can easily "imagine himself being caught up in the action of one of them; they might, so far as he knows, have befallen his next door neighbor or a man in the next lane. The theology, the incidents, the zeal, the trust, the wanderings, the adventures are all his, and overwhelmingly real."[57] History and story are the same for him. There is no Herodotus in Islam.

One searched Muslim thought in vain for a systematic theology, an analytical philosophy, an empirical history. To these goals the Oriental mind is virtually immune. By contrast, that mind is ever susceptible to the wildest flights of fancy, unreality and mad schemes. Writing in 1923 on "The Near East Tangle" for *The Yale Review*, Macdonald instructs his readers on the psychology of the East:

> . . . the East, for all its supposed calm, fatalism, and apartness, is much more unstable, nervously and emotionally, than the West. We may have our "crime waves," and our young people may seem to have got a bit out of hand; but the brain storms of the East are pandemic, rise to cataclysms, and threaten catastrophe.[59]
>
> The life of *The Arabian Nights* . . . is still the ideal of the Moslem East.[60]

The Oriental mind is radically different from "ours," concludes Macdonald; and "our" understanding — or explanation — of Islam lies in comprehending the psychology of Islam. It is a psychology, as Freud might have said, of the id rather than the ego, impatient of reality, ruled by self-deception.

Utilitarianism in Islam

Insofar as a philosophical perspective is to be found in Islam, argues Macdonald, it is pragmatic and utilitarian. The failure of Muslim culture and the dominance of literalist and pragmatic theology in Islam are directly attributable to this aspect. One might see an apparent contradiction between this utilitarianism and the hegemony of the imagination in Islam. Macdonald's version of Muslim pragmatism, however, is spiritual pragmatism. A Muslim lives in continual fear of the Fire. The Muslim life is nothing more or less than a response to that fear.

All Muslim thought and practice is inspired by pragmatism of the sort described by William James' *Varieties of Religious Experience*. One believes and practices because it is beneficial — rather than because it is true.[61] There is no alternative position. Speculation on matters of metaphysics, ontology and cosmology is regarded as irrelevant and suspect. For example, addressing the issue of the failure of Islam to develop a science of its own, Macdonald observes that philosophical speculation, which is the basis of culture, was simply repressed. This was not due, as some have thought, to the doctrine of predestination. Rather "it is that for Islam the map of life is fixed, the scheme of existence all arranged and for the best. Man needs only to accept and enjoy what the bounty of Allah has prepared. Nothing is left to seek or to improve."[62] The proper response is adjustment and acceptance. Knowledge, as Ibn Khaldun states, falls into two categories: (1) what is necessary for us to know with respect to our final salvation; (2) what is necessary for our living in the world. All else is to be left alone. Even those things which are not hurtful to use but do not fall into either of these categories are to be ignored. Ibn Khaldun holds that such "letting alone" is the same as drawing near to Allah; it is the beauty of *islam*, of submission.[63] This is not Ibn Khaldun's view only:

> knowledge for its own sake has no place; it must be of use for this world or the next. And this is not simply theological; it is in the very nature of the Muslim mind. We can say, "This is an interesting book;" in Arabic you cannot express that idea. . . . Even curiosity, in the highest and finest sense, we cannot render. It is either deep, devoted study and research, or intrusive spying.
>
> Here, beyond question, we have one of the keys to the fatal defect in the Muslim mind. Exceptions, of course, there have been, conscious and unconscious, but the whole trend of usage and weight of influence have gone to limit and destroy free intellectual workings; the object must be plain from the first, and be one of certain classified kinds. Investigation which does not know where it is going to come out, and what it may produce, and does not care, is under the Muslim ban.[64]

This stark utilitarianism is, surprisingly, especially marked in Muslim mysticism. For Macdonald, mysticism in Islam means the experience of the unseen. The mystic in Islam is not consumed by the desire to achieve the end of the distinction between self and God for its own sake. Rather, the nearness of Allah is to be sought so that one may avoid the Fire. This is the view of Ibn Khaldun and even Al-Ghazzali.[65] Al-Ghazzali's famous and influential investigation of the Sufi tradition was pursued, says Macdonald, for utilitarian ends. His great autobiography could not simply stand as a great human document or even as an *apologia pro vita sua*.[66]

The utilitarian orientation pervades the mind of Islam. It necessarily rules its educational philosophy. Macdonald recounts an interview with the head of the Al-Azhar University. Having demonstrated his *bona fides* with respect to Arabic texts in logic, Macdonald was appalled to discover that the head was not at all interested in pursuing any further lines of inquiry. The education "stops at the tools. It trains the memory and the power of reasoning — always in formal methods — and then gives to neither any adequate material on which to work."[67]

What of education for the masses? The notion of general education, says Macdonald, has never gained footing in Islam precisely because of the fundamental spiritual pragmatism which regards knowledge apart from that conducive to living in the world of Allah's creation and avoiding the Fire of Allah's Judgment as wasteful of time and energy.[68]

Nor was art possible, if by art one means the creation of forms corresponding in some way to beauty and truth. The artist in Islam is an artisan, a member of a guild, a simple maker of things, just as the student or scholar in Islam is a simple repeater of words. "There was never any such thing as Arab architecture, and when we speak of Muslim architecture, all that can be meant under that phrase is the architecture developed by Muslim purposes in Muslim countries by non-Muslim builders."[69] Islam has no respect for art for it is not conducive to salvation or helpful in this world. The artisan has an altogether different justification.

The three spheres of learning in Islamic cultures — the university schools, the primary schools (*kuttub*) and the guilds — are not concerned with knowledge. Should the pursuit of "unattached, free, useless — as it would seem — speculations, which are the food of the true intellectual life," appear, it would (and did) find no home in Islam. " . . . [W]hen the subjects taught in a university have to justify their existence at the bar of usefulness, it is ill with the future of that university, and with the civilization which it represents."[70] There were exceptions. Ibn Khaldun criticized the mere repetition and compilation of past authorities and encouraged the pedagogy of understanding. "But alas for Islam! Few have been the Muslims who have taken Ibn Khaldun's advice." Indeed, even Ibn Khaldun felt it necessary to defend his treatment of many topics as specifically relevant to this life or the gain of the world to come despite his evident interest in "unprofitable things."[71]

It is only in the last years, says Macdonald, in which Islam had to respond to western encroachment and in which the Christian educational missions were active, that the pedagogy of understanding has challenged utilitarian imitation. In this progress it is in fact the mission schools and colleges at first and latterly the goverment schools which have begun to alter the course of learning.[72]

The history of Muslim culture, such as it is, is one of sporadic renaissances (in the Abbasid, Fatimid and Spanish Umayyad dynasties), each brief and forced, and none Arabian in origin. " . . . Islam has never been able to show any definite thread of progress, one period leading to another, all being a part of a steady forward drift."[73] It is true that the Islamic world found, kept and transmitted the Greek philosophical tradition to Europe, who is for this reason in her debt. Yet Macdonald concludes that because of Muslim utilitarian thinking no attempt of any lasting influence was made to change, alter and incorporate that tradition within the Muslim revelation. Rather it was simply held as an enclave for a time and eventually yielded up altogether. It was the Christian West which made use of the philosophical contributions of Greece in the development of its science — a task never seriously attempted in Islam. It was Christianity which now permitted, now encouraged, the notion "that it is man's duty to seek to fathom [nature's] mysteries, and to make ever clearer its workings as those of God." Islam simply accepted as given, if incomprehensible, the universe of Allah's will "without considering it too carefully."[74]

The Failure of Reason

Macdonald's explanation of Islam is in large part an explanation of its failure to sanctify reason as a redeeming quality of, and means of approach to, God. Islam never addressed seriously nor resolved the question of faith and reason. The general picture is, instead, of disjointed and imported theories, of theologies tentatively explored and rejected, of reason discredited and ignored, of lifeless forms of dogma and law on the one hand and wild imaginings and brainstorms on the other.

The Doctrine of the Difference of Allah

For Muhammad, Macdonald argues, there is but one reality, Allah. He is different from man in every respect. He is unqualified by any power save His own. Reason, then, could never hope to approach Allah on its own terms nor on His. All metaphysical systems must fail in Islam, and they all did fail. Says Macdonald, "The thinkers of Islam had been through them all, and had come out with empty hands. Reason, however subtle, could find no means of passing from 'me' to 'thee,' from the effect to the cause.'[75] There were, in short, no mediating causes and no mediators between God and man. This was Muhammad's doing, although Macdonald also sees clear influence from a particular Christian theology to be a cause of Muhammad's and Islam's overbalancing on the side of Allah.[76]

This utter otherness of Allah contrasts strangely with the anthropomorphic imagery of the Qur'an: Allah, for example, sits on His Throne. The orthodox response to the contrast, says Macdonald, is to discourage further enquiry: "the meaning of these [anthropomorphic] expressions is not to be asked. How Allah can be and do such things you must leave alone, and, above all, you must not make any comparison between Allah and men. You must not think that anything Allah does is really measurable in terms of our thought. That is where the doctrine of the Difference of Allah essentially comes in.'[77] He summarizes the doctrine in this way:

> [beyond other qualities of Allah] is the great possibility . . . that every logically possible thing is open to him, while nothing is incumbent upon him. This is the great possibility for man as well, for it means that every slightest element in the life of man is absolutely in the hand of Allah. When combined with the doctrine of Allah's difference, it reaches religious nihilism, or rather anarchy. There is no unity in the world, moral or physical or metaphysical; all hangs from the individual will of Allah.[78]

This anarchy is, again, rooted in the experience of Muhammad. Muhammad had the genuine religious experiences of a saint; but he also taught the uncompromised absoluteness of Allah and the slavery of men. When in the course of events the two ideas came into conflict, however, the doctrine of the Difference of Allah asserted itself, rendering further argument, theology and philosophy useless in the face of the incomprehensible nature of Allah's relationship with the world: " . . . religion became a theology of the most closely argued, invulnerable, but also impossible type.'[79]

One response which arose in Muslim thought was mystical pantheism. There was, observes Macdonald, no alternative for the devout soul. If, as the doctrine of Difference stated, Allah is utterly incomprehensible and unapproachable, then religious life is pointless. The fact is that the great Muslims were devout souls. Pantheism thus became a more powerful thrust in Islam than it ever did in Christianity. Christianity provided, in its fundamental doctrine of incarnation and in the trinitarian view, a theology of relationship rather than difference between man and God and between world and God. For Islam,

> In the struggle to bring God and his creation together, the creation had to become an aspect of the creator, and finally to vanish into him. Only in this way could the crass dualism be overcome, and that monism which is the basis or result of all mysticism be reached.[80]

This is true even for Muhammad, despite his insistence upon the utter otherness of Allah. The paradox did not trouble Muhammad's brain ("oriental to the core"); and Allah "could be throned apart in unapproachable grandeur yet be near to every human heart."[81] Indeed, concludes Macdonald, whenever the genuinely devout religious life comes into contact with the "scheme of Muslim theology," it must break. "For it, within Islam itself, there is no place. The enormous handicap of the dogmatic system is too great; and if it would live its life, it must wander out into the heresies either of the mystic or the philosopher."[82]

It is evident, says Macdonald, "how barren philosophy, in the strict sense, was in Islam itself, how little, if any, change or advance was made from the Greek positions." To Muslim thinkers fell the burden of conveying this philosophy of the Greeks to the West. But they conveyed it without understanding it; and, indeed, they confused it. That it was the school of the Neo-Platonist Plotinus which gained the upper hand is simply indicative of the "elective genius of [Islam's] oriental fervours. . . ."[83]

It can be said, he notes, that there are two systems of philosophy in Islam. One is a "very curious compound of Aristotelianism and Neo-Platonism." The other is atomism, to which we shall turn below. The former is the result of "a quite overwhelming bit of literary mischief." Macdonald suggests that in the ninth century A.D. a Syrian Christian of Emessa compiled a collection of excerpts from Plotinus' *Enneads*, translated them into Arabic, and entitled the result *The Theology of Aristotle*. Muslims "took this audacity quite solemnly. Here was a solution at last of the century-old problem. The labour of reconciling Aristotle and Plato . . . was accomplished by the stroke of an oriental pen."[84] This literary fraud led to the acceptance of Neo-Platonism and the Aristotelianism of the later Peripatetic Schools as the essential Greek philosophy. As philosophy, that is as an approach to truth, Muslim thinkers held that it must be in agreement with the Qur'an. That the resultant hodge-podge could serve as the foundation for such clarity of thought as seen in the work of Ibn Rushd, Ibn Sina and Al-Farabi is, states Macdonald, incontrovertible evidence of the sanity of the human mind. He observes,

> But is it not wonderful that, dealing with such materials and contradic-
> tions, they developed a tendency to mysticism. There were many things
> which they felt compelled to hold which could only be defended and
> rationalized in that cloudy air and slanting light. Especially, no one but a
> mystic would bring together the emanations of Plotinus, the ideas of
> Plato, the spheres of Aristotle and the seven-storied heaven of
> Muhammad.[85]

All of this was aided not a little by the typical Oriental disdain for confirmation of sources, by "a childlike acceptance of tradition" combined with "the narrowest of deduction."[86]

Neither internal nor external traditions served Islam well in the problems of faith and reason. Islam never resolved those problems. It contributed, further, to its own confusion by the importation and misperception of non-Islamic philosophical traditions. Here is yet another example of the failure of Islam to produce a culture.

Islamic Atomism

Yet there is in the peculiar Islamic doctrine of atomism a possible Muslim philosophy. It is not wholly Islamic, as Macdonald finally concluded. But in the end it won the day as the only orthodox philosophical position which explained the relationship between Allah and His world.

The doctrine of atomism is the work of the school of Al-Ashari. Given the doctrine of Allah's Difference and Unity, no reality other than Allah need or may be posited. All events, therefore, are the direct result of Allah's work and will. The world is Allah's perpetual creation, arrangement and annihilation of "atoms." There are neither interme-diary bodies nor self-sustaining states. Both time and space are atomistic in this sense, and are not self-sustaining. No atom has continuing existence in and of itself; its existence is wholly dependent upon the direct action of Allah. The Aristotelian accidents are the atoms of

Allah's creation. Aristotelian substance does not exist. Macdonald observes that according to this system all philosophy, including ethics, in the strict sense is impossible. There is no "nature," no "personality," no "will" to understand. Each is a direct and miraculous creation of Allah.[87]

No being other than Allah may be said to act. Macdonald illustrated this point in his Lamson lectures by lifting a book. He commented, "In no sense can it be said, then, for example, if I lift this book that that act belongs to me." The Muslim theologians regard the world and each act in it as "a miracle always and constantly going on . . . .[A]ll through the existence of the world — from moment to moment — there is this miraculous creation . . . ."[88] Allah has created the movement of the hand, has created "you cannot say a movement, but, rather a series of books, as it goes upon its way until it lands here."[89] It is like a cinematograph, a rapid and unending series of creations.[90]

Whence came this remarkable theory, "this grotesque . . . tremendously thorough conception and application of the atomic scheme?"[91] In his later writings, notably *The Hebrew Philosophical Genius* and his essay on "Continuous Recreation and Atomic Time," Macdonald is drawn to non-Muslim sources to explain the atomic philosophy. In the latter essay he notes suggestive similarities between Muslim atomism and two Buddhist schools, the Sautrantica and the Vaibashika. It struck him as remarkable that the same idea of non-continuity as a quality of the world itself should lead on the one hand, in the case of Islam, to a belief in the utter reality of Allah, and on the other, in the case of Buddhist philosophy, to the utter emptiness of being itself, divine or worldly (*anicca*).[92] The "original contribution," then, is itself derived and grotesque.

Reason and the People

Islam, we must conclude, does not possess any philosophy worthy of the name. Yet its (ultimately fruitless) efforts to develop a reasoned defense of Muhammad's experience had significant influence for Islam as a Church. These efforts to integrate borrowed systems led to ever-increasing degrees of sophistry, convoluted argumentation and obscurantism. From these exercises the masses were excluded, first by incomprehension and then, in addition by deliberation. Macdonald comments extensively on this division between the truths of the philosophers and theologians on the one hand and the religious life of the ordinary Muslim on the other. The failure of Islam is in part directly attributable to this division.[93]

The great intellectuals of Islam lived and studied at the courts of the Abbasids, the Fatimids, the Spanish Ummayads. They took no interest in the mass of Muslims. "To that democracy Islam has never come. Hampered by scholastic snobbishness, it has never learned that the abiding victories of science are won in the village school . . . ."[94] This "economy of teaching" principle is to be found even in the work of Al-Ghazzali. The truth cannot be borne: the masses could never be taught. With Averroes the discrimination of levels of truth "hardened . . . into the philosophical doctrine of the two-fold truth." The truth for the masses flatly contradicted the truths of the intellectuals, and this, notes Macdonald, was thought to be the right and proper state of affairs.[95] It is true, he notes, that the religion of the masses tends universally to be a religion of phrases, of little-understood words. But the Islamic intellectuals sought to defend rather than to rectify this situation.[96]

The situation was made worse by one of its inevitable historical consequences, the vast chasm which arose between the colloquial Arabic of the people and the language of the learned. "The great hope of the Arabic speaking races," he concludes, "lies in the rise of an Arabic literature written in the language spoken by these peoples. At present their older literature is as remote from them as Latin to an Italian or Spaniard." A beginning has been made, notes Macdonald; but it is limited to "stories, jests and satirical verses." The Arabic world awaits its Dante, its Chaucer, still. When he comes there will be a renaissance "as tremendous as that of Europe." The comparison implied between the medieval world of Europe and the present of Islam is quite intentional.[97]

The Triumph of Mysticism

Macdonald's explanation of Islam is in part of an explanation of the failure of reason. The other side of the coin is the triumph of mysticism. By mysticism Macdonald means experience of the supernatural, of the world of the unseen. Thus Islam is, for Macdonald, a religion in which reason is finally dismissed in favor of the direct knowledge of the other world. Here is the foundation of its beliefs and practices. This, he argues, was true from the very beginning, that is, in the experience of Muhammad.

Muhammad as a Mystic

Macdonald writes,

> . . . adrift on the mystic sea . . . [Muhammad] could not have compared, defined nor explained his wavering thoughts . . . . So, then, I take it that the essential and characteristic elements in the prophetship, in the creed, in the personality of Muhammad all lead us back to something unhealthy, ununified; but to something also in its earlier phases and through the greater part of its life and growth absolutely sincere — absolutely, entirely real.[98]

Muhammad's proclamation of Islam is, then, the proclamation of his knowledge of Allah as derived from direct experience of a supernatural power of overwhelming grandeur and awesomeness. All that survived in Islam lived in the fevered brain of Muhammad the trance-medium.[99] "Muhammad," says Macdonald, "was simply a god-intoxicated poet. The feeling of Allah overwhelmed him, and that feeling he sought to express in all those different phrases" of the Qur'an.[100]

Allah was accessible to Muhammad not through reason but through direct experience. The nature and forms of this experience are our present concern. Muhammad never doubted that the world of Allah, and of the unseen in general, was accessible to variously altered forms of consciousness — a view with which Macdonald himself is in sympathy to some degree. Dreams, for example, were for Muhammad sure and certain occasions for the giving of guidance and truth. Prophecy too, that is direct knowledge and expression of the unseen power's will, was in principle accessible to anyone.[101] [102] Muhammad believed that "any one who gave himself to the thought of God would receive from God rest, calm and strength. 'Our hearts are restless until we rest in Thee,' were the words, you see, both of Augustine and Muhammad."[103] It was not only rest but knowledge which came from Allah directly. This mystical notion arose in the mind of Muhammad himself and was established thenceforward in Islamic belief.[104]

Islamic Mysticism and the Reality of the Unseen

Islam is the institutionalization of the experience of the unseen. Muhammad is its model, not as theological genius, ethical teacher or cultural hero, but as mystic, as one who knew Allah and the world of the unseen directly. This mystical Islam is the burden of Macdonald's Haskell lectures of 1906. He introduces these lectures by stating that the religious life of Islam is his subject, that is the experience of the unseen in Islam. He seeks, he notes, to explain this religious life with the aid of major Muslim thinkers, the parallel to be found in William James' lectures *Varieties of Religious Experience,* and the researches of the Society of Psychical Research. The religious life of Islam is the life of mystical and supernatural experience. Macdonald holds, as we have seen, that the Oriental mind is particularly suggestible, and susceptible to this sort of experience; "it has retained a very lively feeling of contact with an actual spiritual world, self-existent and in no process of dependent becoming."[105]

The Western parallels to this religious life are to be found in the study of the occult, in researches into trance-mediumship, "veridical hallucinations," and the like, rather than in the area of ethics or metaphysics. Macdonald declares that at last part of this body of phenomena is plausible. He regards telepathy and telekinesis as proved; on the other hand he remains unconvinced by arguments for "communications by discarnate spirits."[106] His view of the spiritualism of Islam is thus that it is plausible; it is also mechanical. Macdonald appreciates romantic religion, of which this supernaturalism is an expression: ". . . it is fundamental to all human nature. . . ."[107] But taken alone it is insufficient, incomplete revelation. I shall comment further on this point.

Macdonald's appreciation of James is evident; and like James he links the religious experience of the unseen to a broadly pragmatic and utilitarian attitude. James' *Varieties*[108] is a defense of religious experience — in the sense of the experience of the unseen — whether it is as vague as a felt presence in a darkened room or as formal as the mystical philosophy of Meister Eckhart. His defense is pragmatic; that is, those who have this experience are, very frequently, better people for having had it. The issue is not, for James, whether the object of such an experience exists, but what its effects upon the person are. Does the experience enable the person to work in the world, to wrestle with his fate, or perhaps even to achieve happiness? James concludes that the religious experience, in its varieties, is on the whole a good, because useful, thing. In the case of Islam Macdonald agrees entirely. He cites James' Third Lecture:

> Were one asked [says James] to characterize the life of religion in the broadest and most general terms possible, one might say that it consists of the belief that there is an unseen order, and that our supreme good lies in harmoniously adjusting ourselves thereto. This belief and this adjustment are the religious attitude in the soul.[109]

The text of *The Religious Attitude and Life in Islam* is devoted to explaining the experience of the unseen in Islam. This is tantamount for him to an explanation of the religious life of Islam. He pursues the enquiry under three headings: (a) a metaphysical explanation of the beliefs of the Orient about the unseen world; (b) a psychological explanation and account of the nature and causes of this experience; and (c) an account of the path commended for the development of the experience of the unseen.

As for the metaphysical aspects, the Oriental knows that there is a barrier between the seen and the unseen. But it is, so to speak, a shell of the "merest film," easily penetrable. For the West, on the contrary, the shell is impenetrable. True, "the strict theologian of Islam would tell [us] that there was no such shell at all; that all action and reaction spring from the will of God." But the "wayfaring" man in Islam knows perfectly well that the supernatural has often peered through this film at him. "Our ghost-stories and strange experiences are everyday things for him which he never dreams of investigating, for he never doubts them." Anything is possible for the Oriental; "The supernatural is so near that it may touch him at any moment."[110]

As for the psychological aspects, there are many occasions for such an experience. Dreams are, of course, powerfully significant. They are really a "minor form of revelation."[111] Despite the belief that Allah is impossibly remote, Different, the Muslim knows that the spiritual world and Allah are near to every human heart.[112] It is also true that devilish and deceptive ideas are planted during dreams. But that is simply the other side of the supernatural coin.[113] Dreams are the "means of access to the unseen world open to all, the universal crack in the shell of which I spoke."[114]

The entire range of extrasensory perception and powers was of enormous significance to the thinkers of Islam. Ibn Khaldun proposed that physical effects have psychical causes. This was simply an explication of the detailed operation of a self-evident truth, that "man can still have contact with God."[115] There is no distinction between superstition and religion in Islam, concludes Macdonald; and therefore every event which we would designate as occult, supernatural or ghostly takes its rightful place in the universal scheme of things. It is the task of historians and theologians to explain the details of this scheme.[116] The world of the *Arabian Nights* was and remains the "real" world of Islam.[117]

As for the path to religious experience, Macdonald argues that just as the strength of Islam lies in the mystical experience of the unseen, so the spiritual path of the Sufi, of the darwish fraternities, constitutes the strongest and most long-lived of Islamic institutions.[118]

> From the earliest times there was an element in the Muslim church which was repelled equally by traditional teaching and by intellectual reasoning. It felt that the essence of religion lay elsewhere; that the seat and organ of religion was in the heart. In process of time, all Islam became permeate with this conception, in different degrees and various forms. More widely than ever with Christianity, Islam became and is a mystical faith. All — the simple believer, the theologians of the schools, the philosophers — came in one form or another to the essential mystical positions.[119]

It was Al-Ghazzali who turned the tables on the intellectuals. The ultimate religious truth for him was not the teaching of the savants but the direct experience of Allah. The Sufi control of the natural inclination to the unseen showed the way.[120] The only guide for religion, then, was the skill, developed and disciplined, of being conscious only of God.

After all the forays and sorties in philosophy and law, the crass materialist monotheism of Muhammad yielded finally to the Muhammadan experience of the Face of Allah.[121] This, notes Macdonald, "is one of the strongest developments in all the history of religion. The wheel came full circle and seems now nailed in its place."[122] Islam, then and now, is frankly agnostic, frankly supernatural. The prophets, the soothsayers, the dreamers, the wizards, the familiar spirits, the saints, all find their place in its scheme. "Practically, the conception of the mystical, saintly life and the organization of darwish fraternities cover all Islam and are the stimulants and vehicles of Muslim piety."[123] Philosophy, law and their schools are "nothing but aberrations at the moment."[124] Any modern distrust among Muslims of religious emotion is superficial only.[125]

In sum, the religious life of Islam is dominated and defined by the experience of the invisible world. To this world the pragmatic Muslim, like James' believer, seeks to adjust.[126] Islam will survive not because of Muhammad's model of Muslim ethical discrimination, still less by its ability to reconcile its tradition with the modern movements of the twentieth century. Its future lies down the mystical path, for along that path it has travelled with whatever success it has achieved. But Macdonald believes that Christianity lies at the end of that path, waiting to conduct the Muslim to the Christian marriage of reason and faith. Islam's strength is its mysticism. It is, of course, also its weakness in comparison with Christianity.[127]

Islam: A Christian Heresy

There is in Macdonald's explanation of Islam a striking irony. The orthodox Muslim perspective on Christianity and Judaism is that each is a perversion, a heresy, of Islam. Macdonald believed that Islam was a Christian heresy and, almost, a parody of Old Testament prophecy. The former conclusion will occupy us for a moment.

It has already been suggested that in the status of Muhammad as the first of all creatures and in the doctrine of the Qur'an as the uncreated Word of Allah we have clear indications of the influence of a Logos doctrine of Christ. In addition, the perennial thrust toward the ascetic life, often in the form of reformation within Islam, is, Macdonald argues, the direct result of the Muslim contact with Christian hermits. Denounce them and their other-worldliness Muhammad might; but they continued to sway Islam as they had swayed heathen Arabia — and Muhammad himself.[129] Their fundamental commitment to the idea that only God was real and the world illusion had an irrevocable influence upon Islam and its mystical nature. Sufism itself is the result of Christian influence.[130] In general, the significant theological, nay religious, aspects of Islam are confused derivatives of Christianity.

Both the Qur'an and the Speech of Allah are believed to be eternal. The Qur'an is a manifestation here upon earth of that Speech, written with letters, pronounced with sounds. Of the Qur'an one may say, it is the Word of God. These two doctrines, Macdonald concludes, are dependent upon the Christian doctrine of the Logos.[131]

Again, the pervasive notion in Islamic mysticism that the Muslim can achieve a degree, perhaps absolute, of consciousness of Allah is a product of the influence of Christian mysticism and the monophysite doctrine of God in Christ. "That heresy assigns one nature to Christ, and in certain forms practically means that a particular man was taken and made divine as a whole, in his whole nature"; and it holds out the promise that all may be made divine. The Christian Plotinian tradition "augumented this influence subtantially."[132] This mystical humanity was also an idea of Buddhist origin; and Macdonald was sensitive to the possibility of Buddhist influence with respect to the atomism of Islamic philosophy.[133]

But it is a peculiar Christian influence which dominates Islam. A striking illustration of the Muslim version of Christianity, notes Macdonald, is to be seen in Islam's idea of the Christian teaching of the Trinity. The doctrine which Islam rejects is, as many have observed, a peculiar version of orthodox Christian teaching — that is, the notion that there are three divinities, rather than the Nicene and Athanasian teachings of three persons and one nature. In this instance it may not have been Muhammad's confused brain which gives the explanation. We have learned, says Macdonald, of a remote sect in the Syrian desert among tribes calling themselves Christian who held a doctrine of the Trinity very like the one Muhammad condemned.[134] What Muhammad rejected, therefore, was not true Christianity.

All of this suggests not only considerable confusion in the mind of Islam concerning its relationship to Christianity and the relationship of Muhammad and the Qur'an to Allah, but a good deal about the origins of Islam and the role of Muhammad. This is Macdonald's advice to Christians seeking to understand Islam:

> It may help . . . to remember that Islam essentially in its origin and through its theological development has been and is a Christian heresy —though, it may be, a deadly one. Heresies can purge themselves and be reabsorbed into the Church.[135]

Muhammad may be treated "as the Church treats Origen or Arius or even the Abbot Joachim,"[136] that is, as a heretic who took his insights beyond the orthodox understanding of Christian revelation. Missionary work was a proper and necessary response of the Church to its heretical communities. Macdonald believed that Islam was one of those communities.

Islam, the Hebrew Tradition and Christianity

Macdonald found Islam to be logically incomprehensible, contradictory and irrational. Only his sympathy for romantic religion enabled him to treat Islam as a legitimate tradition of mystical experience. In order to fully understand what Macdonald was about we must see that he set the study of Islam in the context of comparison and contrast with the Christian tradition and its Hebraic prophetic roots.

Muslim Supernaturalism and Christian Incarnation

In describing the "soil" out of which Islamic, Old Testament and Semitic prophecy as a whole arise, Macdonald notes the general sense of the reality of the unseen. But it is not all the same. In the Haskell lectures Macdonald nailed his colors to the mast:

> In these lectures, as I shall not often have opportunity for comparison still less for apologetics, let me seize this one to say, as fixedly and broadly as in me is, that, while the soil of Semitic prophecy is one, I know nowhere in the Semitic world any appearance like that of the great prophets of the Hebrews. They stand as clear from their soil as love in Christian marriage from the lust of the flesh, and the relation is much the same.[137]

It is, I think, the burden of his work to make this metaphor clear.

In Macdonald's view the unique nature of Hebrew prophecy may best be illustrated in the difference between Allah and Jehovah — one may as well say God; for Macdonald does not think of Allah as God, as Jehovah, or even as Yahweh.[138] Allah is the only reality of Islam; but in Christianity, as in the Old Testament prophets, the reality of God neither removes Him from His children nor identifies Him with their religious emotion. This difference is the essential difference between Muslim supernaturalism and the Christian doctrine of Incarnation.[139]

In a revealing essay, "God — A Unit or A Unity?"[140] Macdonald argues against recent, and by implication past, attempts among Christian thinkers to challenge the Christian trinitarian position. There is, he says, a lesson to be learned from Islam. There are in Islam three characteristic and mutually contradictory positions with respect to the nature and work of Allah. First, Allah is wholly other and apart. Second, Allah is closer to us than we are to ourselves. The problems of rationalization arose when it became necessary to explain the relationship between Allah's qualities and His essence. Muslim philosophical theology was faced with a formidable task. It responded by emphasizing the Difference of Allah. Allah's qualities are, it argued, utterly unlike human qualities. Thus Allah is impassable, that is, devoid of emotion or feeling. Allah has no reason which we can comprehend, only an incomprehensible will which must be obeyed. Even good and evil are only expressions of Allah's will and are thus empty of any intrinsic value.[141] In short, human analogies have no necessary or possible connection with Allah. The difference is complete and total. It is impossible in Islam to speak meaningfully of the Love, the Mercy of Allah. What that Love, that Mercy consist of is utterly beyond the reach or grasp of human experience, desire or thought. They have nothing whatever to do with human qualities of the people, of the darwish fraternities or of the Sufis; but whenever *kalam*, theology, is pursued, such a conclusion is inevitable. Even the great Al-Ghazzali follows this trail of argument, though it flies in the face of his mystic consciousness of Allah.[142]

Such utter inaccessibility and unknowableness makes for dead religion. By contrast the Christian doctrine of the Trinity brings God to our lives in Christ without sacrificing his wholly otherness. Here is one of Macdonald's several paeans to the Trinity:

> [the doctrine of the Trinity] renders possible sympathy, affection, trust, love; [it] makes God knowable — that is how the Son reveals the Father to us; [it] makes us the Sons of God, partakers in the divine nature, and not simply the creatures of His hand; [it] finds within the Christian Church the Holy Ghost, the Comforter, the Lord and Giver of Life; and [it] yet preserves the One God — Father, Son and Holy Ghost — as conscious, knowing, feeling, willing Being.[143]

When Islam could not accept the doctrine of Difference in its starkness it chose pantheism. The pendulum swings between Al-Ghazzali's pantheism and dogmatic unitarianism. But for him who searches in the great space "between materialism and pantheism, the presentation that still expresses most adequately the mystery behind our lives, is that in Christian Trinity, and the words that come the nearest are those of the Nicene Creed."[144]

Why is the Nicene, trinitarian formulation unacceptable to Islam? Macdonald observes that Muhammad rejected any notion of divine paternity and human sonship. Yet both pre-Muslim and Hebrew pro-

phetic traditions shared the ancient belief in divine spouses and fore-
bears. Muhammad, and Islam, rejected these ideas; the Hebrew
prophets did not: "When the great change came for the Hebrews,
which lifted them out of Semitic heathenism and made them different
from every other people of the earth, it did not eliminate such conceptions."[145] This highly significant facet of Hebrew prophecy laid the
foundation for the Christian notion of spiritual birth, and the concomitant notion of the man-God relationship as one of parent to child. Nor,
insists Macdonald, was this language simply metaphorical. "The doctrine of the Sonship of Christ is really the doctrine that God is a true
personality and not an absolute unity." This was the expression of the
Hebrew genius, and for this reason it was never afraid to understand
God anthropomorphically.[146] Nor, says Macdonald, should we be.[147] But
"theologizing Islam" condemned "its Allah to negations and unthinka-
bleness. The unity and the unreasoned will of Allah were saved, but for
the thinking and devout Muslim the universe was left a mystery and its
problems remained unsolved."[148] It is this deficiency in Islam which, as
Macdonald noted, made the Gospel of John, with its emphasis on the
paternity of God and the Sonship of Christ and all people, so attractive
to Muslims.[149]

Christianity may add to Islam, then, the solution to the problem of
agnosticism on the one hand and pantheism on the other. Its doctrine of
the Trinity shows that God is neither limited to his creation nor absent
from it: "the yearning of the modern mystic for absolute contact with
his Lord can be satisfied, and yet the personality of both can be
saved."[150] Islam has no understanding of the present working of the
divine in human life. There is, in the Islamic mystical tradition, a sense
of the weird, of the unseen; but this is far different from the Christian
notion of service for God in the world, of the possibility of change and
development in the Christian life of the spirit. The "great revelation for
Islam which Christianity brings," he concludes, is that God is not far
off, that the paradox of the utterly unknowable and utterly present God
may be resolved in the doctrine of the Incarnation.[151]

Prophecy in Islam and the Old Testament

Macdonald's comparison of Islam and Christianity rests upon his
understanding of the prophetic tradition, and its conception of the

personality of God in the Old Testament. He argues that while prophecy as the experience of the unseen is to be found in strength in both
the Islamic and Old Testament traditions, they diverge at the point of
the preservation of the personality of the prophet. The link between the
mystic and the prophecy suggested in both traditions makes the usual
distinction between mysticism and prophecy defended in Old Testament studies meaningless.[152] But Muhammad was not of the "goodly
fellowship of the Hebrew prophets."[153]

The most obvious distinction between the prophetic literature of the
Hebrew tradition and that of Islam is the fact that the latter was poetic.
There is no poetry *per se* among the writings of the great Hebrew
prophets. In Macdonald's understanding this Hebraic prophecy is free
of the supernaturalism which inflected Islam. Poetry is "magical utterance, inspired by powers from the Unseen, and the poet is in part
soothsayer, in part an adviser and admonisher, and in part a hurler of
magical formulae against his enemies."[154] The only example of such a
combination of poetry and prophecy in the Old Testament is the case of
Balaam, who stood in a real and effective relationship with the unseen
world and spoke whether he willed or not. This single instance contrasts
sharply with the proliferation of poetic prophets in Arabia: " the poet of
the Arabs drew knowledge, wisdom, skill and destroying utterance
from his relationship to the Jinn."[155]

It was the "nightmare" of Muhammad's earlier career that he was
"simply a poet possessed by a Jinni." And, says Macdonald, this is only a
little less than the truth, as his opponents observed. "He was in truth a
poet of the old Arab type, without skill of verse, and with all his being
given to the prophetic side of poetry." Add his jumbled recollections of
Jewish and Christian concepts, Macdonald concludes, and you have the
"key to Muhammad."[156]

Macdonald's case rests upon the fact that Muhammad's early utterances were identical in form to those of a class of prophets known as *kahin*
(related etymologically to the Hebrew *Kohen*, "priest"). This poetic
form, which was unmetered rhyme (*saj*), was not the only poetic form
extant at the time of the soothsayers who revealed the truth of the
present and the future under the pressure of a trance-like experience of
fit, in which the power of the unseen was irresistible. Muhammad's
early utterances were, says Macdonald, genuine duplicates of the *kahin*
tradition. In his latter period he retained the form, although without

benefit of the state of ecstatic utterance, because it served his purposes.[157] Undoubtedly he regretted the need to continue in the *saj* form
for it connected him in the ears of some of his hearers with the old
Arabian heathenism which it was his mission to destroy. Nevertheless,
in the end Muhammad must be reckoned a sort of soothsayer who
became convinced that his inspiration was from Allah and not from a
Jinn.[158] But he was not an ordinary *kahin*; what separates him from the
mass of the older sort of prophecy is analogous to what separated Amos
and Hosea from the older prophets of the Old Testament, such as
Balaam or the ecstatic prophets in whose company Saul was found.[159]

Macdonald showed a considerable interest in the mechanics of
Muhammad's prophetic experience. Earlier scholars had attempted to
prove that Muhammad was either epileptic or cataleptic (Weil and
Margoliouth respectively). Springer suggested that hysteria was a more
satisfactory explanation. Macdonald finds a more fruitful line of
research, as we have seen, in the sort of investigations James and the
Society for Psychical Research conducted. Muhammad, he says, may
have learned self-hypnosis. He spoke automatically, like the automatic
speaker or writer who acts at the command of some unseen external
power.[160] With the exception of self-hypnosis[161] these examples serve to
show that Muhammad was sincerely taken by his prophecy, at least in
his early period. His prophecy is a sort of extra-sensory perception; it is
not ethical monotheism. It resembles the "varieties of religious experience" and trans-empirical knowledge; but parallels, with respect to
content of teaching, to the sense of truth and goodness, which one might
expect with the Old Testament prophets, simply do not exist.[162] Amos
was made the mouthpiece of Yahweh; but he was not an automatic
speaker nor an ecstatic *kahin*. He was in control; he spoke the words of
Yahweh as one fully conscious and alive to his surroundings and responsibilities. Moreover, his message was one of ethical power, of the
judgement of a righteous God.

Here, then, lies the uniqueness of the Hebrew prophetic tradition.
There arose a class of prophets who combined those "common human
phenomena" of experience of the unseen "with a certain great moral
earnestness and a certain definite object. The seeing of their great seers
was not limited to trivialities, but widened into the great purposes of
God. It is there that the difference in the case of the Hebrews lies."[163]

"With you only," Jehovah says to Israel, "have I been on intimate personal terms, out of all the families of the earth." This is no terrifying and non-moral unseen power but the very personality of Jehovah, of God.[164] For Islam, as Macdonald's entire corpus attempts to prove, there is no such relationship. Allah is not God.

Islam, Christianity and Brotherhood

Not only did the great prophets of the Old Testament know consciously the personality of God, they also were not blinded to their responsibilities in this world by the experience of the other. Islam, on the other hand, could focus on nothing but the other world, "the unending hereafter with its sharply divided weal or woe."[165]

Christianity, as the successor to Old Testament prophecy, incorporated the Hebrew focus on history and community in the very roots of its structure. It proclaimed a doctrine of brotherhood which was an expression of its experience of God; this doctrine, says Macdonald, announced a notion of brotherhood quite different from the Muslim idea. For Islam the focus upon the final and otherworldly judgement meant that people were members of one "house" or another, the *Dar-al-Islam* or the *Dar-al-Harb*. The theologians thus understood brotherhood to be limited to those who were within the *Dar-al-Islam*. There is no notion that all men and women are by virtue of their being in the world the children of God. The obligations of Islam, then, are first to Allah and then to other Muslims; but for the rest there are no obligations, except the minimal concern for the Peoples of the Book. The concept of universal service and sacrifice, says Macdonald, does not exist in theologizing Islam. The Islamic mystical tradition is typically divergent; for it shares the insight of the Gospel of John with its explicit teaching of universal brotherhood.

Christianity may add to Islam what Islam cannot produce for itself, the twin concepts of universal brotherhood and universal service. Indeed, the popularity of the Johannine teachings among Muslims suggests that there is a serious lacuna in the Muslim understanding of God to which most Muslims are themselves quite sensitive and which they wish to bridge. Christianity offers life in the service of Christ rather than world-denying fear of the Fire. For Muslims who have accepted it, this idea has been "like a breath of fresh, cold air," amid the dusty formalism and otherworldliness of Islam.[166]

Christian Missions and Islam

At this point I wish to describe in more detail the position adumbrated above, namely that Macdonald understood his endeavors as Islamicist and Semiticist in the context of Christian missions. It need hardly be said that he was a scholar; but his scholarship must be seen to be in the service of the mission to Islam. There were reasons why Islam needed Christian missions. Those, I think have already been described. I wish now to focus on Macdonald's definition and defense of the missionary enterprise itself.

The Present State of Islam

Islam had problems and possibilities. Addressing the problems in his St. Louis speech, Macdonald attempted to make the case that Islam could not then or ever serve as the basis for civilization. The grip of Islam on all sides of the Muslim life is the probable cause. "When theology, philosophy, science, law — the church and state in all their phases of activity — are allowed to develop separately, much else will be possible." The situation would be further improved if the doctrine of atomism were overthrown; for only in that circumstance would the philosophical *sine qua non*, the notion of a reign of order and regularity and the possibility of continuous thought and argument, be possible. Moreover, civilization could hardly be expected to flourish in a context of intellectual snobbishness, of the unbridged gap between the learned and the people, when the village school is an object of ridicule and art is the preserve of hide-bound guilds, when learning is limited to the lawyers.[167]

Yet Islam is vigorous, active and dynamic. It was obvious to Macdonald that the intellectuals of the West had yet to learn this elemental truth. The study of "Muhammadanism," he notes, is limited as a field of research to the History of Religion; "that is practically all the recognition which the whole Muslim world has had, a world which, at the present time, is going through a great awakening, and which stands with Christendom and the civilization of China as one of the three great existing and militant civilizations."[168] It is purest folly to ignore these realities. "[I]gnorant depreciation and extravagant worship must yield to patient appreciation, and that can only be reached by the students of Europe and [the European students] of Islam recognizing their mutual dependence and joining their forces."[169] It is for the student "to remember that Islam is a present reality and the Muslim faith a living organism, a knowledge of whose laws may be life or death for us who are in another camp." For Islam is militant. The cause of civilization will be secure only when "mutual understanding" or unification is achieved.[170]

As for modern Islamic intellectual developments, Macdonald identifies the schools of Ghazzali and Wahhabi (and through him Ibn Taymiya and Ibn Hanbal) as the strongest and most viable. The latter moves toward simple monotheism, the former toward, agnostic mysticism. Looking about for alternatives, Macdonald sees no hope whatever in European materialism, which is on the rise. Also the legal formalism of Shari'ah and Fiqh, though still the source to which an enormous proportion of Muslim theologians turn, is a dubious basis for the religious life. Pantheistic mysticism is widely popular, especially among Persians and Turks. But even as in the days of Ibn Taymiya, the people are overburdened with superstition. Of philosophy in the strict sense there is not a trace, even of that melange of Neo-Platonism and Aristotelianism.[171]

Macdonald identifies three routes toward possible reform of what is, in fact, a failed reason. First, since the economy of teaching has failed so spectacularly, popular education must be built up and widely extended to all classes of society. Second, the principle of *taqlid*, of slavery of the student to the master, must be brought to an end. Third, Muslims must at last turn to the study of the world as a realm of law and order, of natural law; "it must experiment and test rather than build lofty hypotheses." But, Macdonald asks, can "the Oriental mind thus deny itself?"[172]

With respect to the geopolitical realities of the early twentieth century, Macdonald observes that Islam has found these realities not all to its liking, but has not failed to respond. He offers three observations. First, the advance of Christendom on Muslim lands has been met with flight. There are those, despairing in the face of the growth of modern culture, who, like the Senusites, have withdrawn ever deeper into the desert, anxious to avoid all contact with the non-Muslim world.[173] Second, some have made militant declaration of undying opposition to the new civilization. "If active warfare were possible, they would embrace it and die in the last ditch." Instead, they praise the old books and live the old life insofar as they can. The Ulama of Egypt, the followers of the Mahdi in the Sudan, the Al-Azhar are examples of this response. This movement has attracted the nationalist fervor of some Muslims, notably those of Egypt. The contrast with Turkey is striking; and here the third response may be found, though not only here. This Turkish group is prepared to "assimilate the civilization of Christendom, to come within the circle of modern life, and to acknowledge publicly that Islam is incompatible, root and branch, with the irresistible forces of modernity." The Young Turk Committee, Macdonald argues, is committed to this path. In Egypt, on the other hand, there are those who recognize the need to come to terms with the modern world; but they insist that Islam in its essential characteristics must be preserved.[174]

Is there any cause for genuine hope in these movements? No, says Macdonald, so long as they hold to the "essential Islam";

> Where . . . are the germinant ideas, where the plans of life and thought which hold the future? No one, looking at essential Islam, can believe that they are there. The great curves of progress touch but seldom its surfaces.[175]

Essential Islam is vestigial; it does not share any significant portion of modern life. The Young Turks are right: in order to live in the twentieth century one must give up Islam. They must think of Turkey, not Islam.[176] Whether the Turkish experiment works, says Macdonald, will depend on the patience and courage of its reformers. We, in the West, "must have patience. We must give them a chance to show what they can do — that is the last word, must be the last word of any one who speaks upon Islam and its possibilities. There is a long road lying ahead before anything is to be reached that will be worth reaching, but I believe that the road has now been entered."[177] The history of the Turkish experiment showed Macdonald how clearly it lay outside "essential Islam." Islam did not respond to the summons to support Germany during the First World War. Nationalism was, and is, more important than Islam.[178]

Finally, the present vigor in the Islamic world, though evident,[179] is due to stimulation from the West; it is not endemic.

> For over a century [writes Macdonald] the intellectual, moral, economic and political life of the Moslem peoples has been stimulated from

the West through schools of all kinds, through Christian Missions, through trade intercourse, through political experience .... The process of shaking the Moslem world awake was at first very slow and seemed almost hopeless, but towards the end of the last century it went with geometric progression and no one can say now that that world is not awake.[180]

But there is very little, if any, genuine creative life in Islam in the modern age; it is all reactive, all defensive.

The Attitude of the Christian Missionary

It is to Macdonald's credit that he urged upon all missionaries a sympathetic attitude toward Muslims. In this he stands in sharp relief against many of his contemporaries. The sympathy he commended to his audience in the Lamson lectures was no mere good feeling; it should be informed, he argued, by a close and disciplined study of the theology and philosophy of the tradition. Moreover, the points of agreement must be stressed; and only a learned and understanding person could be successful in that field:[181]

> The missionary to them must emphatically be a large, all-round man of personality, and, if possible of mystical tendency. He must be able to realize that when Muslims accept Christianity they will have to make it over for themselves; they will have to construct their own theology; and it is his business to supply them with general ideas, with conceptions of character and conduct, and to help them discreetly in the development of their own system. By no means should he attempt to force any system upon them or be surprised at any deviations which they may develop.[182]

The "surprise" he may experience should be met with reflection on the many "uncouth ways in which the doctrines of Christianity are often presented."[183] He must, furthermore, know the popular language; for this is the language of the people of his field. He need not even be conversant with the classical literature of Islam; for they themselves do not know it.[184] It is, also, fruitless to engage in controversy with Muslims. For controversy simply breeds hostility. Indeed, "often he will find that it is not best to attack Muhammadanism directly, but to let the new ideas eat away its foundation. An attack, however valid and logical, arouses resistance."[185] Rather it is better to allow the source of Christian truth, the Bible, to speak for itself. It all lies, he says, "in the attitude."[186]

Macdonald's words on the Muslim's understanding of the Bible are no mere gesture. For he holds that all men and women are naturally Christian.[187] Islam, he notes, believes that all children are born Muslims. Their parents pervert their natural affinity for Islam with teachings of the Christians, Jews and Magians. This belief stands in contrast to the Christian idea that all are children of God, and further that in the Kingdom of God the child is the true citizen not because he is born into one group but because the dignity and respect inherent in childhood are hallmarks of that citizenship.[188] But Macdonald goes further: "The human soul, when unbiased by systems and prejudices, is naturally Christian." "[S]uch freedom has been the mark of Sufi'ism at all times."[189]

Macdonald deplores the too familiar militancy of Christian missions to Muslims:

> . . . I regret that in the recent renewal of interest in Muslim missions [he wrote in 1909] there has been so much warlike denunciation and beating of the crusading drum. The Muslim world knows of it and takes its attitude from it, and the young men who go out under its influence cannot easily return to the sanity, sympathy and charity which the spirit of their Master requires.[190]

On his extended visit to the Muslim world (prior to the delivery of the Lamson lectures) Macdonald discovered that his sympathy for the tradition of the saints attracted the admiration of his Muslim acquaintances. He was said to have behaved "like a religious-minded man and a gentleman." In this spirit his dealings with Muslims were thoroughly cordial and friendly.[191] Such an attitude should be possible for the missionary of strong personality and sympathetic genius.[192] For the way to understanding Islam "is the sincere way of sympathy; the broad way of unity; the honest way of endeavoring to understand from within."[193]

Yet the status of the Muslim converts to Christianity suggested that this way had not been followed. They were widely regarded still as natives, as "Oriental" Christians. This "second-class" status is not an outgrowth of Christianity *per se*, argues Macdonald, but of the combination of the "necessarily dominant European race with Christianity." Here was a serious problem for the missionary. In fact Christianity, in the modern world at least, has never been able to obliterate the distinctions of race. Islam has had much greater success in this respect. That is its danger and its glory.[194] But the European Christian treats the Oriental, Christian or not, with disdain, unconscionable rudeness and a thoroughly repulsive condescension. The way to understanding is through sympathy, knowledge, courtesy and intelligence. It is also the way of love; for none of these other qualities can exist unless the missionary is "genuinely in love with the people of his field; likes them and theirs; is in many respects one of them."[195] "The paradox, in truth, of the missionary's life is that he must have a liking for his people and their queerest little ways even while he is trying to change them."[196]

As the last quotation clearly indicates, Macdonald's sympathy is flavored rather strongly with condescension. He argues that the missionary must not think of his people as childish or ridiculous. The proper attitude is to think of them as "child-like." He writes:

> How, to illustrate, would we handle a child who had the ideas of a child about fairies or about Santa Claus, or who was somewhat weak-kneed on the subject of fact? We certainly would not talk to him about ridiculousness or childishness or use abusive forms of speech. We would take him as he was; make the best of him; and try to guide him, using those ideas of his as we might, and being sure that they would fade, as they must, into the light of common day.
>
>   That is essentially the problem of the missionary in dealing with the Muslim peoples.[197]

Macdonald's charity and sympathy for the Muslim peoples in the mission field was really that of the adult for the child, the mature person for the undeveloped, the teacher for the pupil. For all his sympathetic understanding of Muslims, for all his objection to the aggressive postures of others in the mission field, Macdonald does not accept the Muslim as an equal, nor even with the respect which one would give a worthy adversary. This is his view of Muslim theology and jurisprudence, of Muslim history and civilization; and it is his view of the individual Muslim. The task of Christianity is to save Muslims from an arrested development and — if it is the opposite of civilization — from barbarism.

Spiritual Mission and Western Materialism

It is essential, Macdonald argues, that the missionary understand the Muslim view of Christianity and Christendom. In brief, this view is that there is no comprehension of true religion in the West. The "Oriental's assured feeling of religious superiority" is a concrete fact of life, however galling it may be.[198] Macdonald offers an illustration in a report of the response of Muslim scholars to a paper devoted to the Qur'an given in Algiers by a European scholar, Karl Vollers. It argued that the Qur'an was not the work of Muhammad (or of Allah) but of subsequent editors and redactors. The response of the Muslims present was clear and unequivocal: Vollers, or indeed any European, could never understand the Qur'an. In the matter of the Qur'an, one scholar told Macdonald, "we will take nothing from a foreigner." In the material and technological side of life they are willing to take almost anything. But in the matters of the spirit Americans and Europeans are simply unlettered. "No Christian can really feel the things of God as [a Muslim] does."[199] Muslims have made up their minds that Westerners are so entirely godless and so given over to material things that they have no mind for the things of the unseen world. In this regard they lack both inclination and aptitude.[200]

The missionary would be well advised, then, first, to take this attitude seriously and, second, to stress the "charismata" of the Christian tradition in order to convince Muslims that Christians too have a sense of the spiritual world. It is not the task of the missionary to turn the Muslim into a "sober-sided Presbyterian or Episcopalian." Rather, the emotional side of religion which Islam and Christianity have in common should be emphasized. The *zikhr*, he argues further, is a model which the Christian missionary may well emulate, converting it into a Christian expression.[201]

The successful mission to the Muslim world therefore will not consist primarily of eleemosynary medical, technical and material assistance. The East, says Macdonald, cares most about theology, about the world of the unseen. When our missionaries go to them with a non-theological temper of mind, he points out, Muslims are suspicious and distrustful. These people say they are religious; yet they talk of technology and not of God. Why should they be trusted? Macdonald urges that the true focus of missions must be evangelical, theological and spiritual. The missionary must proclaim "a definite theological teaching which produces a life-transforming faith." He must preach Christ. Otherwise, the Oriental mind is puzzled and confused.[202]

The paramount issue is this, says Macdonald: can we all be saved, Muslims and Christians, from a world view composed of "philosophic doubt, of common sense attitudes, and of material luxury?"[203] This is what the future may hold. The roots of such a future are deep in Western materialism: they are "the effect of Western civilization in the Eastern world when unaccompanied by Western religion — the only thing which keeps our civilization sweet."[204]

The missionary's task is to preach Christ and the spiritual life. Muslims must be convinced that Christians can be spiritually mature, can recognize the power of religious emotion, of ecstacy in encountering things unspeakable.[205] The temptation to conduct humanitarian projects at the expense of spiritual Christianity must be rejected. These projects must be subordinated to evangelism; otherwise they "put dynamite under all religion."[206] Thus the materialistic threat from the West will be met successfully only if Christianity, Christ and spiritual life are the true heart of the missionary's gospel.[207] Any other approach will play into the hands of the coming valueless culture of the modern world.[208] A purely materialistic world, concludes Macdonald, is "as near hell as anything thinkable." The East is defenseless in every respect in the face of the Western onslaught. It is the task of the missionary for Christ to stand in its way. He must proclaim as a divine fact "the Incarnate Life of the Lord Christ. That this is a frankly supernatural doctrine makes no difficulty for the East; for it a religion must be supernatural; otherwise it is nothing."[209] Further, the missionary must convince the young Muslims that their despair in the face of war, disruption and the decadence of their own tradition can be lifted. The doctrine of Christ is "not war but peace, and is the hope of abiding peace for the world."[210]

Islam cannot save itself or its people:

> Unless all signs deceive [he writes], there lies before the Muslim peoples a terrible religious collapse. Islam as a religion is not holding its own against the unbelief that is flooding to it from the European civilization. Young men are growing up into crass and material forms of atheism, forms that the best intellectual life of Europe has itself thrown off. And as education spreads and deepens, as history vindicates for itself its place, as the moral feeling becomes more watchful and sensitive, so the legend of Muhammad will crumble and his character be seen in its true light. And with Muhammad the entire fabric must go. It is then for the Christian schools and preachers to save these peoples, not only for Christianity but for any religion at all; to vindicate to them the claims upon their lives of religion in the broadest sense.[211]

Islam was part of the problem and not of the solution: "Thus the Muslim peoples are slowly and uneasily becoming aware that the Faith which was their pride and strength — nay, the very essence of their being — is their handicap. Militant and dominant Islam is gone. Can Islam be anything else?[212]

Thus Macdonald justifies Christian missions to Muslims as a saving work. His justification rests comfortably upon his scholarly and interpretive work as an Orientalist. The missionary enterprise constituted the working arm, the practical consequence of his analysis of Islam. As an Orientalist he sought not merely to describe but to save. It was not Islam but Christianity which emerged as the true and saving faith. This conclusion Macdonald urged forcefully on Christians and Muslims as well. However sympathetic his tone and attitude, however repugnant he found aggressive and militant missionizing, he never doubted the need for nor the righteousness of the Christian missionary enterprise. His comprehension of Islam, must, I think, be seen in that light.

Conclusion

I have attempted here to present the work of Duncan Black Macdonald under three rubrics: (1) his effort to explain Islam; (2) his comparative treatment of Islam, the Hebrew prophetic tradition and Christianity; and (3) his justification based on the first two for Christian missions among Muslims. One may now ask whether Macdonald understood Islam. I suggested earlier that his effort began with explanation rather than understanding as a goal. Not surprisingly, he concluded that the weakness of Islam as a religious tradition, as a civilization, and as a resource for true human aspirations greatly overwhelms its strengths. Those strengths lie solely in the area of religious experience, in the knowledge of the unseen — and here the inability to bring faith and reason together crippled Islam from the beginning. He explains Islam, only to explain it away. Sympathy for the child-like Muslim, with his queer little ways, he may have; understanding of Islam or of the Muslim, and a shared sense of the presence of transcendent and spiritual reality, are conspicuously absent.

Wilfred Cantwell Smith has suggested two different ways of testing for understanding in the study of religious traditions.[213] First, one should ask whether the conclusions of the study are agreed to by each of (at least) three persons, viz., a member(s) of the tradition under study, a member(s) of at least one other religious tradition, and a person(s) trained in academic discipline. If the conclusion suggested is seen to be true to all, the chances are very good that some significant level of understanding is present. Does Macdonald's conclusion pass the test? No, it does not. No devout Muslim, I think, could possibly agree with Macdonald's view of Muhammad; nor would he see himself as a child who believes in Santa Claus. The second person(s) would agree with Macdonald only if he were, for example, a Christian of the sort who holds to an exclusive claim of God's revelation. I would argue that, since such a claim contradicts what God has revealed of His own nature, this person does not really understand his own tradition. The third, academic, sort of person would be forced to object to Macdonald's comparative treatment of the Old Testament prophets and Christianity on the one hand and Islam on the other. He claimed to be an Arabist, an Islamicist, an historian; on this crucial question he became a theologian of missions.

The second test we may apply concerns the way in which different traditions might think of each other. One can, says Smith, begin by talking about "it." One may then progress to "we" talking about "they," and to "we" talking to "they." This may become "we" talking with "you." If there is mutual comprehension and sympathy, it could emerge that "we" are all talking with each other about "us." That final stage is one of understanding. Does Macdonald move us along this road? No. What Macdonald desires is that Muslims, "they," cease in a profound way to be "they" and become the "we" of the earlier stages, and thus precludes any genuine sense of talking with each other about "us." A sacrifice is required; for in Macdonald's view the Muslim must become a Christian in order to be saved. He must cease to be a Muslim — cease to be the servant of God. In a very important sense, then, Macdonald is not "right" in his view of Islam. For he fails to understand and to participate. He judges and, finally, condemns.

NOTES

1. A Glasgowian by birth, Macdonald spent his entire academic career (1892-1925) at the Hartford Theological Seminary and particularly at the Kennedy School of Missions at that institution. He continued as "Honorary Consulting Professor of Muhammadanism" until his death in 1943. He was the author of five books, three on Islam and two on the Hebrew tradition (the latter written during his retirement). He was a regular contributor to and served on the editorial board of *The Moslem World* (now *The Muslim World*). He contributed more than eighty articles to the Lieden *Encyclopaedia of Islam*, wrote seventeen articles for the eleventh edition of the *Encyclopaedia Brittanica*, and had numerous entries in *The Jewish Encyclopedia*, Hastings' *Encyclopaedia of Religion and Ethics*, and *A New Standard Bible Dictionary*. He wrote a number of essays on *The Arabian Nights*. He was an influential figure among Islamicists and students of missions in his time; and his work is still respected today. Cf. J. Jermain Rodine, "The Legacy of Duncan Black Macdonald," *Occasional Bulletin of Missionary Research,* vol. 4, no. 4 (October, 1980).

2. Duncan Black Macdonald, *Aspects of Islam* (Hartford-Lamson Lectures, 1909) (Freeport, New York: Books for Libraries Press, 1971; orig. 1911), p. 20.

3. *Ibid.*, p. 262, cf. pp. 269-70.

4. *Ibid.*, pp. 284-5.

5. Duncan Black Macdonald, "The Problems of Muhammadanism," *Hartford Seminary Record,* XV:2 (February, 1905), pp. 90-91.

6. Duncan Black Macdonald, *Development of Muslim Theology, Jurisprudence and Constitutional Theory* (New York: Charles Scribner's Sons, 1903), p. 150.

7. *Aspects*, pp. 55-6.

8. *Ibid.*, p. 60.

9. *Ibid.*, p. 62, cf. pp. 63-4.

10. *Ibid.*, p. 66, cf. pp. 63-5.

11. *Ibid.*, p. 69.

12. Cf. *Ibid.*, p. 72; and cf. Duncan Black Macdonald, "Immortality in Islam," in *Religion and the Future Life*, ed. E. Hershey Sneath (New York: Fleming H. Revell Company, 1922), pp. 299-301.

13. *Aspects*, pp. 72-3.

14. *Ibid.*, pp. 73-4.

15. *Ibid.*, p. 74.

16. Qur'an 11:109; *Aspects*, p. 75.

17. *Ibid.*

18. *Ibid.*, p. 77.

19. "Problems," p. 79.

20. *Aspects*, p. 100.

21. *Ibid.*, pp. 103-4, cf. Duncan Black Macdonald, "What Christianity May Add to

Islam," *The Moslem World*, VIII:4 (October, 1918), p. 348, and "Immortality," pp. 315-6.

22. *Aspects*, pp. 110-11.

23. *Ibid.*, p. 258.

24. *Ibid.*, pp. 259-60.

25. "Immortality," p. 296.

26. "Problems," p. 79.

27. *Aspects*, p. 77.

28. *Ibid.*, p. 78.

29. *Ibid.*, pp. 78-9.

30. *Ibid.*, p. 80.

31. *Ibid.*, p. 81.

32. *Ibid.*, p. 87.

33. *Ibid.*, p. 105.

34. *Ibid.*, p. 108.

35. *Ibid.*

36. *Ibid.*, pp. 111, 222-3.

37. "Problems," p. 80.

38. *Development*, p. 262.

39. Duncan Black Macdonald, *The Religious Attitude and Life in Islam*, "being the Haskell Lectures on Comparative Religion delivered before the University of Chicago in 1906," (New York: AMS Press, 1970, orig. Chicago, 1909), pp. 6-7.

40. *Ibid.*

41. *Ibid.*, pp. 7-8.

42. *Ibid.*, p. 10.

43. *Ibid.*, p. 11.

44. *Aspects.*, pp. 10-11.

45. *Ibid.*, pp. 23-4.

46. *Ibid.*, pp. 36-7.

47. *Ibid.*, pp. 37-8.

48. *Ibid.*, p. 52; cf. *Development*, pp. 31-2, 39-49, 212.

49. *Aspects*, pp. 53-4.

50. *Ibid.*

51. *Ibid.*, p. 122.

52. *Ibid.*, pp. 223-4.

53. *Ibid.*, pp. 228-9.

54. *Ibid.*, p. 231.

55. *Ibid.*, p. 238.

56. *Ibid.*, p. 239.

57. *Ibid.*, pp. 282-3.

58. *Ibid.*, pp. 349-50.

59. Duncan Black Macdonald, "The Near East Tangle," *The Yale Review*, XII:2 (January, 1923), pp. 345-8.

60. *Ibid.*, pp. 346-7.

61. "Problems," p. 21.

62. *Ibid.*, p. 89.

63. *Life,* pp. 11 -123.

64. *Ibid.*

65. *Ibid.*, pp. 123 ff.

66. *Ibid.*, p. 174, cf., pp. 180 f, 192.

67. *Aspects*, pp. 288-9

68. *Ibid.*, pp.

69. *Ibid.*, p. 307

70. *Ibid.*, pp. 308-9; cf. *Life*, pp. 19 ff.

71. *Aspects*, pp. 310-19.

72. *Ibid.*, pp. 319-20.

73. "What Christianity May Add to Islam," p. 345.

74. *Ibid.*, pp. 345-6.

75. *Life*, 131.

76. Cf. *Aspects,* pp. 124-5.

77. *Ibid.*, pp. 133, 136.

78. *Ibid.*, pp. 141-2.

79. Duncan Black Macdonald, "The Vital Forces of Christianity and Islam: Concluding Study," in *The Vital Forces of Christianity and Islam: Six Studies by Missionaries to the Moslems*, with an Introduction by the Rev. S. M. Zwemer, D.D., and a Concluding Study by Professor Duncan B. Macdonald, D.D. (New York: Oxford University Press (Humphrey Milford), 1915), p. 224.

80. *Life*, pp. 39-40.

81. *Ibid.*

82. *Ibid.*, p. 301.

83. "Problems," p. 81.

84. *Aspects*, pp. 142-3.

85. *Development*, pp. 163-4.

86. *Ibid*.; cf. *Life*, p. 42, *Aspects*, pp. 97, 99-100.

87. Cf. *Development*, pp. 200-7, and Duncan Black Macdonald, "Continuous Recreation and Atomic Time," *The Moslem World*, XVIII:1 (January 1928), pp. 6-28.

88. *Aspects*, pp. 136-7.

89. *Ibid*., pp. 137-8.

90. *Ibid*., p. 138.

91. *Ibid*., pp. 143-4.

92. "Atomic Time," pp. 6-28; cf. Duncan Black Macdonald, *The Hebrew Philosophical Genius: A Vindication* (Princeton: Princeton University Press, 1936), p. 136.

93. Cf. *Development*, p. 206.

94. *Development*, pp. 153-4; cf. "Problems," pp. 91-4, *Aspects*, p. 321.

95. *Life*, pp. 227-8.

96. *Aspects*, pp. 45, 115.

97. *Ibid*., pp. 356-7.

98. *Ibid*., p. 76.

99. *Ibid*., pp. 184-5.

100. *Ibid*., pp. 185-7.

101. *Ibid*., p. 187.

102. See Macdonald's account of Ibn Sayyad, a boy with prophetic characteristics very similar to Muhammad's, whom Muhammad investigated out of fear of competition. *Life*, pp. 34-6, *Aspects*, p. 68.

103. *Aspects*, pp. 189-190.

104. *Ibid*., p. 190.

105. *Life*, pp. vii-viii.

106. *Ibid*.; cf. Duncan Black Macdonald, *The Hebrew Literary Genius: Being an Introduction to the Reading of the Old Testament* (Princeton: Princeton University Press, 1933), pp. 86 ff.

107. *Literary Genius*, p. 145.

108. William James, *Varieties of Religious Experience* (New York: Modern Library, 1902).

109. *Life*, p. 1-2.

110. *Ibid*., pp. 8-9; cf. *Aspects*, 345-7.

111. *Life*, pp. 70-78.

112. Cf. Duncan Black Macdonald, "From the Arabian Nights to Spirit," *The Moslem World*, IX:4 (October, 1919), pp. 336-48, and "The Development of the Idea of Spirit in

Islam," *The Moslem World*, XXII:1 (January, 1932), pp. 25-42 and XXII:2 (April, 1932), pp. 153-68.

113. *Life*, pp. 79-80.

114. *Ibid.*, pp. 93-4, 106-7; cf. *Aspects*, pp. 173-4.

115. *Life*, 130-1.

116. Cf. *Ibid.*, pp. 106-7, 110-1, 116-7, 118 *et passim.*

117. *Ibid.*, p. 126.

118. Cf. *Aspects*, pp. 171, 182-3.

119. *Life*, p. 159.

120. Cf. *Development*, pp. 215-6, 232-3, *Aspects*, pp. 192, 197-9, "Immortality," pp. 318-19.

121. Cf. *Aspects*, p. 188.

122. *Life*, 189-190.

123. Cf. *Aspects*, p. 209.

124. *Life*, pp. 124-5.

125. Cf. *Aspects*, p. 184.

126. *Life*, p. 302; cf. *Aspects*, pp. 145-6, 148-9.

127. *Aspects*, pp. 111-3, 114.

128. Cf. *Development*, p. 146.

129. "Problems," p. 79; cf. *Development*, pp. 125 ff.

130. *Development*, pp. 128 ff., 30, 131, 177-8.

131. *Aspects*, pp. 106-7.

132. *Ibid.*, pp. 190-1.

133. *Ibid.*, pp. 191-2.

134. Duncan Black Macdonald, "The War and the Missionary Outlook in Moslem Lands," in *The Missionary Outlook in the Light of the War*, The Committee on the War and the Religious Outlook (New York: Association Press, 1920), pp. 153-4.

136. Duncan Black Macdonald, "The Christian Message is Peace," *The Moslem World*, XXII:4 (October, 1933), p. 27.

137. *Life*, pp. 13-4.

138. Cf. *Literary Genius*, p. 2.

139. Cf. *Aspects*, pp. 43-4.

140. Duncan Black Macdonald, "God — A Unit or A Unity?" *The Moslem World*, III:1 (Janaury, 1913).

141. Cf. "What Christianity May Add to Islam," pp. 340-1.

142. "God," pp. 14-20; cf. "What Christianity May Add to Islam," pp. 340-1.

143. "God," p. 20.

144. *Ibid.*

145. Duncan Black Macdonald, "Begotten Not Made," *The Moslem World*, VI:1 (January, 1916), p. 24; cf. *Life*, pp. 37-8.

146. Cf. *Literary Genius*, pp. 49-50, 148 *et passim*.

147. *Ibid.*, p. 144.

148. *Ibid.*, p. 27.

149. *Ibid.*, cf. "Vital Forces," pp. 235-8.

150. "What Christianity May Add to Islam," pp. 341-2.

151. "Peace," pp. 328-9.

151. "Peace," pp. 238-9.

152. Duncan Black Macdonald, "The Doctrine of Revelation in Islam," *The Moslem World*, VII:2 *(April, 1917), pp. 116-7.*

153. *Life*, p. 14.

154. *Ibid.*, pp. 6-7.

155. *Ibid.*, pp. 17 ff.

156. *Ibid.*, p. 20, cf. pp. 23-4, 28.

157. *Ibid.*, pp. 44-5.

158. *Ibid.*, p. 33.

159. *Ibid.*, pp. 37 ff.

160. *Ibid.*, pp. 46-7.

161. Cf. *ibid.*, pp. 68-9.

162. Cf. *ibid.*, p. 67, and *Literary Genius*, p. xvii.

163. *Literary Genius*, pp. 84-5.

164. *Ibid.*

165. *Life*, p. 15.

166. "What Christianity May Add to Islam, pp. 344-5.

167. "Problems," pp. 95-6.

168. *Ibid.*, p. 96.

169. *Ibid.*, p. 97.

170. *Development*, p. 6.

171. *Ibid.*, pp. 285 ff.

172. *Ibid.*, pp. 285-7.

173. *Aspects*, pp. 253-4.

174. *Ibid.*, pp. 254-5, cf. pp. 125 ff.

175. *Ibid.*, p. 257.

176. *Ibid.*, p. 277.

177. *Ibid.*, pp. 361-2.

178. Duncan Black Macdonald, "The Disruption of Islam," The *Yale Review,* VI:I (October, 1916), pp. 101-116; cf. " War" pp. 139-41.

179. Cf. "What Christianity May Add to Islam," p. 340.

180. "War," pp. 138-9.

181. *Aspects*, pp. 21-2.

182. *Ibid.*, pp. 1-2.

183. *Ibid.*, p. 3.

184. *Ibid.*, pp. 5-6.

185. *Ibid.*, p. 13.

186. *Ibid.*, p. 23.

187. "Vital Forces," pp. 234-5.

186. Cf. "What Christianity May Add to Islam," p. 348.

189. "Vital Forces," pp. 234-5.

190. *Aspects*, p. 18; cf. "Peace," p. 328.

191. *Ibid.*, pp. 21, 24-5, 28; cf. "Vital Forces," pp. 215-6.

192. *Aspects*, p. 29.

193. *Ibid.*, p. 30.

194. *Ibid.*, pp. 286-7; cf. "War," pp. 150-1.

195. *Aspects*, pp. 357-8.

196. *Ibid.*, p. 359, italics in original.

197. *Ibid.*, pp. 259-60.

198. *Ibid.*, pp. 39-40.

199. *Ibid.*, pp. 40-1, cf. pp. 42, 323-4, 347-8; and "Tangle," p. 347.

200. *Aspects*, p. 347-8.

201. "War," pp. 152-3. For Macdonald's sympathetic treatment of the darwish fraternities, cf. *Aspects*, pp. 22-3, 49, 150, 154, 162, 164, 167-8, 169, 176-7, 180, and "Vital Forces," pp. 219-221.

202. Duncan Black Macdonald, "The Essence of Christian Missions," *The Moslem World*, XXII:4 (October, 1932), p. 328.

203. *Aspects*, pp. 256-7.

204. "War," pp. 144-5.

205. *Ibid.*, pp. 149-50.

206. *Ibid.*, p. 150.

207. *Ibid.*, pp. 151-2.

208. Duncan Black Macdonald, Christian Literature for Moslems," *The Moslem World*, XIII:4 (October, 1923), p. 340 *et passim.*

209. "Essence," pp. 329-30.

210. "Peace," p. 329.

211. *Aspects*, pp. 12-3.

212. *Ibid.*, pp. 252-3.

213. Wilfred Cantwell Smith, "Comparative Religion: Whither — And Why?" in *The History of Religions,* ed. Mircea Eliade and Joseph Kitagawa (Chicago: University of Chicago Press, 1959), pp. 31-58. Cf. pp. 34, 52.

6

SIR HAMILTON ALEXANDER ROSKEEN GIBB

Ziya-ul-Hasan Faruqi

We are fully aware of the efforts and achievements of the Orientalists in their valuable studies of the cultures, civilizations and religions of the East, achievements that have given to Orientalism the status and respectability of a recognized academic discipline.

The Orientalists dug out a good deal of learning buried in the thick mists of the past; discovered rare and precious manuscripts of books, studied, edited and published them along with their notes and comments; they also published translations of some of these materials in different languages, making them available to scholars and researchers in their respective fields of religion, history and civilization. They used modern research methods in their work, subject always to change and further improvement. This, in turn, lent respectability to their recourse, in their studies of other cultures and civilizations, to the techniques of modern disciplines such as linguistics, philology and social sciences, and to modern methods in history and philosophy. This led also to the development of Orientalism as an inter-disciplinary branch of learning.

We concede the valuable services of the Orientalists in promoting the cause of knowledge. But, we feel pained to note a good deal of subjectivity in their academic endeavors, otherwise so commendable in so many respects. They claimed that they were objective but hardly any one of them was able to suppress his mental reservations and rise above his religious and cultural prejudices; and this is particularly notable in their studies of Islam and Islamic law, of the Qur'an and Prophet Muhammad. Indeed, they are not only subjective; their deep-rooted prejudices are pronounced.

For historical and political reasons, among the Orientalists there are both Christians and Jews. The former, however, outnumber the latter. The story of hatred and animosity towards Islam and the Prophet of Islam, inherited by them, is spread over a period of almost fourteen hundred years. It consists of many ups and downs; its characters have

177

kept on changing; there have been changes too in its plot. But the basic theme of the story has remained unchanged.

Since the third decade of the present century, and particularly after World War II, there seems to have been an appreciable change in the approach of the Orientalists, for reasons political as well as economic. But, academically, a marked decline in the standard of work is also noticeable over the same period. Broadly learned Orientalists such as those of the nineteenth and early twentieth century are not seen today, with the exception perhaps of one man, the extent and variety of whose knowledge, erudition, discerning insight and sharp intellect are beyond doubt, and commended by all. But, unfortunately, even he is not totally unbiased, and the concepts and ideas inherited by him from some of the early masters of Orientalism are reflected, though not in so pronounced or easily detectable a manner, in some of his writings. He is Sir Hamilton Alexander Roskeen Gibb, more familiarly, H.A.R. Gibb, the subject of this study.

Born on January 2, 1895, in Alexandria where his father was employed as farm manager in a land reclamation company, Sir Hamilton was educated in Edinburgh, Scotland, first at the Royal High School there and then at the University where his main subject was Semitic languages (Hebrew, Arabic and Aramaic). In World War I he served in the Royal Field Artillery and saw active service in France and Italy. After the war, in 1919, on his request, a 'war privilege' Ordinary M.A. degree was awarded to him. Then he went to the School of Oriental Studies, newly established in London. He was appointed lecturer in Arabic in 1921 under Sir Thomas Arnold. In 1922 he obtained the degree of Master of Arts in Arabic from the University of London. In 1926-27 he made his first prolonged visit to the Middle East and began his study of contemporary Arabic literature, having previously spent two long vacations in North Africa. In 1929 he was appointed reader in Arabic history and literature at the University of London (tenable in the then School of Oriental Studies) and in 1930, on the death of Sir Thomas Arnold, succeeded him in the Chair of Arabic at the University of London.

He also succeeded Sir Thomas Arnold as the British editor of *Encyclopaedia of Islam*, and became one of the original editors of the revised edition, retiring in 1956. He contributed many articles to both editions.[1] As Professor of Arabic, he joined the University of Oxford in 1937, where he stayed until 1955. The same year (1955) there was an invitation for him to join Harvard as University Professor and James Richard Jowett Professor of Arabic, which he accepted. In 1957 he became the Director of the Center for Middle Eastern Studies at Harvard, and worked in that capacity until 1964, the year in which he was struck down by illness and never fully recovered from the physical effects. "The remaining years of his life (he died in 1971) were spent in Oxford, where he was devotedly cared for by Lady Gibb (Helen Jessie Stark, known to her friends as Ella) until her untimely death in 1969. These were years of great privation, of an incapacity courageously and patiently — even willingly — borne with no trace of self-pity or word of complaint."[2]

Professor Gibb's scholarship and academic achievements were universally recognized. He received many honors and was member of a number of learned societies. It was because of his worldwide reputation as an Arabist that he was selected as a foundation member of the Fuad I Academy of the Arabic language, Cairo. He was an Associate Member of the Institute d'Egypte and member of the Arabic academies of Damascus and Baghdad.

Professor Gibb is the author of a number of books and learned articles. His reviews of books represent the best in him as a scholar of diversified academic interests and penetrating intellect. Below, in order of publication, is a list of some of his works: 1) *The Arab Conquests in Central Asia* (London, 1923); 2) *Arabic Literature* (London, 1926; revised edition, Oxford, 1963); 3) *Ibn Batutta, Travels in Asia and Africa* (London, 1929); 4) *Damascus Chronicles of the Crusades* (London, 1932); 5) *Modern Trends in Islam* (Chicago, 1947); 6) *Mohammedanism* (London, 1949); 7) *Islamic Society and the West,* Vol. I, Part I (London, 1950), Part II (London, 1957), (with Harold Bowen); 8) *The Travels of Ibn Batutta,* Vol. 1 (Cambridge, 1958), Vol. II (1961); 9) *Studies on the Civilization of Islam,* eds., S.J. Shaw and W.R. Polk (Boston, 1962); 10) *The Life of Saladin from the works of 'Imaduddin and Baha'ad-Din* (Oxford), 1973).

In the West, Professor Gibb is ranked as one of the foremost Islamic scholars, meaning that he was one of those Orientalists who devoted the best years of their lives to the study of Islam, Islamic civilization, Arabic language and literature. His profound scholarship, coupled with historical insight and analytical approach, is also acknowledged by those Muslim scholars who have studied his works with care and interest. And there is no doubt that some of these works (books and articles) are marked by great erudition, a unique ability to explain and interpret, freshness and originality of ideas, sharp and keen intellect, and deep humanity and understanding.

Gibb's articles on different subjects concerning Islam, its history, culture, systems, movements, religious thought, etc., are so fertile with new ideas that some of them have served as texts for further elaboration by others, leading, in some cases, to what have been claimed as independent works. The titles of some of his articles published at intervals in reputed journals of the world and included in the valuable collection of his articles, *Studies on the Civilization of Islam*, are as follows: 1) "An Interpretation of Islamic History"; 2) "Social Significance of the Shu'u-biya"; 3) "The Evolution of Government in Early Islam"; 4) "The Armies of Saladin"; 5) "Al-Mawardi's Theory of the Caliphate"; 6) "The Islamic Background of Ibn Khaldun's Political Theory"; and 7) "The Structure of Religious Thought in Islam."

Besides these, he wrote a number of scholarly articles on the development of modern Arabic literature, e.g. "The Nineteenth Century"; "Manfaluti and the new Style"; "Egyptian Modernists"; "The Egyptian Novel"; "Nish'ah al-Insha' il-adabi," and "Bada'at-Talit an-Nathri." These important articles are sufficient to justify his distinguished place among contemporary Orientalists. In fact, he had a profound feel for the Arabic language and Arab artistic creation as displayed in Arabic literature. His article, "Islamic Biographical Literature,"[3] is an indication of how strongly he believed that neither Arabic literature nor Islamic history could be studied in isolation from the other without distortion of the underlying reality, since both were expressions of a living society. Ibn Khaldun's *Muqaddimah*, for its originality of ideas and concepts as well as for its literacy and artistic beauty, had captivated his heart and mind and throughout his intellectual life remained for him a source of inspiration and delight. He has described him as ". . . the lively, direct, colourful, brilliantly imaginative, exuberantly eloquent Ibn Khaldun, whose ideas stream out in long cascades, sometimes indeed tumbling into excited incohesion, but for the most part held together by a taut and beautifully modulated structure of prose, controlled by precise and refined mechanisms of co-ordination and subordination, and articulated with a trained elegance that gives to every word the exact degree of emphasis required by his argument."[4]

However, Gibb's main concern was history and culture, with great emphasis on *historical thinking*. He regarded history as a search for the patterns in the web of human life. To him the real historian was one who tried first to discover and then to investigate the patterns that were already there, "woven into the web of human life in time past by the actions of innumerable individuals." But, one would hardly concur with all his interpretations and conclusions. At some places in his writings, he seems not to have escaped certain preconceived notions and reads and explains historical events in their light. Moreover, in the case of the personality of Muhammad, he does not rise above the level of his contemporaries. It seems to have been beyond his comprehension to see in Muhammad a divinely inspired Prophet ordained to give mankind a message of hope and happiness in all walks of human life. And, there-fore, to him Muhammad was a statesman, a military strategist and a patriot in the style of the contemporary West.

In one of his best articles, "An Interpretation of Islamic History," published in the *Journal of World History*, 1:1 (Paris, 1953), he writes with full conviction that:

> Since, however, inescapable economic forces made any permanent sta-bilization of inner-Arabian conditions virtually impossible, the mere suppression of Bedouin opposition — with the implication that the forces of Islam would be used up in an interminable and sterile struggle with the tribesmen — was an inadequate solution for the problem set by them. It was necessary to find the terms on which the tribesmen as a whole could be swung, if not up to the first level of assimilation, at least on the level of identifying Islam with their own interests. Hence the trial expeditions deliberately organized by Abu Bakr after Muhammad's death, when groups of tribesmen were despatched under Meccan commanders towards the frontiers of Syria.[5]

Earlier, in his *Mohammedanism* (chapter 2, 'Mohammed') Gibb had written on the subject in much the same vein, though in different and more cautious words:

> . . . whether deliberately guided by Mohammed in this direction or under the unconscious play of forces which swept him along in their current, the Islamic movement became to an increasing degree, a focus of Arab feeling . . . Mohammed seems to have been aware of this tendency. It may have partially contributed to (and been confirmed by) his measures against the Jewish tribes. And whether or not the story be true that in 628 he sent summons to the Roman Emperor, the Persian King of Kings, and other ruling princes, he was certainly contemplating some action against

the Byzantine power in the north before his death in 632. The almost immediate launching of the first expeditions towards Syria by his successor Abu Bakr can hardly be explained otherwise.[7]

Further, in one of the earlier passages in the book he had remarked: "At Medina he (Muhammad) sat astride Mecca's vital trade route to the north. All his expeditions against the Bedouin tribes seem to be part of a master plan, elaborated with great skill and insight, to take advantage of this position and blockade Mecca into surrendering."[8]

This approach to interpreting history is purely economic and materialistic. In it, one finds no reference to the historic role of the impact of the reformative and revolutionary teachings of Islam on the minds of any section of the Arab tribesmen. It simply seeks to have one believe, in a roundabout way, that the moral and spiritual precepts of Islam could not attract the tribesmen of Arabia. Rather, when they found that their material and worldly interests would be best served if they stuck fast to the fold of Islam, they started identifying themselves with Islam. Professor Gibb, it seems, first formulated a notion and then interpreted the Islamic conquests in Syria, Persia and Egypt to justify it. It may also be deduced that, consciously or unconsciously, he was toeing the line drawn by Caetani and other Orientalists charmed and seduced by the agnostic and materialistic tendencies of their time. It is noteworthy that here, like most of his predecessors in the field of Orientalism, Professor Gibb also does not care to refer to the threatening postures of the Byzantine power against the Muslim Arabs at the time of the Prophet Muhammad and after. In our view, this approach is opposed to the methodology used in modern historiography, and sadly diminishes the historical objectivity which the modern West so proudly accords itself.

The same approach and attitude are witnessed in Gibb's treatment of the subject of Hadith. With his characteristically fascinating style and dialectical method, he seems to try to convince his readers that the prophetic tradition is nothing more than forgery and fabrication, artificially created to suit expediency. He argues:

> By the end of the first century, separate and diverging rules of law were being applied in different cities and provinces, based on the independent interpretation of local teachers, and complicated by survivals of customary law and administrative regulations. The religious leaders saw in this a danger, especially when local rules appeared to diverge from the ethical principles of the Koran. *The Method by which they proceeded was to*

produce 'Traditions' from contemporaries of the Prophet which related to the decisions
of Muhammad on specific points, and to claim for these binding authority scarcely
inferior to that of the Koran[9] (italics ours).

Continuing this line, when he deals with the emergence of Hadith as
a new science with its principles of collection, criticism, classification
and co-ordination, and its general acceptance as the second source of
law, Gibb dubs the lot as merely an "artificial creation."[10] It would not
be correct to say that he was totally unaware of the history of the
development of Hadith literature, or that he had never heard of the
'uswah-'i-hasna as mentioned in the Qur'an itself. One is, therefore,
naturally led to conclude that, by his explanation and use of such phrases
as "artificial creation," he deliberately attempts to deprecate the religious and legislative value of Hadith for his Muslim readers who,
because of its being so closely related to their Prophet, consider it as one
of the very bases of Islamic culture, which has enabled it to sustain itself
in spite of the absence of any formal organization, in all later centuries
in the face of political pressures, intellectual adventurism, mystical
deviations and the inflow of new ideas and peoples.

In fact, Professor Gibb's understanding of Hadith is substantially the
same as that of some of his predecessors like Ignaz Goldziher, David S.
Margoliouth and Henri Lammens, the weaknesses of which have
already been pointed out by Muslim scholars.[11]

It is interesting to note the Professor Gibb was very much impressed
by and had developed a liking for the person and achievements of Sultan
Salah ad-Din, known in the West as Saladin. He made a searching study
of this unusual 'Islamic' personality of the twelfth century. His articles,
"The Armies of Saladin," combine true scholarship and understanding
with modern research techniques to give a finely detailed history of
outstanding quality. To date, perhaps, no Muslim *'alim* or intellectual
has produced a work of such a high standard on the subject. His article
"The Achievement of Saladin," however, stands out *par excellence*. In it
he proves that Sultan Salah Ad-Din was not one of those individuals
whose achievements can be attributed to the complex of circumstances
within which they have to act. He was not the creature but the creator
of his circumstances. His career indeed involved distinctive moral and
religious elements, and it was this only that could explain how he was
able to vindicate the honor of Islam in that period of political disintegra-
tion and moral decline.

Professor Gibb writes: "It is rarely indeed in medieval history that we have at our disposal authentic materials from which positive conclusions, that will stand up to rigorous historical criticism, can be drawn . . . (But) for the life and achievements of Saladin we possess, by a fortunate conjunction, five contemporary sources in Arabic."[12] These were, according to him, Ibn 'Ali Taiy, Ibn Al-Athir (al-Kamil fit-Tarikh), Qadi Baha'uddin Ibn Shaddad (an-Nawadir as-Sultaniyah), 'Imaduddin (al-Barq al-Shami), and Al-Qadi Al-Fadil. He examined these five sources very minutely and critically, and in all aspects, and concluded that "no Muslim prince had for centuries been confronted with the problem of maintaining an army continuously in the field for three years against an active and enterprising enemy. The military feudal system was entirely inadequate to such a campaign . . ."[13] Although neither warrior nor governor by training or inclination, the reasons for Saladin's success lay in his capacity to inspire and gather round himself

> all the elements and forces making for the unity of Islam against the invaders. And this he did, not so much by the example of his personal courage and resolution — which were undeniable — as by his unselfishness, his humility and generosity, his moral vindication of Islam against both its enemies and its professed adherents. He was no simpleton, but for all that an utterly simple and transparently honest man. He baffled his enemies, internal and external, because they expected to find him animated by the same motives as they were, and playing the political game as they played it. Guileless himself, he never expected and seldom understood guile in others . . . .[14]

We believe that no Christian historian or biographer has ever presented, after a thorough investigation and critical examination based on the principles of historical criticism of contemporary sources, so beautiful a pen-portrait of Sultan Salah Ad-Din.

But it is unfortunate that a great scholar like Gibb, who was so objectively considerate in his studies on Islamic history and Arabic literature, tends to display something of a sort of disloyalty to his own historical insight and academic objectivity at different places in his writings on subjects related to the Qur'an and the life of Prophet Muhammad. This tendency in such writings of his can only be explained by his having inherited the traditions of prejudice and subjectivity from his religio-cultural environment and from his predecessors in the field.

Before elaborating this with examples, it seems proper to quote a statement that he made as a confession of his belief. In his foreword to

Modern Trends in Islam he wrote,

> In these days, when we are enveloped in an atmosphere charged with
> propaganda, it is the duty of every investigator to define precisely to
> himself and to his audience the principles which determine his point of
> view. Speaking in the first person, therefore, I make bold to say that the
> metaphors in which Christian doctrine is traditionally enshrined satisfy
> me intellectually as expressing symbolically the highest range of spiritual
> truth which I can conceive, provided that they are interpreted not in
> terms of anthropomorphic dogma but as general concepts, related to our
> changing views of the nature of the universe.[15]

Apart from what Professor Gibb actually means to convey to his
readers in respect of his belief in 'Christian doctrine,' this much is clear:
that in spite of all the provisos mentioned by him in this statement, he
was a believer in Christianity as literally and traditionally understood,
although not necessarily in all its metaphors and symbols.

There is nothing wrong in his believing in Christianity. Everyone is,
and should be, entitled to a belief which satisfies him spiritually and
intellectually. It were better Gibb conceded this entitlement to Muslims
also. It was expected of him that while writing on the Qur'an and the
life of the Prophet he would do justice and give due regard to the
religious sentiments and susceptibilities of the Muslims. But he did not
do so. On the contrary, one is led to feel that his Christianness swung
him to the point where he had to disregard objectivity and that basic
approach in the study of comparative religion which, centuries before, a
Muslim scientist and scholar, Al-Biruni (362-433 A.H./972-1051 A.D.)
had used in compiling his *al-Athar al-Bawiyah* and *Kitab al-Hind*.

Writing on others' religious beliefs, traditions and social institutions
is not prohibited. But the fair way in all such writings is to state the view
of the adherents of the religion under study

> in its entirety so fully and clearly as to have no room for complaint of
> misrepresentation. If the writer holds another view, or if he wishes to
> refer to still other views, he would be fully justified in introducing all
> this, separately and distinctly, after he had stated (the former's tradi-
> tional view). But unfortunately this logical and natural order of repres-
> entation is seldom followed and is often inverted, with the result that
> unless he is well instructed the reader will, in effect, be subjected to some
> 'indoctrination' or at least to such confusion that he will be unable to
> distinguish between native tradition and the opinion of the writer.[16]

It is surprising to find a scholar of the stature of Gibb, whose
erudition and scholarly seriousmindedness is also acknowledged by his

Muslim readers, sometimes neglecting to observe such basic elements of scientific study.

Professor Gibb's book on Islam is entitled *Mohammedanism*. D.S. Margoliouth's book of the same title was published in 1911. After the lapse of more than thirty-five years, Gibb considered it wise to publish "a restatement of the subject . . . rather than a reedition of the original work."[17] The reason for this undertaking was, according to himself, not only "the discovery of new facts and the increase of understanding which results from the broadening and deepening research,"[18] but also the change in the spiritual and imaginative environment usually suffered between one generation and the next.[19] He further says: "Every work of this kind reflects not only the factual kowledge but also the intellectual and emotional limitations of its period, even when every effort is made to eliminate prejudgement and prejudice."[20]

He accepted that "Muslims dislike the terms Mohammedan and Mohammedanism."[21] Still, he deliberately chose 'Mohammedanism' as the title of his book on Islam, for in his opinion the term in itself is not unjustified. His arguments were: 1) There was a time when Muslims themselves called their community *al-'ummah al-Muhammadiyah* and; 2) when the Muslims affirm their faith by reciting the *Kalimah*, the significance of the second part of this article of faith, with all its implications, is markedly and fully alive in their minds as "the first may be assented to by many besides Muslims."[22] Since the time of Muhammad no one who did not believe in the prophethood of Muhammad has been allowed to consider himself as Muslim. "Conversely, the orthodox exponents of Islam have generally maintained that no one who publicly professes these articles can be declared a non-Muslim."[23]

Are these arguments not fantastic? Do they not testify to the hollowness of his assertion on this count that the age of D.S. Margoliouth suffered from its emotional limitations and intellectual environment? Muslims, as the Qur'an has denominated them, like to be called Muslims, not 'Mohammedans', but Gibb asserted that they may also be justifiably called 'Mohammedans.' Thus one cannot but conclude that the centuries old prejudices of the Christian world still persist and are reflected in one form or the other in the works of Christian writers.

On the very first page of this book Professor Gibb says: "The word *Islam, finally* adopted by Mohammed as the distinctive name of the faith which he preached,"[24] . . . etc., etc. In fact, his view of Islam as the name of Prophet Muhammad's faith which he preached from the very first day of his prophethood presupposes the discussion in chapter 3 of *Mohammedanism*, on the origin of 'The Koran.' Surmising as to how the concept of *tawhid* could have developed in Prophet Muhammad's mind, he asserts that the Qur'anic idea of *tawhid* was basically related to the belief of those "so-called *hanifs*,"[25] of whom little is known.

According to Professor Gibb, Prophet Muhammad glorified in the name (*hanif*) and attached it "as a distinctive epithet to Abraham," who was "neither Jew nor Christian."[26] In his opinion there was a variant reading of the Qur'an verse[27] which suggested that the doctrine preached by Prophet Muhammad was initially denoted by the word *Hanifiyah*. It was only later that he adopted the word *Islam* for his doctrine. We are unable to trace any mention of, or reference to any variant reading of the said verse in *Bayan al-Qur'an* (at-Tabari), *Tafsir-i-Kabir* (ar-Razi), *Durr al-Manthur* (as-Suyuti), *Ruh al-Ma'ani* (al-Alusi) and *Fath al-Bayan* (Siddiq Hasan Qannawji) while Gibb himself does not indicate any source. It seems that the learned author, taking advantage of some weak *rewayat* or mere conjecture of his own, considered it necessary to impress upon his readers' minds that it was all Prophet Muhammad's doing to call his doctrine first *Hanifiyah* and then replace it by *Islam* as the name of his faith.

In fact, this is all seen due to an overly vivid imagination and also to the author's belief that the Qur'an is nothing more than a mere compilation of Muhammad's own religious ideas, as they gradually developed in response to his ever changing circumstances. Chapter three opens with the following sentence:

> The Koran is the record of those formal utterances and discourses which Muhammad and his followers accepted as directly inspired.

Since the dawn of the principles of historical criticism in the academic world in the West, the Orientalists have been busily preoccupied in establishing the Judaeo-Christian origin of the Qur'an. The theme has been subjected to incessant and serious conjectures, from which historical, literary and theological conclusions of farreaching consequences have been drawn. And, then, these conjectures and conclusions have been repeated in so many ways, and in such a manner that, among the Christian and other non-Muslim peoples, they generally enjoy the dignity of facts. But, despite all this, the idea remains as it was two hundred years ago, i.e. merely hypothesis.

Is it not surprising and interesting that the Christian West, with all its material and intellectual resources coupled with rigorous application of principles of modern research methodology and historical criticism, has completely failed to provide, in the historical sense, any convincing and decisive evidence to prove that the Prophet of Islam borrowed extensively from the Old and the New Testaments and that the Qur'an is merely "a record of his formal utterances and discourses? The only surviving contemporary evidence is that of the Qur'an itself, and it rules out any possibility in most categorical terms'"[28] of borrowing from any external source. But this evidence is too often brushed aside as it negates the very purpose of the Orientalists.

There is no paucity of reliable documents and authentic details about the life of Prophet Muhammad. Much of Hadith literature in this respect is genuine. But perhaps Professor Gibb considers it his duty to confuse his readers on this count. He rather too glibly 'sets aside' the biographical details concerning the period from the childhood of the Prophet Muhammad to the proclamation that he was a prophet divinely ordained, observing:

> of his early life and circumstances little is known with certainty. That he was born . . . into a cadet branch of one of the leading families of Mecca, was left an orphan in early life and brought up by an uncle, engaged in the caravan trade, became commercial agent to a widow named Khadija, married her and had children . . . all this is commonplace and gives no hint of future greatness. The anecdotal detail with which pious tradition delighted to fill out these bare outlines must be provisionally set aside.[29]

The learned author does not find any measure of greatness in Prophet Muhammad's purity of conduct in pre-Islamic Meccan society, then steeped in debauchery, licentiousness and other vices; nor in his uncompromising honesty and unblemished integrity, which were so famed that even his staunchest opponents recognized his moral excellence and called him *Amin*; nor in his wisdom and insight when called upon to settle matters of historical significance; nor in his anguish and anxiety about the moral degeneration of his people, his deep concern for the weak, the oppressed and the strangers who were not entitled to any civic rights in Mecca and suffered much at the hands of the strong and the privileged and, in general, his spiritual suffering and disquietude over the moral decadence of the social environment around him. To Gibb all these traits of Prophet Muhammad's early character contained nothing unique and distinctive given the circumstances of his upbringing. He simply ignored them and said that of Muhammad's early life and circumstances nothing was known with certainty and that "he succeeded because he was a Meccan."[30]

Now, when a great scholar of gentle disposition like Professor Gibb, ranked as one of the greatest Islamic scholars that Christendom has ever produced and said to have studied Islam as a Christian in search of a common spirituality in the teachings of the two great religions, insists that the Qur'an owes its origin to the Judaeo-Christian traditions, refuses to see any spiritual dimension in the early or later parts of Muhammad's life and fails to comprehend the Islamic concept of prophethood and prophetic mission as adumbrated in the Qur'an, it can be well imagined what novel ideas in regard to the Qur'an and the life of the Prophet and, in general, to the teachings, history, culture and civilization of Islam have been put forward by second rank Orientalists.

NOTES

1. Ann K.S. Lambton, "Obituaries: Sir Hamilton Alexander Roskeen Gibb," *Bulletin of the School of Oriental and African Studies*, XXXV, Part I (1972), pp. 338-339.

2. *Ibid.*, p. 339.

3. *Historians of the Middle East*, eds., Bernard Lewis and P.M. Holt (London: Oxford University Press, 1962), pp. 54-58.

4. H.A.R. Gibb, Review of Franz Rosenthal's translations of Ibn Khaldun's *Muqaddimah, Speculum*, XXXV (1960), p. 139.

5. H.A.R. Gibb, *Studies on the Civilization of Islam*, eds., Stanford J. Shaw and William R. Polk (Boston: Beacon Press, 1962), pp. 5-6.

6. *Ibid.*

7. H.A.R. Gibb, *Mohammedanism*, fifth edition (New York: Oxford University Press, 1962), p. 31.

8. *Ibid.*, pp. 29. All this reminds Gibb's readers, particularly his Muslim readers, of some of the writings of the Italian Orientalist, Prince Leone Caetani, who, under the impact of the general materialistic and rational tendency of his time and his deep interest in economics, geography and geology, accounted for the rise and spread of Islam in terms of inevitable economic and geographical factors. Besides these he also mentioned other factors, e.g. 'the power of resistance of the Arabs, the sensuality and the avidity of the Bedouin . . . who is the least religious and who loves plunder and depredation; the failure in general of the preaching of Muhammad who could influence only a small minority with a true religious sense; the gradual 'degeneration' of Islam into a political movement after the migration of the Prophet to Medina and the contemporary decadence and deterioration of the empires of Persia and Byzantium. All these elements led to the successful campaigns of Islam, a large part of the followers of which consisted of the Bedouins, who were pure and simple plunderers and for the love of booty and adventure and for the enjoyment of unbridled license. In this movement we should not search for any religious impulse no more no less than we can search for any religious element in the invasion of the German hordes that crossed the frontiers of the Roman Empire or that of the Tatars who flooded Asia in the twelfth century. The Arabs carried on their conquests only with material means and with moral virtues inborn in their nature and to which Islam had nothing to add. Islam was just a temporary phase. (*Studii di storia orientale*, volume I (Rome: 1911), pp. 368-369; see also Reyazul Hasan, "Prince Leone Caetani — A Great Italian Orientalist (1869-1935)," *Hamdard Islamicus*, V:1 (Spring, 1982), pp. 63-64.

9. Gibb, *Studies on the Civilization of Islam*, p. 15.

10. *Ibid.*, p. 16.

11. See Shibli Nu'mani, *Sirat-un-Nabi*, volume I, seventh edition (Azamgarh: Darul Musannifin, 1971); S. Sulaiman Nadwi, *Maqalat-i-Sulaimani*, volume II (Azamgarh: Darul-Musannifin, 1968) and Fazlur Rahman, *Islam* (Chicago: University of Chicago Press, 1966).

12. Gibb, *Studies on the Civilization of Islam*, pp. 91-92.

13. *Ibid.*, p. 104.

14. *Ibid.*, p. 99.

15. H.A.R. Gibb, *Modern Trends in Islam* (Chicago: University of Chicago Press, 1945), p. xi.

16. A.L. Tibawi, "English-Speaking Orientalists," *The Muslim World*, LIII:3 (July 1963), p. 191.

17. Gibb, *Mohammedanism,* p. v.

18. *Ibid*.

19. *Ibid*.

20. *Ibid*.

21. *Ibid*., p. 2.

22. *Ibid*.

23. *Ibid*.

24. *Ibid*., p. 1.

25. *Ibid*., p. 28.

26. *Ibid*.

27. *The Qur'an* III: 67.

28. Tibawi, "English Speaking Orientalists," p. 104.

29. Gibb, *Mohammedanism*, p. 24.

30. *Ibid*., p. 25.

7

GUSTAVE E. VON GRUNEBAUM
AND THE MIMESIS OF ISLAM

Bryan S. Turner

The Orientalist version of Islam is defined by a limited, but highly persistent, bundle of interpretative themes which have the effect of bringing into question the authenticity of Islam as religion and culture.[1] There is firstly the dominant theme of historical decay, retreat and decadence because of which the explosive rise of Islamic society was followed by an equally rapid and total decline. The consequence is that Islam is a religion which either fails to fulfill some latent promise or which represents some retardation of the prophetic monotheism of the Abrahamic faith. The 'failure' of Islam is secondly located within a broadly teleological conception of history in which the unfolding of Islam and its interruption are explained by reference to certain innate and ineradicable features of the 'Muslim mentality,' the favored characteristic being Leibnitz's 'Mahommedan Fate.' In its socio-logical version, this conception of an inherent flaw in Islamic social structure concentrates on alleged gaps in the 'civil society' of Islam. The social stationariness and economic stagnation of Islamic society are thus connected with the absence of autonomous urban communities, a bour-geois capitalist class, achievement motivation and a systematic, but flexible, legal system.[2] Thirdly, there is the Orientalist notion that Islam, if not exactly a defective form of Pauline Christianity, is then at least a parasitic and arid religion. The expansion and appeal of Islam can thus be partly explained by its alleged simplicity, both in theological formulation and ritual practice. While Islam is typically held to be merely dependent on the Judaeo-Christian tradition in spiritual terms, Islamic philosophy and natural theology are themselves highly depend-ent on Greek philosophy. In addition, Islamic philosophy is dependent on decadent forms of Hellenism, namely the Neo-Platonic compilations of Plotinus. Finally, while the Orientalist is professionally immersed in his subject, there is characteristically an emotional gap and cultural hostility which alienates the Orientalist from Islam, producing a covert antipathy towards the Orient. The personal distance between Oriental-ist and Orient serves to reinforce the notion of the uniqueness of the

West and the unbridgeable gulf separating Orient and Occident. These persistent themes within the Orientalist discourse by which 'Islam'[3] is constructed and represented were deeply embedded in the diverse scholarly *ouevre* of Gustave von Grunebaum, who has become the object of both academic glorification and critical scorn.[4]

G.E. von Grunebaum (1909-1972) was born in Vienna on September 1, 1909 and received his Ph.D. from the University of Vienna in 1931. Having taught at the University of Vienna, he emigrated in 1938 to the United States, where he subsequently taught at the Asia Institute, New York (1938-43), the University of Chicago (1943-57) and, as Director of the Near Eastern Center, at the University of California, Los Angeles (1957-72).[5] The early publications of von Grunebaum were primarily concerned with issues in Arabic poetry[6] but, while he never abandoned his interest in Arab literature, he became known as the author of a number of influential studies of macro-cultural problems relating to the unity of Islamic history and society. These macro-cultural studies included *Medieval Islam* (1946),[7] *Islam* (1955),[8] and *Classical Islam* (1970).[9] He was also editor of and contributor to *Unity and Variety in Muslim Civilization* (1955)[10] and *The Dream and Human Societies* (1966).[11] A bibliography of his scholarly publications lists 172 items covering the years 1936 to 1970.[12] Gustave von Grunebaum can thus be regarded as a typically productive member of the European migration to the United States in the period of fascist ascendancy.[13]

Unlike the majority of academic Orientalists steeped in the scholastic minutia of such problems as Averroes' interpretation of Aristotle's view of tragic poetry, von Grunebaum came to appreciate the relevance of anthropological and sociological studies in the analysis of Islam. He was, for example, perceptively critical of Max Weber's commentary on the role of Islamic towns in *Economy and Society*.[14] It was, however, the cultural anthropology of A.L. Kroeber which von Grunebaum adopted as a perspective on his favorite theme, that of Islamicate cultural diversity and integration.

Kroeber (1876-1960), in developing the geographical notion of *Kulturprovinz* in his studies of the North American Indian, concentrated on the notion of 'culture' as a superorganic entity which was largely independent of material culture and developed according to processes which were immanent principles.[15] Kroeber, whatever his views on the Plains Indians of North America, was not exactly a sympathetic student of

Islamic culture. Islam, according to Kroeber,

> lacks some of the most significant features of other great civilizations. It
> had no infancy and no real growth . . . There is nothing new, nothing
> specific to it . . . Ideologically, the peculiarities of Islam are restrictions.[16]

Von Grunebaum also adopted the conceptual apparatus of Robert
Redfield's studies of folk society which distinguished between the 'great
tradition' of the scribes and the elite, and the 'little tradition' of the
village and the illiterate mass; this dichotomy made an appearance, for
example, in von Grunebaum's commentary on the adjustments in
Islamic society of the orthodox culture to the local cult tradition.[17]
While there are these overt interests in cultural anthropology, von
Grunebaum's work appears to depend more on Hegel's idealism than on
Kroeber's culturalism.

As with many nineteenth-century philosophers and historians, Hegel
was impressed by the vigor and vitality of early Islam, but impressed
also by its 'failure' to fulfill that early promise. Islam lacked that
dialectical process by which human communities could in history
achieve self-consciousness. The result was that

> Islam has long vanished from the stage of history at large, and has
> retreated into Oriental ease and repose.[18]

Like Hegel, von Grunebaum was the historian of Islamic decadence and
retreat. In the preface, for example, of his *Classical Islam* von Grunebaum informs us that its very title

> implies a judgment. The classical represents a model. It is, in fact, a
> model whose reconstruction is by definition an obligation and an
> impossibility.[19]

Islamic history is the history of the divergence of an ideal community
based on holy law, prophetic guidance and uniform commitment to
certain religious norms from the actuality of imperial fragmentation,
the separation of legal prescription from social practice and the loss of a
state legitimated by sacred principles. The decline of Islam from an
ideal embodiment of religious virtue was, in von Grunebaum's view,
crucially bound up with the problem of a sacred law tradition which
could not be developed to meet entirely new circumstances and exigencies of social development. Thus,

The steady decay that, beginning as early as the ninth century, ate away the strength of Islam and had, by the middle of the tenth, ruined the central authority of Baghdad beyond repair compelled acquiescence in conditions only too far removed from those postulated by political theory. It may be doubted whether the caliphate as designed by the legists ever had any real existence, but in the eleventh century the discrepancy between reality and ideal had become so flagrant it could no longer be overlooked by the body of believers . . . The believer was thought under obligation to obey whosoever held sway, be his power *de jure* or merely *de facto*.[20]

This alleged hiatus between religious ideal and power politics as manifest in the gaps in the *shari'a* is a constant theme of Orientalism and closely related to the argument that in Islam there is no sound principle of opposition to illegal politics. It was, for example, fundamental to Max Weber's view that the gap between legal ideal and empirical reality could only be plugged by irrational *fatwa*; the same Orientalist thesis emerged in Bernard Lewis' argument concerning the absence of oppositional principles in Islam.[21] For von Grunebaum, the rigidity of law and the gap between norm and practice manifests not the absence of a principle of legitimate resistance but, rather, the teleological failure of Islam. Islam suffered from conservativism and lack of cultural integration:

Arrested in its growth during the eleventh century, it has remained an unfulfilled promise. It lost the power of subjecting the innumerable elements to an organizing idea more comprehensive than the desire for individual salvation. It stagnated in self-inflicted sterility.[22]

While von Grunebaum has been characterized as the theorist of decay, in fact his 'Islam' is an endless repetition of the same, an unchanging religious reality. As a fixed cultural form, Islam constantly erected barriers and defenses around itself in order to maintain its sacral identity against external interventions. Hence,

the adjectives that von Grunebaum unites with the word Islam (medieval, classical, modern) are neutral or even super-redundant: there is no difference between classical Islam and medieval Islam, or just Islam.[23]

Illustrations and examples can, therefore, be taken indiscriminately and at random from any Islamic society and from any point in history to demonstrate the unchanging nature of Islamic reality. This indiscriminate selection of evidence and total disregard for precise periodization perfectly illustrate this Hegelianized version of Islam in which any one item of culture is expressive of the totality.[24] One single poem can illuminate the whole of Islamic culture. The endlessly repetitious nature of Islamic history is, for von Grunebaum, one further dimension of Islam's capacity for cultural mimicry and social imitation. Islam is consequently treated as an endless borrowing from its pagan Arabic past, from Judaeo-Christian monotheistic theology, from Hellenistic logic and from Chinese technology. On the whole, Islamic society was wholly uncreative and almost without influence. Byzantine iconoclasm was not the product of Islamic influences;[25] the conventions of Arabic composition in poetry have made for "repetitiousness and a certain lack of invention."[26] The need to maintain the authority of revelation over reason put definite limits on the impact of Greek science and philosophy on Islam.

> Where theory ran no risk of becoming dangerous, investigation went ahead: optics, botany, pharmacology and empirical medicine are all deeply indebted to Islamic research. But the conceptual framework of late classical thought, and even Galen's anatomy and Hellenistic astrology, remained untouched though certain parts were known to be superseded.[27]

In philosophical matters, the Islamic theorists remained entirely mimetic. Rational thought was confined to the elite; the philosophers were essentially translators, merely a vehicle of Greek thought.[28] Islamic history is thus the history of failure, unfulfilled promises and cultural limitation. In terms of three fundamental criteria of civilization, Islam can be seen to be a major failure:

> Mastery of nature, public morality and the condition of the common man have been suggested as measures of backwardness or achievement of a civilization. It does not require elaborate demonstration that, by these standards, the Islamic world has but a small contribution to make. There never has been a concerted effort in Islam to put natural resources to such use as would insure progressive control of the physical conditions of life. Inventions, discoveries, and improvements might be accepted but hardly ever were searched for.[29]

Despite the fact that Orientalists normally hold that despotism in Islamic society was the product of large scale irrigation works designed to insure "progressive control over the physical conditions of life,"[30] von Grunebaum here decides to ignore those developments in experimental science and technology which were apparently characteristic of Islam.

When von Grunebaum turned to problems of Islam as religious belief and practice, we find once more the notorious charge that Islam is arid, simply and emotionally unsatisfying. In his study of ritual, it is interesting to note that von Grunebaum employs the implicitly contemptuous notion of 'Muhammadan festivals.' In this discussion of the "five pillars of Islam," von Grunebaum's main argument is that the simplicity of Islamic practices creates a gap within which saint worship and the cult of the Prophet could develop to satisfy the emotional needs of the laity. From the point of view of a cultured Westerner, however, Islam appears somewhat underdeveloped liturgically and ritually. The reason for this is not hard to discover:

> Islam was born in one of the backward areas of the ancient world. The radical monotheism of its doctrine and the puritanism of its mood, combined with the esthetic limitations of the Muslim cultural heritage, left the believer satisfied with an arid, if physically exacting liturgy.[31]

Because Islam had no clergy, there was no social group of liturgical specialists with an interest in ritual elaboration and innovation. Islam, from inception, was intended to be a 'laymans faith and, therefore, the beliefs and practices of the religion are "few and simple,"[32] namely *shahada, salat, saum* and *hajj*. The implication of this view is that Islam is an undemanding religion, placing few psychological burdens on the religious consciousness. Islam lacks, therefore, precisely that social leverage which is held to be characteristic of the Protestant ethic. Islam is a religion of cultural and psychological containment. Hence, in a passage which reads like a copy of Hegel's discourse on the Orient in the philosophy of history, von Grunebaum concludes his study of medieval Islam with the authoritative pronouncement that

> The Muslim's world is at rest, and he is at rest within it. His immediacy to God and his acceptance of the divine order were never, during the Middle Ages, seriously disturbed. Resignation and submission to the inevitable and abdication of searching reason before the inscrutable were rewarded by the consciousness of fitting perfectly and naturally into the great preordained scheme of things that embraces mankind as it embraces the genii, the angels and the stars. The Muslim knows and accepts man's limitations.[33]

In short, von Grunebaum leaves us, as the conclusion to his study of medieval Islam, with a thesis that is highly recurrent in Orientalism: that the failure of Islam was in the last analysis a failure of mind and will. The sense of fatalism in a world determined by the iron laws of divine omnipotence conditioned the human spirit to "peace and repose."[34] In the West, the emergence of the modern world is marked by a declaration of the active mind, namely, "I think, therefore I am," in the Cartesian revolution of philosophic skepticism.

A range of criticisms could be mounted against the Kroeberian perspective of von Grunebaum. There are, for example, problems associated with the privileged status he accords to the analysis of poetry in the understanding of Islam; despite references to the 'little tradition,' there is little space in his history of Islam for everyday life and the world of the common people. Rather than considering detailed criticisms, there are two very general objections to von Grunebaum's analysis which can be considered. Firstly, he examines Islam from the outside and indeed regards it as an academic duty to sit in judgment over Islam. It is not simply that he brings external criteria to Islam, but that he considers Islam in terms of elitist, normative and exacting Western criteria. The standards which signify the 'failure' of Islam would in fact also signify the failure of Christianity. The gap between the ideal of a Christian community and the realities of political life as indicated in the controversy surrounding the church-sect typology and the compromise with state power and political violence would be a case in point. Put simply, von Grunebaum's perspective is colored by prejudice and ultimately by an "almost virulent dislike of Islam."[35]

Secondly, there is a striking relationship between von Grunebaum's style and the repetitious, mimetic character which he ascribes to Islam. His discourse is peppered by erudite references, by quotations from a variety of philosophical and linguistic sources and by a curious mixture of social anthropology and philology. Despite his apparent commitment to social science, there is curiously little significant intellectual development in his work, little change in his account of classical Islam and little modernization of his views on Islamic literature. Von Grunebaum not only repeats himself, but reproduces all the mimetic themes of Orientalism. The stationariness of von Grunebaum's discourse is ironically a facsimile of the social stationariness which allegedly characterizes Islam and a mimicry of that very intellectual repose which supposedly characterized the Muslim mind.

NOTES

1. For a general statement on Orientalism see Bryan B. Turner, *Marx and the End of Orientalism* (London: George Allen & Unwin, 1978) and Edward Said, *Orientalism* (New York: Vintage Books, 1978).

2. For an analysis of this problem, Bryan S. Turner, "The Middle Classes and Entrepreneurship in Capitalist Development," *Arab Studies Quarterly*, I (1979), pp. 113-134.

3. On the construction of Islam see Edward W. Said, *Covering Islam* (New York: Pantheon Books, 1981).

4. The contrast is provided by Amin Banani, "Islam and the West, G.E. von Grunebaum, Toward Relating Islamic Studies to Universal Cultural History," *International Journal of Middle East Studies*, 6:2 (1975), pp. 140-147 and David Waines, "Cultural Anthropology and Islam, the Contribution of G.E. von Grunebaum," *Review of Middle East Studies*, 2 (1976), pp. 113-123.

5. Franz Rosenthal, "In Memoriam," *International Journal of Middle Studies*, 4:3 (1973), pp. 355-358.

6. G.E. von Grunebaum, *Die Wirklichkeit Weite der fruharabischen Dichtung. Eine literaturwissenschaftliche Unterschung* (Vienna: Selbsverlag des Orientalischen Institutes der Universitat, 1937).

7. G.E. von Grunebaum, *Medieval Islam, a Study in Cultural Orientation* (Chicago: University of Chicago Press, 1946).

8. G.E. von Grunebaum, *Islam: Essays in the Nature and Growth of a Cultural Tradition* (London: Routledge & Kegan Paul, 1955).

9. G.E. von Grunebaum, *Classical Islam, A History 600-1258,* trans. from German by Katherine Watson (Chicago: Aldine Pub. Co., 1970).

10. G.E. von Grunebaum, ed., *Unity and Variety in Muslim Civilization* (Chicago: University of Chicago Press, 1955).

11. G.E. von Grunebaum and Roger Caillois, eds., *The Dream and Human Societies* (Berkeley and Los Angeles: University of California Press, 1966).

12. G.L. Tikku, ed., *Islam and its Cultural Divergence, Studies in Honor of Gustave E. von Grunebaum* (Urban, Chicago: University of Illinois Press, 1971).

13. Donald Fleming and Bernard Bailyn, eds., *The Intellectual Migration: Europe and America 1930-1960* (Cambridge, Mass: Belknap Press, 1969); Franz Neumann, Henri Peyre et al, *The Cultural Migration: the European Scholar in America* (Philadelphia: University of Pennsylvania Press, 1953).

14. Von Grunebaum, *Medieval Islam*, p. 174.

15. On Alfred Kroeber's influence see Abdallah Laroui, "For a Methodology of Islamic Studies. Islam seen by G. von Grunebaum," *Diogenes*, 81-84 (1973), pp. 12-39.

16. Alfred L. Kroeber, *The Nature of Culture* (Chicago: University of Chicago Press, 1952), p. 381.

17. Von Grunebaum, *Unity and Variety*, p. 28.

18. G.W.F. Hegel, *The Philosophy of History* (New York: Dover Publications, 1956), p. 360.

19. Von Grunebaum, *Classical Islam*, p. 7.

20. Von Grunebaum, *Medieval Islam*, p. 168.

21. For a critique, Bryan S. Turner, "Determinant Structures and Contingent Revolut-ons: Critical Comments on Vatikiotis," ed., *Revolution in the Middle East, Review of Middle East Studies*, 3 (1977), p. 1-17.

22. Von Grunebaum, *Medieval Islam*, p. 322.

23. Laroui, "For a Methodology," p. 27.

24. On 'expressive totality' in the Hegelian tradition, Louis Althusser and Etienne Balibar, *Reading Capital* (London: NLB, 1970), p. 17.

25. G.E. von Grunebaum, "Byzantine Iconoclasm and the Influence of the Islamic Environment," *History of Religions*, 2:1 (1962), pp. 1-10.

26. G.E. von Grunebaum, "The Concept of Plagiarism in Arabic Theory," *Journal of Near Eastern Studies,* 3 (1944), pp. 234-253.

27. Von Grunebaum, *Classical Islam*, p. 135.

28. This is the basic theme of De Lacy O'Leary, *How Greek Science Passed to the Arabs* (London: Routledge and Kegan Paul, 1949).

29. Von Grunebaum, *Medieval Islam,* p. 343.

30. The question of 'hydraulic societies' is fully developed in Anne M. Bailey and Joseph K. Llobera, eds., *The Asiatic Mode of Production* (London: Routledge & Kegan Paul, 1981).

31. G.E. von Grunebaum, *Muhammadan Festivals* (London: Abelard-Schuman, 1958), p. 3.

32. *Ibid.*, p. 5.

33. Von Grunebaum, *Medieval Islam*, p. 346.

34. *Ibid.*, p. 347.

35. Said, *Orientalism*, p. 297.

8

'ALONGSIDEDNESS — IN GOOD FAITH?': AN ESSAY ON KENNETH CRAGG

Jamil Qureshi

D r. Cragg's earlier works[1] have the feel of critical manuals about separate elements of Muslim belief and practice, addressed either to those in missionary work or to Christian minorities in Muslim-majority areas who need to put up a more active, informed resistance to that circumstance. The later works,[2] especially the two book-length essays on the Qur'an, contain more sustained arguments, variations still on the aversion characteristic of all Western-Christian approaches to Islam — that it is a law as well as a faith, that it requires political form and sanctions force. The enterprise is undertaken, avowedly, in a spirit of inter-religious humility, a patient 'alongsidedness,' an exchange both ways of honest, caring criticism. It is not Dr. Cragg's purpose that Muslims should change their religious allegiance. He desires only to bear Christian witness so that, while explaining Muslim belief and practice, he may demonstrate how near Islam comes to Christian sentiments. Whether those who call themselves Muslim continue to do so is not important — what matters is that they feel those Christian sentiments.[3] To bear Christian witness is, for a Christian, an unquestionable right, even a duty. But to do so in the act of explaining Islam is suspect — Dr. Cragg is open to the charge of attempting not conversion but 'subversion,' the political metaphor having a particular bitter-sweet relevance for our general argument.

I do not question the sincerity of Dr. Cragg's intent but his truth in its fullfilment. His efforts to be courteous and understanding often feel —in the experience of this Muslim reader — like the manners of a man much less concerned with the thoughts and feelings of others than with his own reputation of courteousness in their view of him, a rather sticky, shallow courtesy that mars even his best perceptions.[4] The reader might well feel such personal remarks (even if justified, which has yet to be shown) quite improper in an academic context. But I must insist on a certain (I hope properly measured) implacability in this response to Dr. Cragg's work. My object is to illustrate and then share the quality of 'alongsidedness' Dr. Cragg in fact brings to bear upon

Islam. Some attack, some defense and defensiveness, are inevitable in this pursuit. Yet personal vindictiveness or vindication are not at issue since the alongsidedness concerned is not peculiar to Dr. Cragg but typical of Western/European alongsidedness with any other culture or value-system, though most especially with Islam.

Dr. Cragg is some way removed, it is true, from that quite extraordinary arrogance that could blithely dismiss nine-tenths of the world as 'heathen' and 'uncivilized,' but not so very far. The missionaries of the nineteenth century were courteous and honorable, so too (for the most part) the colonists — the former content to have colonization as a means of access, the latter content with Christian mission as a pretext for taking power. There were, no doubt, exceptional wicked individuals, and times and places where wickedness was exceptionally intense, but surely no one believes that, on the whole, missionaries or colonists ever represented their activity to themselves as wicked or destructive in purpose. They believed that they came to civilize and, where possible, Christianize. They came, in short, to teach the colonized people how to view themselves, for just as they found the 'natives' unfit to govern themselves, so too they found them unfit to entertain any *general* notions about their own cultural or religious values. Despite every posture or intent to the contrary, and despite the absence of a background of overt coercion — covert military and economic pressure is still a present reality — Dr. Cragg is securely in this line of entrepreneurial scholarship. The implicit aim is to save Islam from the Muslims, for them, not as a museum relic — that scholarly enlightenment belongs to the colonial period — but as a living reality, re-lived through the Christian idea of the nature of God or, at least, through the strenuous Promethean questioning of minds alive to the intellectual reach and technological competence of Europeanized man.

My emphasis above on *general* ideas is important. Any specific techniques or crafts that the native had developed might be worthy of respect but not his general ideas of values, nor their mutual relation. For example: a Muslim may add significantly to Dr. Cragg's knowledge of the particulars of, say, *salat* (prayer), but to his (Cragg's) view of the *general* meaning for the Muslim of the Muslim prayer, the Muslim's view is not adequate, perhaps not even reliable, certainly not definitive. *Salat* is the most conspicuous external feature of practiced Islam and Dr. Cragg returns many times to the subject. He notes the postures of prayer in *The Dome and The Rock*;[5] his interpretive descriptions of the same, some ten years later in *The Mind of the Quran*,[6] is one of the best things in all his work on Islam. He is well aware that *salat* cannot and should not be isolated from the whole of Muslim *ibadat* (worship). In the Qur'an, it is usually linked with paying *zakat* (welfare-tax), freeing slaves, ransoming captives, and struggling in the way of God. In longer Qur'anic contexts, prayer is associated with remembering the transcience of all human effort, however directed, and with the narratives of the Messengers calling the faithful and the unfaithful to the remembrance of God; it is, in sum, associated with seeking freedom from self-interest and self-will and freedom (serenity) in surrender to God's will.

The Prophet of Islam instituted the details of the ritual not out of any personal caprice but in obedience to the Qur'anic requirement that Muslims observe prayer. That requirement is not cheapened by Dr. Cragg. He shows that he clearly understands that *salat* is intended to recall and enable man's double responsibility: his upright power in the world given for his use and prostrate humility before God. But this understanding does not affect Dr. Cragg's general assessment of Muslim prayer. That derives from his general assessment of Islam which precedes any study (and thereby precludes any honest experience) of it. Islam is a revealed law, that is, it tells people what is right and wrong, it tells them what to do,[7] and this law *requires* prayer. Prayer in Islam is obligatory. That, for Dr. Cragg, is the controlling generalization whence all his comment on *salat* is directed. Now there is, in Islam as in every religion, spontaneous, extra-ritual prayer called *du'a*, distinct from *salat*. Of course Dr. Cragg is aware of this — he is a diligent translator and anthologizer of prayers of this kind[8] — and evidently it presents a problem if it is to be assimilated to the notion that in Islam prayer is obligatory. The longest treatment of the problem is in *The Dome and the Rock* — I quote as fully as space permits:

> No observer of Muslim *salat* can fail to sense the feeling of merit, or if the word were not so clumsy, meritoriousness about it. We must beware of stating this over crudely . . . But it follows from the obligatory character of Muslim ritual that its performance is praiseworthy . . . It is difficult for minds schooled to Christian concepts of grace and redemption to appreciate fully the extent to which this is inevitably the case in the Muslim soul . . . . The whole basis of our acceptance with God lies in that of which we are no other than repentant recipients. God's is both the

initiative and the accomplishment of our salvation and our works of gratitude follow, not that we may qualify with him for favour, but because undeserved favour has already been bestowed. [In the Muslim reckoning the] shifting of the onus for our relationship with God to a fulfilment of obligation, a bringing of tribute, a performance of ritual duty, makes meritoriousness central . . . . .[Muslim worship lacks the sacramental dimension, and] that to which it is responsive in God is majesty and law, authority and greatness . . . . .[It has to be conceded that:] Fulfilment of the rital obligation in Islam does qualify for God's favour, but gives no ground for presumption about its being granted. [Dr. Cragg here translates and quotes *du'a*]: The petition reads: O God, I ask thy succour, I implore thy guidance, I pray thy forgiveness, I repent unto thee. In thee I believe, upon thee I rely. To thee I ascribe all praise: I thank thee and am not among them who belie thee and thy gifts.' . . . Thus it is clear that Muslim reliance on the merit of religious performance does not obviate self-reproach and humility. On the contrary. Still, the Christian task is to carry these merciful instincts after self-abasement into their full and real significance as tokens of the truth in Christ that our relationship with God cannot be other than one of dependence upon mercy. It will be found in the end that loyalty to that principle must take us to the cross. Islam has halted at a half-way house, reaching to the recognition of unworthiness yet relying on the accrediting of worth, remaining in the status of creditors Godward and yet using the language of debtors.[9]

Elsewhere, the quality of Dr. Cragg's attention to his subject is superior to the commentary noted. However, the courtesy gestures and the linking of thoughts in the language of this passage show in a very tangible way what, elsewhere, is difficult to isolate from larger and longer exchanges of thought and attitude. The effort to be conciliatory in "if the word (meritoriousness) were not so clumsy" follows the thorough confidence of "no observer can fail to sense . . ."; similarly, the judicious "We must beware of stating this over crudely . . ." is followed by the categorical, apparently irrefutable "but it *follows* from . . . that its performance *is* . . ." The whole show is, of course, quite beyond the Christian pale (meritoriousness and prayer not being a feasible conjunction in the Christian mind) and requires much sympathetic stretching of the imagination "to appreciate fully the extent," etc. Christians feel in debt to God because, they believe, He took the initiative and died for them through his Son, a debt that cannot ever be fully repaid.

Muslims, however, when they pray seek to get into credit. Christians respond through prayer to God's mercy, Muslims only to His sovereignty: the King demands (and looks with favor upon) tribute. There is some hope for Muslims in that they dare not *presume* that God has marked up their credit point; nevertheless, they strongly suppose that "fulfilment of the ritual obligation *does* qualify for favour." The sticking point comes with the non-obligatory petition, duly translated. Dr. Cragg concedes, but only negatively: "Muslim reliance on the merit of religious performance does not obviate self-reproach and humility. On the contrary." Plainly, on the sticking point, Dr. Cragg is stuck. "On the contrary" is dangling because its meaning is not something that Dr. Cragg can bear to write out into the argument — namely, that the obligatoriness of *salat* does *not* necessarily entail meritoriousness. He has then no choice but to shrug ("Still"), for the argument is lost, and go on anyway: "Still, the Christian task is . . . ." The last sentences are odious in the extreme; the sanctimoniousness of "loyalty to that principle must take us to the cross" can be measured in the unashamed indecency of Dr. Cragg's conclusion: Muslims know (use) the language of self-reproach and humility but they do not know what it means. It could be argued that there is no religious devotion whatever that lacks some notion of self-reproach and humility: turning to God implies it. There is a special degree of it, perhaps, in Christian prayer, and a special quality of psychological and emotional satisfaction obtained from it, that so obscures this fact that, for Dr. Cragg, to know the meaning of self-reproach and humility means knowing *Christianly* or not at all.

It would be no good defending *salat* by admitting that there is absenteeism from and in the act of prayer, that certain individuals do only go through the motions of prayer in the hope of being well thought of, but that such failure of concentration of intent (*niyat*) is a *universal* human imperfection. Dr. Cragg's criterion for judging *salat* is Christian prayer, which is not required as evidence of belonging to Christian faith, being instead a voluntary turning of the individual soul to God. The familiar caricature of the Sunday service — the pious, priestly gaze wandering surreptitiously from a moralizing text to uplifted female bosoms in the congregation, the faithful themselves ranked in social pride or envy, some alert in rigid duty, some honestly asleep, all vaguely clogged up in an atmosphere thick with every manner of religious prop — embroidered ceremonial robes and cloths, symbols in stone and wood and glass, incense — and above all, the relief and release of stirring hymns, before they all escape at last, their weekly duty done to their individual souls as well as to their corporate Christian identity —this caricature might serve to jeer back at the meritoriousness Dr. Cragg finds in Muslim prayer, and a memory of it might well have prevented a little the Christian pride in his comment. But he would still insist on his argument that Islam formally *demands* the five daily prayers, Christianity at most encourages formalized prayer, never setting too much spiritual store by it.

But the obligatoriness of prayer in Islam is not the most general characteristic to be noted of it: its obligatoriness must, necessarily, be an 'Islamic' obligatoriness. For an authentic inter-religious humility, that fact ought to be the starting-point and goal of inquiry, not something incidental. As Dr. Cragg himself notes, prayer is urged in the Qur'an as part of a broad pattern of *ibadat*, also obligatory. Thus, paying the welfare due, remembering and declaring that there is no god but God, lauding the mercy of God in the twin miracles of Creation and Revelation and, its counterpart, seeking the forgiveness of God, are all obligatory. The obligation does not derive from any kind of priestly class as, in Islam, the individual Muslim must be his own priest — with all that that means in responsibility to faith and religion. It derives rather from the Qur'an which, in Muslim belief, is the word of God. Fulfilment of obligations to God is the definition of *islam* or submission; 'dutifulness' is then a less apt term to describe a Muslim response to obligations to God than 'gratitude' or 'affirmation.' Self-evidently, God does not need praise, it is the Muslim who needs to praise God,[10] to thereby affirm his dependence upon the Divine. Thus the observance of *salat* is approximately equivalent, in the Christian service, to singing hymns in God's praise. Pharisaical observance is known in all religions — quite independently of whether the observances required are obligatory or voluntary. In the Qur'an, it is regarded as a spiritual disease (also a political malaise) and called *nifaq*, usually rendered in English 'hypocrisy,' though 'hollowness' might do as well. Since there is no compulsion in religion,[11] there is no foolproof defense against *nifaq* except in the sincerity and inwardness of the Muslim's submission, and since it is mentioned innumerable times in the Qur'an that God sees into the heart, we may suppose that sincerity and inwardness of devotion were fully understood *at the outset* of Islam.[12]

The several elements of *ibadat* do work, as a mutually supportive system, to locate and rehabilitate *nifaq*. A Muslim in whose daily life *salat* is a strong and conspicuous thread is less likely to neglect his responsibilities as father, brother, neighbor, guardian, leader; as these responsibilities are also obligatory, in the same way as *salat*, he should know that *salat* is not, of itself, sufficient guarantee of his *islam*. The converse is equally important: namely, to serve the common good in abstraction from *salat* risks willful satisfaction in one's own dynamism and hasty self-congratulation for 'good deeds' that, sooner rather than later, renounce God and, sooner rather than later, turn against their own intent. No good deed is good *and* Muslim unless accompanied by a concentration of intent that knows it inwardly as part of 'struggling in the way of God': the Muslim's daily 'hours' are regular sustenance for that intent as well as a regular and (for some) strenuous demand upon it. Further, while the different capacities and circumstances of individual Muslims determine the different degree of their service (good deeds), the relation of each to God is universal, invariable, all are alike in being slaves. None is nearer God save in and by his God-fearing. *Salat* is then a levelling of righteous pride in success as well as an uplifting and consolation for the ignominies and inadequacies of daily failure: *salat* is the one obligation that can be fulfilled by all and, if the place is clean enough, it can be fulfilled anywhere: there is no need of a stony church hush.

How is it that, as I describe it, *salat* is for self-criticizing, and Dr. Cragg finds that it is for self-esteeming? Nothing that I have said above of the institution of prayer in Islam is missing in Dr. Cragg's observations somewhere in his work.[13] The difference comes only from the generalization ordering the description. Dr. Cragg *begins* with an attitude opposed to Islam, disposed (whatever his conscious intention) to avoid the whole truth, and make a detrimental presentation where possible. A crude example is that above where, in order to sustain the thesis of meritoriousness, he must represent God in Islam as the Western caricature of the 'Oriental despot,' a king awaiting tribute. The attitude is typically European rather than Christian: Muslims know the language of self-reproach and humility but not its 'real' meaning; the Red Indians had no property laws, so how could it offend them if land or resources which they previously 'had' were expropriated; Africans had no democracy and no vote, so how could it be said that colonization deprived

them of freedom in any 'real' sense; Palestinians never quite had a
legally distinct national government, so why not Israel?

Doubtless this will seem Third World peevishness. But not so. Europeans have been traditionally reluctant to concede to others any capacity for general ideas outside the European system. If the notion of
self-reproach is integrated differently in Islam than in Christianity, it
follows that in Islam it has not yet developed fully. Islam is a somewhat
deficient, immature Christianity. Islam 'fails' to give the right priority
to self-reproach — inconceivable that Christianity actually overdoes it,
tempting its believers to exaggerate and linger in what may be called (in
Kierkegaard's sense of 'aesthetic') aesthetic religiosity, mock humility,
so much in love with its own voluntary gesture of self-abasement. Dr.
Cragg happily forgets that Islam is not more 'primitive' than Christianity, actually it came *after* Christianity had been around to mold ways of
thinking and feeling and living for six hundred years — that Islam
acknowledges Christianity and sees in it several errors of emphasis and
meaning the require forthright reappraisal. However, it is an instinct
with Europeans (the Romans had the same attitude to the Jews and
Christians) to believe their civilization the most advanced, the most
experienced, the most evolved. Again and again, Dr. Cragg finds
himself working on the hypothesis that Christianity happened *after*
Islam. In *The Privilege of Man*, he even notices that he is doing this, but
does it anyway:[14]

> Christianity, historically, contrasts clearly and unmistakably with both
> of them [i.e. Judaisim and Islam], though with the same commitment to
> the Divine sovereignty and the same human dominion. It parts with the
> particularism of Israel and it diverges from the power invocation of
> Islam. Its new covenant by its open character breaks out of the ethnic
> framework and by its gentle quality abjures and disallows the sanction of
> force and the persuasion of political authority.
>
> It may seem anachronistic to write in the present tense in these terms
> before Islam existed. But it will be clear in all that follows there were
> deep 'Islamic' issues in the very making of Christianity and it is in no
> essential way anticipatory to see them side by side. See below.

What 'see below' directs us to is the argument that the crucifixion is the
only adequate response to the question of power. From the Islamic
viewpoint, and from Christian practice, which preceded it, this was *not*
an adequate response: see below.

II

It is impracticable to analyze each of Dr. Cragg's particular commentaries on Islam in the detail we have afforded to that above on *salat*. I propose instead to state briefly his general program of criticism, evaluate it from a Muslim viewpoint and then discuss its major elements. That general program derives from the single premise that Islam is not Christianity and should be, a premise issuing from the Christian hope, not consciously aggressive, that it could be. For the purposes of discussion we can open that premise out to show its major elements.

1. Christianity sees the unvindicated suffering of the Messenger as the supreme proof of Divine mercy and the supreme attribute of the Divine nature. The crucified Messenger seeks neither to combat nor prevent nor silence evil, but rather to transform, to redeem it. Islam altogether lacks this notion of the redemption of evil, seeking instead its forcible containment or elimination. The central Christian symbol —the unclenched hands nailed open, the arms forced out in a wide embrace, the bodily form wounded and giving, the cross where human cruelty and Divine kindness are eternally interchanged — has no equivalent in Islam. In place of the cross, there is the Hijrah, the migration from suffering into statehood.[15] In its founding history (that is, in its Scripture, the Qur'an, and the acts of its Apostle) Islam sanctioned the use of force to establish an 'Islamic state' and 'Islamic law.' State and law require (and may compel) outward conformity, a 'patterned piety,' but what of the inner recesses of the heart where state and law cannot reach? For those who reject the order of the 'obedience community' or who, if they must seem to obey, disobey inwardly, Islam has no response. It thus lacks a proper understanding of the true nature and dimensions of evil.[16] Islam is spiritually naive and cannot console the inward refusal of God, the tragedy of self-damnation.

2. Those Christians who can accept that Jesus was the Son of God can affirm that, through his sacrifice, God intervenes positively in the world of human sinfulness. God therein assures man that henceforth (and retrospectively too, somehow) His relation to man is that of ever-patient Father awaiting the return of a penitent child. The cross makes Old Testament law profoundly irrelevant: questions of *how* to be good are insignificant beside the greater question of *whether* to be good. Precisely that *whether* option is invited by man's indebtedness following the Divine sacrifice: the cross proves how inexplicably and rootedly

evil man is, but it proves at the same time with what gentle earnest God awaits man's repentance.[17] Islam, however, has a different notion of the Divine. God in the Qur'an is transcendent, inscrutable; His Mercy is in the creation of man for right guidance, in the giving of right guidance (revelation), and in the wide creation and abundance of nature so that, using it, man may remember and be rightly guided. Islam is confidently addressed to community and state, with rules to keep community and state in order. But it is a naive confidence — for Islam supposes that a community obedient to Divine law will thereby be able to dispose individual Muslim souls rightly toward God. It fails to address the individual in his proper 'person.' This is, supremely, the area of competence of the Christian Gospel.[18] Christianity cares more profoundly about sin and suffering — God comes down to prove it — because it conceives both more realistically, that is, tragically.

3. On the modern agnostic temper, spreading from the West: Dr. Cragg has not written with much explanatory zeal[19] about the vastly preponderant majority of the non-religious for whom human dignity is defined in terms of increased buying power. He writes more fully, however, and sympathetically, of the conscientious minority[20] who assert, through their refusal of God, what they believe to be a true moral heroism in facing up sincerely to the void. They reject traditional religion as harmful delusion that leads to obscurantism, superstition and repression of human instincts and intellect. They do not consider the existence of God an important question even if it were capable of answer.[21] The steady freedom from doctrinaire concepts and precepts, the evolving flexibility of commitment — if I may so call it — that the Christian world has enjoyed, is certainly, Dr. Cragg thinks, the origin of this feeling of skepticism. But it is also the main hope for its conversion and ultimate solace. Nothing could be less appropriate to the modern mood than Islam,[22] for in Islam there is no possibility of an interrogation of God, no room for doubters. A more Christian Islam, a more exclusively inward Islam, if such is possible, will open a door from within and, through the mystery of doubt and sin, let the person 'in' to God.

4. The Old Testament prophets who speak of their travail and perplexity in presenting the Divine message to human recalcitrance, as well as crucified Jesus, are significantly absent from the Qur'an. But it is their unrequited ministry that most deeply touches the sceptical, rebel-

lious soul and so brings it to God. It is they who, by confronting to the end the tragedy of human evil, represent most fully what the task and possible achievement of conversion to God is.[23] The Prophet of Islam was not of this temper. Orthodox (Sunni) Islam, according to Dr. Cragg, sees suffering as an obstacle and not as a means to salvation. It praises an authoritarian God, sovereign and transcendent, it obeys a law imposed from on high. The faithful are vindicated by success in this life if they will but collectively establish and collectively observe the law.[24] Dr. Cragg accepts that there are many millions in the modern world who, if they are to be moved at all towards God, must be moved 'Qur'anically.' It is therefore urgent that the teachings of the Qur'an be properly interpreted for modern times — that is the motive of his two books on the Muslim Scripture. The general theme of *Counsels in Contemporary Islam* is the bewilderment in semi-secular Muslim states (which owe their existence to the expulsion or retreat of European imperial powers) as they try to define means and goals for a truly Islamic community, bonded willy-nilly to political and economic structures inherited from non-Islamic, indeed anti-Islamic, administrations. Industrialization, West-dependent, is urgently necessary to contain the needs of vast population growth; with it come secularization and Westernization. It follows that a separation of the (devotional) 'Makkan' from the (political) 'Madinan' phase of Islam is inevitable, is already happening.[25] Better then to understand more deeply the implications of the Makka phase before it emerged into confident statehood in Madina. It is for this reason, not for the motive of religious aggrandizement, that the Christian message must come 'alongside' the faith of the Muslim. Muslim and Christian should, in praise or petition, come 'alive to God,' and if the Muslim will leave out of his rubric "and Muhammad is the Apostle of God," and the Christian leave out "through Jesus Christ Our Lord,"[26] might they not kneel at their prayers side by side? Dr. Cragg's anthology of prayers and meditations from both faiths, *Alive to God*, is his evidence that they might indeed, if only they would.

III

Whatever his conscious intentions, Dr. Cragg is plainly evaluating Islam against Christianity. He measures the life of Jesus which, Christians believe, ended on the cross, with that of the Prophet Muhammad which ended with the secure foundation (in equivalent terms) of 'church' and 'state.' A more honest and fruitful comparison would surely measure the evolution of the Christian churches within the pax Romana against Qur'an and Sunnah. For the Sunnah (the example of the Prophet and the Companions) represents the earthly expression, interpretation, and perpetuation of the meaning of the Qur'an: very roughly the same relation obtains, with the addition of official priesthood and corresponding institutions, between the early Christian churches and the meaning of the life of Christ. But surely, somewhere in twenty years of reflection and published commentary on Islam, Dr. Cragg must have come across this rather obvious point? To my knowledge, he has treated the point directly only once — and then cursorily, as well as emotively:[27]

> . . . The Church, for all its brave Gospel about a universal sonship and a supra-racial family, has in fact allowed history to give it sharply national form and deeply cultural monopoly of race. Are not long stretches of 'the new covenant' as privately ethnic as the old? Are there not whole eras of the Christian Church, both eastern and Western, Constantinian and Roman, Byzantine and Lutheran, taking a fully Islamic character vis-a-vis the political order? Is not the doctrine of the two realms a sort of Meccan/Medinan theme without a Hijrah?
>
> It must be so conceded. Nor does Christian faith mean that these great 'principalities,' these organs of human existence, as it calls them, are in any way negligible or irrelevant. On the contrary, it acknowledges their irreducible role in the order of the human world and gives them relative and due validity within the larger whole. But, when it is true to its own Gospel, it does not entrust them with the whole onus of the Divine Kingdom. It sees the state as holding the ring for the inward forces of righteousness, attaining or at least attempting, such justice as its nature allows, within which other instruments of truth and value may undertake their inalienable tasks. It sees nationhood, likewise, a necessary context and sanction of the good life, but not itself the crux, still less the guarantor of it. Political kingdoms and popular identities, the realms of power and blood, are inescapable factors with which it is imperative to reckon both as proper agents and menacing rivals of men's final loyalty under God. But there must always be, not only with them, but strenuously over against them, the rights of God as the only true condition of man. The whole essence of the Christian distinctiveness, in new testament for old, is the Cross not the Hijrah, in the counter choice that both salutes and rejects the Jewish and the Islamic, lies in the conviction of sonship [i.e. to God], in nature and through grace, as the ultimate religious experience . . . Reality, in the Christian view, has to do, not

finally with nations or lands, or goods, or forces, or laws, or techniques, or ideas, or power, or politics, but with people in all these, alienated, frustrated, exiled, bartered, depraved or deprived, but capable also of being creative, compassionate, responsible, free and alive. For such is 'the adoption of sons.'

In Islam, it is true, power (victorious or not) is not of itself the Divine Kingdom; it is there, like all the things of this world, all without exception, to test the soul, to give it scope and means for surrender. Nevertheless, state care, the right use of power, are in Islam as a religious responsibility, a calling to the religious; they fall within the realms of 'inner forces,' as Dr. Cragg calls them, not outside. The concept of secularity is non-existent in original Islam, so too the distinction between lay and ecclesiastical authority. Because of its "robust handling of the theme of power," its naive, sanguine confidence that political and military means could serve to bring men to accept the sovereignty of God, Islam (according to Dr. Cragg) fails to reach the inner person. This is the core of Western-Christian hostility to Islam, and the problem deserves careful sorting out. It hinges on the meanings of 'person.'

From the long quotation above it is clear that Dr. Cragg understands by 'person' a capability, a potentiality for good or ill, spiritually independent of any circumstances limiting or guiding that potentiality. The 'person' is then the individual's absolute freedom to affirm or deny his relatedness to the Divine. The crucifixion was addressed to this freedom, offering a new dimension of relatedness ('sonship') inviting the potentiality for good or ill to choose the good. Acts of suffering and self-immolation can be used for political ends, but are not then addressed to the 'person,' they are not intended to change him in his 'person,' only to persuade his allegiance. The New Testament Jesus was not, however, protesting a cause against the Roman or Jewish authorities when he accepted the cross. He was taking on and seeking to redeem, to annul spiritually, not only their cruelties but also the political aspiration of the oppressed among his supporters. Though executed for political reasons, his acceptance of death was not a political act; rather it made the political as such irrelevant: he suffered to the end for the truth that a man should and can love his enemies even in the utmost of their enmity.

In this way the Divine capacity of love for all sinners is realized and demonstrated. This meaning of the cross did not sink in immediately: it found solid advocacy only after the resurrection, in the acts of the apostles and in the experience of the early church. It seems to me inconceivable that the Romans (who had no state religion until Constantine) would have gone to the expense and trouble of trying to wipe out the Christians if at least some groups of them (remembering Jesus' response to the moneylenders in the temple) had not provoked or participated in insubordination, somehow threatened political disloyalty. Whatever the precise facts, it is known that the Christians were obliged to find some institutional space at the peripheries of Roman power in order to practice their faith. This they did by clubbing together as funerary societies, permitted under Roman law. They felt obliged too to formally protest, indeed insist upon, their loyalty to the Emperor. Among the faithful, that loyalty never extended to accepting his claims to divinity. Dr. Cragg quotes one such protest and then comments:[28]

> 'What man is more concerned about the Empire than we are? Who loves him more honestly than we? For we pray incessantly for him that he may be granted long life and that he may rule the nations with a just sword and know an age of peace and plenty in his Empire. Then we pray for the welfare of the army and for the blessing of mankind and of the world. But we cannot sacrifice to the Emperor in the temple. For who may pay divine honours to a man of flesh and blood?'
>
> Spoken around the year A.D. 250, on behalf of a Christian community by one of its leaders, these words state with typical forthrightness the attitude of the Church of the first three Christian centuries to the Empire. They embody the classic Christian concepts of the relation of faith to citizenship, of Church to State, of the spiritual to the political — a ready obedience in all things lawful and honest, together with a fierce, uncompromising hostility to any state demands which flouted the rights of God. The primitive Church had no desire either to subvert or disobey the imperial, civil power, even though identified, as that power was, with such monsters as Nero and Domitian. But with that docility and acknowledgement of citizen-duty went this quite heroic defiance in what had to do with faith and worship.

By Dr. Cragg's own argument it is clear that the early church did not consider the monstrous cruelties of imperial rule as of its own doing and so of its realm of competence or active concern. The evil and sin was in the person of a vicious emperor or of vicious officers who carried out his whims. The duty of the church (and true victory for the cross) lay in passionate readiness to comfort the victims, to set personal examples of sacrifice and good conduct for personal imitation — not in any form of political dissent. This is the classic Christian concept of what and where sin is, so inadequate from the Muslim viewpoint. What it means is that the Christians were, as willing or unwilling participants, free to collectively benefit from imperial rule; they were able to stand by (and suffer within) as Roman authority did what it had the power to do and what its power required it to do, without having to, so to speak, actively unwish or unseat that power.

Is the typical Christian 'person' then a being of relatively comfortable conscience, seeing that his field of active operation is so narrow? He is, but only if the 'Christian' in his 'person' is morally paralyzed. If the Christian in him is well, his instinct must ever be to fall to his knees in repentance for (the tragedy of) the world's sinfulness and for his part in it. To sustain the way of the cross as a model for living, the whole paraphernalia of Christian melancholy is logically implied — hatred of the worldly and the bodily insofar as these drag the 'inner person' down into sin. When fully alive, the Christian is not spiritually gladdened except in successful acts of renunciation or in moments of sharing such acts with others; nor is he ever spiritually content unless his work enables an uninterrupted succession of such acts and moments. From within, this probably feels like spiritual alertness and dynamism; from the outside (and there has been an increasing amount of outside inside Christians since the Renaissance) it looks like restlessness complicated by sexual and psychological self-torture. The ideal of the Christian 'person,' its sublime, is not dynamic or restless or introspective; rather, the image of composure, of heart-stillness, at peace with the Divine Compassion, perfectly confident that the Fatherliness of the Father has an assurance for every political or social difference, a gentle answer for each of His 'sons,' if they will but acknowledge their relatedness and put the question. Islam has always been forward to honor such saintly repose (which is in the grace of God) whether of Muslim or Christian or Buddhist or Hindu allegiance. But the ideal is not our concern here; no one would claim that Christian/European civilization in any serious way resembles the life of its founder or of its saints.

The incongruity between European/Christian achievement and the original impulse of Christianity is recognized by Dr. Cragg in the remark that there is a Makka/Madina in that achievement, though no

Hijrah see quotation above). However, he gives no indication about what 'Madina' for Christians is supposed to have been — unless he means by it any entrustment whatever of the 'person' to non-personal forces. Such entrustment is inescapable — only a very few are capable of monastic life, and even then there is a necessary regime to be observed governing relations inside the monastery so that its work with the temptations outside can be effectively Christ-like. The Roman Empire and classical Greece are, I suggest, the Christian's 'Madina' — conceived not as historical or geographical locations but as intellectual bearings. It may be presumptuous to claim the connection as a historical fact;[29] nevertheless, it is a useful hypothesis without which the incongruity cannot be explained. Suppose, then, that there is a European or Greek-Roman 'person' alongside the Christian, just as there was an expansion of Europe alongside the expansion of Christianity: what are his attributes?

His most conspicuous, brilliant quality is epitomized in the famous slogan "Man is the measure of all things." The use of tools, of signs, of mental structures independent of sensible objects, distinguishes and separates man from the given world. This separateness is felt even in the most primitive societies, though to a lower degree: man is imaged as a more or less powerful element in a closed framework of natural-social-religious laws that cannot be questioned (let alone opposed) without shattering the whole order, natural and supernatural — these two being not very satisfactorily differentiated. The Greek doctrine of Ideas (Forms) gave to this vague feeling of being powerfully, differently alive, a special dignity and a logical home. The doctrine emerged from the observation of permanent relations (mostly obviously, number) between objects themselves transitory; for while particular objects might perish, their relations were experienced and observed to recur. The recurrence of the relations was of less significance than the implied fact of their absolute (logical) independence. Relations were *universal*. Extending relations to cover qualities as well as quantities meant that it was possible to think 'justice' or 'goodness' independently of any act or instance of 'justice' or 'goodness.' Man's separateness from the natural, given world was thus secured in the access that rational discourse gave him to universal ideas. But discourse is not a solo activity: it needs at least two thinkers or, better, an academy. Man the measure of all things can thus also measure his own measuring. Discourse, the means of measurement, can intervene to protect the ideas from the individual caprice of any irresponsible (illogical) idea-monger. The teacher was dispensable; the teaching, the discourse, remained so long as somebody, anybody, was willing to learn it by thinking it through. Qualities (especialy moral qualities) could not, self-evidently, admit of a formulation like number or geometry; so the final object of discourse, the complete definition of forms, or Truth, was in principle unattainable. Discourse had, therefore, to be open ended, a potentiality for Truth but not itself the Truth.

The penalty of in this way setting up Man, or rather Discourse, as a thinking vertical in a flat world, is that the world has to be flattened for Discourse to give its performance. Greek thought and art were rational-istic (mathematical), idealistic and unhistorical, typically lacking in respect for the 'minute particular,' for the individual detail, individually perceived. Neither Plato nor Aristotle were able to satisfactorily explain how precisely the eternal Ideas or Forms participate in sensible objects, the world of lived experience. Nor could they satisfactorily formulate the (religious) question of why the Eternal should bother to participate in the transitory. A far more pernicious consequence (from a Muslim viewpoint) of so elevating Discourse was that, though only theoretically, it represented the human capacity of reasoning out (and thus finding or making) order, as an analogue of the Divine. The proud defiance of the attitude, valued as intellectual freedom, is of almost irresistible appeal in modern times: Truth was not known in the past, is not known now, and cannot be known in the future; it can always be sought for — that is the heroism of open endedness.

Various commentators have remarked, in contrast to the mathemati-cally proportioned, ideal, naked forms of Greek sculpture, that in typical Roman statues, the heads are individualistic — lively with the cares of the world, full of busy, moral character — but screwed onto conventional bodies, clothed to show the man's office or job. The Romans gave a practical, legal, external definition to 'person,' gave him particular rights and particular duties, and so all but invented the modern concept of civic or conventional morality, the zealous service, in a particular post, of a central, military and bureaucratic power. The grandiosity of the Roman's notions of state and state office, reflected in their architecture and their brilliant achievements in civil engineering, was repeated in the pompous solemnity and pride with which the citizens strove to carry out their duties: whatever these duties, the vocation was 'Rome.' Whatever the Romans took from the peoples they conquered, they repaid with reliable administration and, of course, good roads. A particular Roman task — from polishing the Imperial breastplate to planning the logistics of a military campaign — might terminate, but the work as such did not, the work of policing and enlarging the state of Rome. The only limits were practical or external. In principle, 'Rome' (in legal or emotional identification with which the Roman located his highest dignity) was a potentiality, a power to do more and to govern more. Like Discourse for the Greeks, for the Romans 'Rome' was open ended.

In contrast to Greek Man or Roman Citizen, all three Abrahamic faiths stress the particularity of the individual human being, a particularity assured by the belief that the One God who created him knows him from within, listens for him, accepts his praise and answers his petition. Christianity is distinguished from Islam or Judaism not, as Dr. Cragg suggests, in the high priority it accords to the 'personal' (there isn't any higher priority than the 'personal' in Islam, Islamically defined), but in its absorption, away from Judaism, of a variety of nature cults, its 'baptism' of primitive adoration for landscape and all creatures great and small. This is evident in the imagery of Christian ritual, and the seasonal quality of its major festivals. Even in medieval painting, rigidly formal and hierarchical though it is, there is a profusion of faces which can only belong to particular men and women, very much themselves, even though their 'station in life' is strongly indicated. When the confines of medieval Christendom were finally burst, the intellectual freedom of the Greeks and the civic confidence and power urge of the Romans were let loose — but accompanied at the outset of the Renaissance, by a more delighted, unashamed appreciation of the sensible world, slighted in different ways by both Greeks and Romans. That delight was too soon diverted, at least as regards the mainstream of European achievement, by the greater force of Greek and Roman attitudes, into experimental science — the discovery of universals adaptable to material ends, Truth in the service of military and economic growth, which is the great engine of European success.

That — somewhat impressionistically — is the Christians' 'Madina.' But there need be no permanent Hijrah, Dr. Cragg will maintain, for the 'Makka,' the faith proper, is all within, the call is from within, the sickness and the sin, and the healing, are all within. If Christians have traveled away from their inspiration, the option to travel back is always there. That is precisely the special risk and special promise of the cross: it may appear only to point upward into cold space or outward beyond the ends of the earth, but in its gentle patient way it also points inward to itself, reminding of the Redeemer. Yet, it seems to me, given that the meaning of the cross is the 'Makka,' the 'Madina' of Greece and Rome is necessarily entailed — the former logically, as the latter was histori-cally in the Roman authority and name of the church. The cross is less an event in the biography of the great teacher, less an example, than it is a challenge or promise, a pure potentiality: it has exactly the logical eternality of the Greek Ideas (an eternality guaranteed in the doctrine of Jesus' divinity). How that ideal is to be embodied in a sustained way in the life of an individual is left open ended. The cross represents an Ideal gesture of will, a gesture of supreme sacrifice and conviction — and yet how does it teach the living of itself? As any good actor or dancer could demonstrate, a gesture is not necessarily limited to an instant, it can be drawn out, elaborated. That elaborating of the Ideal of sacrifice and of conviction is the motive of monkish retreat: for in retreat, the monk, as alone with his will as it is physically possible to be, can interrogate himself about his own inner readiness to follow the cross. His self-interrogation (necessarily solo) is the counterpart of an academy think-ing through a Platonic dialogue. The only way that that readiness can issue into positive achievement is neighborly love — self-sacrifice (not for the sake of perfection of one's will, but) for the sake of others. Here, where Christianity is not unique, there are strong, positive elements of the teacher's life to be lived through, the way of the Prophet Jesus, revered in Islam.

But even here, alas, the quality of the Christian gesture too often overwhelms the Christian deed. Genuine giving requires a victory over one's own neediness to meet the other's inability in his neediness. But if that first victory is a long-studied triumph over one's own will, the preparedness of the giving reduces it to gesture, and the gesture wounds the receiver, stings with its superiority and stinks of sanctimony. (Interestingly, the single instance where English grammar permits the use of 'Christian' as an adjective of negative value is in such phrases as 'Christian duty,' and 'Christian pity'). Planned actions of pity not for a neighbor but for the 'needy,' (the savage, the heathen, etc.), however good the intention or successful the relief, are not heart-uplifting. By contrast, spontaneous personal response to another's need as two lives cross in the givenness of accident, lifts the heart of giver and receiver alike. There is an immediate, natural cheerfulness in it, an exchanged feeling of substantial equality and honor, of alike participation in the giving and receiving of God's plenty. A true Christian is instinctively alert to sanctimonious pride in the ability to be 'giving' and is thus inevitably driven back again into self-interrogation, to make the will ready once more.

Since the passing of medieval Christendom, open enddedness, the critical spirit, the driving forward to progress or change, have constituted the West's dominant image of itself. At the heart of that image is the Idea of man as an infinite potentiality — for pure thought, for discovery of novel experience, for high-minded civic duty for ideal 'personal' sacrifice. That is the Christian/European person in his full 'Makkan'/'Madinan' roundedness and compositeness. So conceived, the person is radically distinct from the given world in which he finds himself, in which he freely acts and freely thinks, the past in general; and he is radically distinct from the acts and thoughts he contributes to that world, his personal past. Because he can freely think and freely will, that potential for doing so is reserved as the defining area or 'skin' of his Real person. All that is, so to speak, outside that skin is 'other.' What is uniquely inside, the gathering unitive power which transforms the manifold outside into a single experience, is the person's Real 'I,' changing and growing to be sure, but nevertheless distinct and irreducible, and always recognizable from within as itself. The substantial content of this wholly liberated 'I' is an obsessive yearning and longing, a desire distinct from any particular goal or object. No worldy goal or object can satisfy such a desire, no achievement is really sufficient, for if it were the desire would perish. The only proper company for a person so defined is either an unattainable Ideal (the intelligible Real of Platonic doctrine as opposed to the fake real of the sensible world) or it is its own desire become abstract and worshipped, literally, as power, as potentiality. For the sake of this liberated-I, the world degenerates to the condition of a passive, horizontal field for its heroic operation — the individual's own realized acts and achieved thoughts are likewise only additions to this field, spread below, waiting to be endlessly traveled over, worked in, explored, exploited. The liberated-I is a stranger wherever the person goes; even with itself it is not at home, but stands tensely, flexing its intellectual or spiritual or military muscle. European technology is its necessary extension. For by dedicating itself to the creation of vastly complex mechanical systems, and correspondingly complex social ones, which separate out and so efficiently fulfill the immediate external needs and duties of the individual, the liberated-I has successfully isolated the 'will,' making it as free as humanly possible to know and enjoy, to just be, itself.

Sometimes, it is true, the liberated-I buckles under the stress of its own busy dynamism and longs for a holiday from itself; it imagines a place where enough is enough, where a man has some things he needs for his use, and not buying power as such. It looks abroad to Africa and Asia, the Far East particularly, and sees 'simplicity' or 'serenity,' 'wholeness' or 'wholesomeness' in cultures that have not sought open endedness for its own sake. But the glamor of being liberated is apparently irresistible, for when it feels busy again and wants to be able to buy, 'simplicity' looks like 'docility,' 'serenity' like 'inertia,' 'wholeness' like 'conceptual imbecility' or 'undifferentiation'; 'wholesomeness' like 'want of artifice and variety.' Islam is not, by Christian/European criteria an open ended way of life, for it deliberately seeks repose, and so is straightway vulnerable to negative caricature. For Dr. Cragg, Islam is an 'obedience community,' it sticks in its orthodoxy, gives itself orders and obeys them. But, it ought to be obvious, since Islam persists, since it has survived conquering and conquest, that it does not live by force of arms; nor, since it has generated a culture and absorbed others, by force of its own habits. How do people 'be Islamic'? What is the Muslim sense of 'person'?

It is firmly opposed to the European/Christian. Islam does not accord priority to the willful, thinking, liberated-I. Rather, this 'I' is seen as merely a fragment, a phase, of full personality. In Islam, the 'person' is a unique composite of all the potential and realized acts of the willful 'I,' within the given conditions of its existence. If the story of an individual's life could be recorded in absolute, Ideal detail, omitting neither intentions nor deeds, and including all of their relevant consequences, foreseen or unforeseen, that story would express — indeed, it would actually be — that individual's 'person' in the full Muslim sense. Every individual knows what he means when he says 'I' — he refers to the self he recognizes from within. But there is another self, including the 'I,' which is known from the outside, that is, known by the 'I' of others and by God. Some few gifted individuals can perhaps recognize themselves at all times in both directions, but all of us do experience, at some time or other, special crises in which the less familiar self presents itself and, far from being a total stranger, is fully recognized. Moreover, this other self is known in the outside, that is, in what the 'I' has left behind, its own past: the crudest experience of this is, perhaps, seeing one's image in an old photograph, or in an old recovered letter, or in a childhood diary or some such thing. The point is that the story is being set down — most of the time we seek escape from that fact, but fact it is, for when the time for Certainty comes, the Qur'an assures believers and non-believers alike, the book will be there, a flawless record, a perfect witness.[30]

The Qur'an and Sunnah together constitute Islamic faith and religion; they are not addressed to the will but to the whole life with the will in it. Salvation is to be hoped for, not for the will alone, but for the whole life. The 'person' in the Christian/European definition is, in every sense, unrealistic: it is mere potentiality, that is, deficient in reality, deficient in history. Observation and experience alike deny the glamorous optimism (or its brooding shadow, melancholy anxiety) of the European emphasis on the will. Is there not sinfulness and goodness in the circumstances that the will must address; is there not an accumulation of either or both in the generations that precede, in the community and institutions that surround, the will; likewise are there not innumerable acts of intended goodness or sinfulness whose real consequences are quite otherwise or quite simply unknown?

From the Muslim viewpoint, to address salvation to the individual will in isolation from the history in which alone it really is (which isolated will then must, logically, be conceived as born sinful to explain the accusation implied in addressing salvation uniquely to it) is a monumental error. The Qur'anic injunctions embrace both the individual will in its immediate relation to God (in *du'a*, for example, or in the personal confession of faith and religion, the *shahada*) and in its immediate relation to all that is 'outside' — family, neighbors, community, law, economy, government, work. Without the Divine injunctions ordering these relations, the will (the liberated-I) must necessarily improvise its own in their place — unless, of course, the particular individual can envisage total renunciation of the real world. To minds schooled in the

West, the whole Muslim code of life will seem, in principle, an impri-
sonment, a denial of freedom. The restrictiveness of medieval Christianity comes to mind with all the terrors of a nightmare. But that
restrictiveness was, while claiming absolute sanction, in fact humanly
improvised. The injunctions or rules of Islam are 'given,' or 'revealed.'
Revelation is simultaneous with the Creation of man and the givenness
of the rules is like the givenness of life, it is an issuing into history,
dynamic within definite conditions and for a definite end: to serve God.
Nothing is likely to convert European antipathy to the Shari'ah, but an
analogy may ease understanding a little:

The rules of language offer a more useful comparison than the
Christian middle ages. Grammar is a definite set of rules, of constraints,
but it enables rather than prevents a full and varied expression of
meaning. Individual words can be coined or imported from other
languages, so too (though to a very limited extent) can new structures.
A grammar evolves, of course. But it does so by a natural process over a
period much longer than any individual life and much wider than any
single generation; attempts to prevent this process invariably fail. The
Shari'ah is just such a grammar, enabling a Muslim life within a Muslim
umma, at a given time and place, to know and express itself both freely
and fully: its forms too have multiplied and evolved by a complex
process of analogy and invention. Tyrannical attempts to freeze that
evolution in the past, and in the present tyrannical attempts to hasten
the importation of foreign structures, explains the 'choking' of the
Muslim world inthe face of the European challenge.

But looked at in concrete terms, personal freedom in Muslim terms
must yet seem to the liberated-I no freedom at all. Let me then take a
concrete example:

To sunbathe more or less nude on a public beach is, apparently, a
freedom necessary to the modern Europeanized woman, part of the
right to live, at times, just for fun. Suppose, for argument's sake, that a
Muslim woman, brought up to be a Muslim, had the opportunity to
sunbathe nude. She would not do it, but how would she reason her
position? Quite simply, she would measure the desire (if any) to so
sunbathe against the achievement to be gained from actually doing it
—because, by Muslim terms, personal freedom extends to the deed and
does not stop at the potential for the deed. She would reason that
sunbathing in this way is either an act of public display (designed to

attract or tease male attention, or feminine envy — since, in general, old or ugly women don't feel the need to do it) or a preparation for an act of display in marginally less public circumstances. Certainly, such display, by drawing male attention, might please her ego (her consciousness of her power to attract) or, if she is married, her husband's ego. But the kind of caring she would then get (one of the real achievements of the display) is surely not addressed to the most valuable or enduring qualities of her person. And the kind of interest she has aroused in another man might, first, provoke from him some unwelcome behavior (welcome, if at all, only to her consciousness of her power to attract) and, second, will most likely divide him, however fleetingly, from his own wife — making him regret his lot and envy her husband's. Measured against its actual consequences, the European freedom of dress or undress is not something that need necessarily appeal to the Muslim woman with a Muslim sense of what personal freedom means.

This is all very well, the liberated-I will retort, but the point is that the Muslim woman hasn't the freedom of choice to reason in this way. The individual must decide; communal piety should not enforce the 'right' behavior.

Here again, the liberated-I prefers an idealized or purely potential freedom to the freedom actually practiced. In actuality freedom is always defined by convention and not by the individual. Not that long ago, nude sunbathing would have been considered eccentric even on the westernmost coast of the United States.

Just so, the liberated-I will resume, but Muslim convention is stricter and, because religiously fixed, incapable of adaptation over a century, let alone a decade!

That is a point of some force and deserves a long answer:

The Qur'an describes itself as the last Divine Revelation, and the Prophet Muhammad as the last of the prophets. What this means for Muslim belief is that the grammar of inter-human relations and of human relations with the Divine (the Qur'an is always about both together), is fixed and, as grammar, will not change to the end of time. The liberated-I will scream at this, of course. But we must refuse to be deafened by its self-confidence and pursue the matter calmly. In the world of plants and animals, innumerable species are scientifically (that is, within definite limits) described as stable societies of miniscule bio-chemical events — such visible adaptation as occurs does so only in response to catastrophes engineered by man playing (for good or ill) his genetic or environmental games. Like all the higher forms, man also long ago achieved stability in his bodily form. Moreover, he has long owned the *nous* to adapt the world to his needs, rather than the other way about — his evolution (seen from the human viewpoint) is cultural or historical, not biological. Technology is a fragment of that cultural evolution and its possibilities do indeed seem infinite — something to please the liberated-I in its quest for ever-greater potentiality. But it is only a fragment. Along with technological advance man has formed patterns of dependence and relation which have altered in their detail and means but not in their role or purpose: thus, the roles of motherhood or of rulership, or the functions of collective economy or collective defense/aggression, have changed greatly in their means, their technology, but they have not disappeared. It is to such general human relations and their functions that Shari'ah is primarily addressed. There is no ruling, in principle, upon technology as such, nor is it, in principle, inhibited in advance of its use in the service of those general relations.

But a grammar is not simply a descriptive list of functions, it is a description also of their right relations. For a number of historical reasons the English language has remained recognizably the same since about the time of Chaucer: certain inflections have disappeared, some words have reduced or englarged in meaning, some have become obsolete, and there have been numerous new words added. But Chaucer could even now make his speech understood and understand the speech of others. This is so only because the major structures have remained the same. A grammar that is stable does not, for that reason, inhibit the generation of an infinite variety of sentences; yet without the grammar, coherence and meaning (the whole point of speaking) would be impossible. The rules prescribed in the Qur'an and Sunnah are prescribed for the major conditions and relations of life, and for the like reason that life may be meaningful. The rules do not of themselves, either by being rules or by being *these* rules (and not others), create conformity or mediocrity; nor do they, of themselves, prevent novelty of feeling or uniqueness of thought and expression. Negatively, they are intended to prevent only that incoherence of relation between persons and between them and God which pitches individual and collective life into barbarism and absurdity. Positively, they are intended to enable the person to obtain and express serenity (or well-being, *falah*) in the conduct of his daily life.

The grammar analogy breaks down, however, when we come to how the rules are learned. In the case of language, the rules are largely given. It is true that if the learner is exposed to 'good' language, he learns 'good' language, otherwise he speaks and writes badly; nevertheless, competence is not related to conscious knowledge of the rules. The rules for life that Islam enjoins are not of this kind. Dr. Cragg makes a nice distinction between 'belonging' and 'believing'[31]: it is not enough simply to belong to Islam, a Muslim must believe it. Returning to the question of modesty of dress for a Muslim woman: it is of course essential that see sees examples in the community of modesty of dress and conduct, but it is also important that she knows what this modesty is meant to achieve and to avoid, and that, above all else, her own 'conformity' is done with the right *niyat*. Mere habit without *niyat*, without concentration of intent, invalidates all acts.

In answer, then, to the taunt that in Islam rules of conduct are religiously fixed and incapable of adaptation, we may say that, first, personal freedom is differently understood in Islam, and that, second, the rules which enable its expression are not 'mere convention,' provided the observance is consciously and religiously attended. Such observance makes the conforming behavior traditional rather than conventional — the difference being that tradition derives from imitation of a great example, set by a great man or woman, and is graceful and secure, whereas convention derives from nobody in particular, it is simply custom which the individual conforming ought to have had the courage to throw aside. In Islam, tradition of course means Tradition, the great example of the Prophet. For just as personal freedom is not an absolute or theoretical potentiality, giving either legal or spiritual license to the will in voluptuous isolation with itself (e.g. in nude sunbathing or guilt-choked introspection), so too the ideal man is not an absolute or theoretical concept, but a whole biography available in extraordinary detail, lived in a dynamic relation with the absolute authority of the One God and the multitude of fully real historical circumstances.

In Islam, it is not the will alone turning, in and of its volition, to God, that is the area of active Divine competence, the means of being saved or not saved. Rather, the whole life is forwarded to the reckoning; there is no wastage in the Creation, Creation was not in jest, the world does not grow or diminish by so much as the weight of an ant but that God knows it and intends it.[32] Salvation is not a foregone conclusion: every individual is commanded to work for it and pray for it, to invoke the Divine Names so that *din* (the religious life) is not a lazy or time-serving conformity, but becomes, when enlivened by *iman*, a solid and sustained embodiment of his *islam*. If the difference between Islam and Christianity can ever be epitomized, it is this: the latter aims at an ideal gesture, an ideal readiness, the former at an ideal achievement, an ideal history. Aesthetic elements are, for that reason, very vigorous in Christian rituals; both musical and visual means aid the worshipper to 'get' religion, to 'get' Jesus, to feel 'saved.' The immediacy of the Divine in the human is a state of mind, to some degree (an outsider simply cannot measure it fairly) disembodied from the ordinary current of living. False and thoroughly inadequate worship can be observed in Islam as well as Christianity; yet, because there is no way of 'getting' *islam*, Muslims are (in general, it must be stressed) spared the extremes of looking and sounding 'holy' and 'saved.'

IV

Christians are conceptually bound to regard the cross as the ultimate in religious experience: the cross is where the Platonic 'Real' and the sensible 'real' intersect. But that is only part of the reason why Dr. Cragg and other Christian commentators are unable to affirm the Prophet of Islam as the prophet of a true religion. Measured against the cross, they see the Hijrah as a betrayal. The Makkan surahs are wonderful indeed, for they address the will, remind of transience, of human finitude and infinity, they commend forgiveness and loving kindness; they are, in short, 'poetic.' But the Madinan surahs are tiresome, long, 'prosaic' — what not to eat and who not to marry, what to do with inheritance and divorce, or with thieves or slaves or 'war booty,' and so on and on. For reasons I have given, Christian commentary has to see in the Makkan/Madinan difference not the historical difference that is there — a difference in real temporal and geographical terms — but its own conceptual duality of the 'really' religious and the 'really' secular. Islam — by a wise intuition, as Dr. Cragg notes — dates its calendar not from the birth of the founder (this too, a Christian notion — Islam completes, not founds) but from the birth of the Madinan *umma* constituted as a state. The Prophet failed his calling: he should have submitted to the Quraysh, seeing that he could not persuade them — as Jesus of the

New Testament did to the intransigence of the Jews. But, in Muslim terms, the Prophet *did* suffer to the end. He was *commanded* to leave Makka, *commanded* to found a Muslim community in Madina. The Arab tribesmen that it was his mission to convert were 'real' persons constituted in tribal loyalties and hatreds, in the peculiar social/economic relations of raiding and trading, of enslaving and ransoming, of arbitrary exclusion of certain clans from water rights or even from basic human rights; these same persons also bought and sold wares in marketplaces, married and remarried or simply 'took' more women, and they borrowed and lent money on interest. The Prophet took on this *jahaliyya* in Madina, and in Madina's relations with Makka, and brought all to a religious use.

The Christian approach to such *jahaliyya* is to annul it in a spiritual sense — to strike at the heart of the problem by addressing to the will of each 'person' the physical, emotional, psychological, spiritual shock of the crucifixion of the Son of God. The shock will embarrass all, 'liberate' a few, leave the rest entrapped in their tragic, sinful darkness. For the Christian view does not admit that this darkness has any potentiality to enlighten itself except in the receiving grace, the potentiality of being 'born again' in Christ. The person as he is constituted in his history has to be broken. But even when broken and born again, the person has still to constitute himself in all the physical and social relations human existence entails — and that, for the Christian, is the tragedy of it, for truly the Christianized soul is lost, wasted in the world. The European approach to *jahaliyya* is to annul it literally, that is, to take firm control of all social, cultural and economic relations, and administrate the new into existence by bold, confident action. The latter approach is brutally 'masculine' in its contempt of what needs change, the former is more 'feminine' in its detestation. From the Western/Christian viewpoint, Islam itself is a *jahaliyya*, Orientalism one of its means of relation.

Dr. Cragg is among the most gentle of Orientalist commentators — most consistently in *The Mind of the Qur'an* — he strives to find as much as he can of Christian emphases and possibilities in the Muslims' Scripture and their worship. But when, as in *The Dome and the Rock*, he is writing primarily for an actively Christian audience, his feelings are embarrassingly strained. The real facts of real Muslim lives either remain for him vague, unpleasant shapes or turn out, on inspection, to be unmistakably like the spiders he had determined to pick up and hold close to — but couldn't. This is clear enough in the whole of 'Precincts and People,' but in the final chapters (e.g. 'or Turk' p. 240-250) on working with Muslims in labors of compassion, it is glaring. The problem for such a man is to feel what he says he believes, namely that spiders don't bite or contaminate, aren't even so very dirty. The truth that we are all God's creatures has little meaning unless we can embody it in feelings that are capable of *exchange*; it has no meaning (or a very sloppy one), if, in reality, we feel as different from them as bees and wasps.

Any truly valid conversion (the only kind Dr. Cragg is interested in) is impossible without visible and mutually felt, mutually exchanged respect for the differences between the persons concerned. Sadly for the spread of Christianity (until very, very recently), that respect for differences has meant separate standards of living for those arrived as Christians, as well as separate privileges and separate places; it has meant also a separate (lesser) degree of personal warmth and a separate (lower) set of advantages for those who converted and so became useful to the first group; above all it involved extraordinary problems for the converted who, though moved and won by the ideas communicated, could not quite share in the barely concealed feelings of the first group (the communicators) towards both themselves and those who remained unconverted. My point is that Christianity, collectively transported, has not and cannot be taken anywhere without the whole apparatus of wretched attitudes attaching to a superior civilization. Pity for ignorance, pity for poverty, pity for sickness, pity for *jahaliyya* is not itself a religious sentiment: it is a psychological, emotional technique for justifying one's freedom from those negatives, and perilously close to sudden, nervous laughter or a tight-hearted coldness. Genuine love for another is instinctively comfortable with the otherness and difference of races and cultures, and concedes the Creator's purposefulness in intending that otherness.[33] We are different, says the Qur'an, so that we may know one from another, none is nearer God save in his God-fearing.

Of course, such criticism of Christian mission/European civilization can be and has been made from within Christianity. But the Christian criticism is always of the same kind — that mission hasn't been genuine enough, its motives (the 'will' again) not satisfactorily analyzed, not deeply enough immersed in the full meaning of the Cross. But a potentially more fruitful shock could be administered to the Christian/Western self by contrasting the mission following the Hijrah and that following the Cross. Consider, given Christianity's commitment to and care for the 'person,' and that of European civilization to full freedom of the individual, how many peoples of the world there are in Africa, in Asia, in the Americas, who feel that they have been culturally inhibited by Christianization as well as by Europeanization; consider too the real quality of personal relations, the quality of real personal freedom in Europe or the U.S. Despite some recent propaganda to this effect, Islam has not spread at the expense of culturally alienating its converts. Do the Muslim peoples anywhere in the world resent the Arabs for what started in their midst? Do they in fact, as Dr. Cragg insists Islam needs to do, feel that Islam vindicated itself politically and militarily at their expense? Is not Islam precisely the positive to, in this respect at least, Christian Europe's negative?

I would claim further, for Islam, that it improved minds and hearts, that the lived ideals of brotherhood, neighborliness, equality and justice before the law, of forgiveness for God's sake to end the current of sin (rather than by exacting punishments complicating that current), were felt and practiced in the daily round of individual lives, and all this in spite of some abominably corrupt and avaricious 'Muslim' dynasties. Not only here and there, but with some considerable consistency, Islam enriched and deepened personal lives, each individual 'will' as constituted in its proper history, as well as enriching the broader concepts within which people's worldly aspirations to happiness are formed. Islam achieved this only and entirely because Muhammad, upon whom be peace and the blessings of God, was commanded the long travail of the Hijrah and *not* the cross.

But Western/Christian attitudes will not soften toward Islam. The medieval polemicists did their work too well. 'Muslim' is a negative adjective in consequence of their Christian diligence in presenting Islam as a heresy: it not only denied the divinity of Jesus, it denied his crucifixion. But for this, the Prophet of Islam might have gained some acceptance in the collective European subconscious. The Qur'an affirms the virgin birth, it affirms the spectacular miracles of healing, it affirms the teaching of the Prophet Jesus that made some Christians tender, compassionate men, God-fearing believers in the Last Day. Is it likely that the Qur'an (non-believers would say the Prophet, insisting that he made it up) would affirm all this and deny the crucifixion? What propaganda advantage accrues to the Qur'anic revelation, or to the Prophethood of its Apostle, by this denial? Dr. Cragg thinks Islam is spiritually too naive to understand the meaning of the cross: the Qur'an/the Prophet made a spiritual mistake in making the inner decision for the Hijrah and so had to deny the meaning of the cross to the Prophet Jesus also. This is hard to take, not least because it is self-contradictory. For it cannot be argued that the Qur'an denied the meaning of the cross to Jesus without presupposing that that meaning was known. It follows that the Hijrah is not so much spiritual mistake (cowardice) as spiritual *lack*. But it is most unlikely that the Prophet Muhammad met all the wrong Christians and so got a deficient explanation of its central event.[34] The problem then remains: why no crucifixion?

Muslims should not be anxious to give offense, but the Qur'anic truth is that it did not happen. Which leaves Muslims at a loss to explain the historical fact that it was and, to a lesser degree, still is, tenaciously believed. There are tentative speculations to be offered about nature cults in Asia Minor with parallel beliefs in a victim-savior, about forms of worship that had internalized sin and, with it, shame and guilt; and there were the Greek Ideas devolving and percolating through the cultural and intellectual unease after Roman conquests: the historical truth is probably unrecoverable; it is in any case, if I may say so, irrelevant to the fact that it is believed, explained and understood, and still believed. The Qur'an denies it: that too is a fact, which can only be made sense of if, by denying it, the Qur'an denies it any spiritual worth or sees in it some spiritual danger.

The Prophet Abraham was commanded to sacrifice his son. Because he loved his son, because he knew the commandment against taking human life, there was great trouble in the Prophet's mind, but there was no doubt that he would do as he was commanded. His faith was absolute, God would restore his son to him in some way that he, being merely human, could not reason out. He was a true prophet, one who had truly 'surrendered,' and so he made ready the sacrifice. But God demands faith, not sacrifice, and prevented the killing of the Prophet's longed-for son. Such readiness to put life and love on the line, in this instance (so Kierkegaard's famous analysis) to put one's ethical principles on the line, is as far as human faith can go — being killed is not a jot further except that all options are then closed. Surely Dr. Cragg does not believe that the Prophet Abraham 'cheated' on his calling or (worse) that God 'cheated' on him? Why then does he believe that the Prophet Muhammad 'cheated' and, at the last minute, took flight from Makka instead of facing it out to the end, i.e. to his murder? It is a fact that all believers, the *muhajirun* who left their Makkan homes and all the securities that these afforded, made a great sacrifice: all that saved them from destitution was faith and the brotherly love of the *ansar*, the Muslims resident in Madina. The Hijrah did not offer vindication, it offered sacrifice — no gain, no booty, no security, was in prospect — nothing was certain except their growing faith. Nor, except in consequence of belief in the One God, were the *muhajirun* an unwelcome political faction in Makka, seeking a political future elsewhere: the Quraysh would have been delighted to welcome them, had they but renounced their faith. Sacrifice unto death is quite fully grasped and trial through suffering quite fully understood in the Quranic narrative and in subsequent Muslim history. The crucifixion is denied in the Qur'an for other reasons than that Islam doesn't know the value of 'suffering to the end.' All the ethical principles that have their basis in self-sacrifice — all that, in practice, humanism takes out of Christianity — have an honored place in Qur'an and Hadith.

The crucifixion is understood by Christians *as redeeming the sin of others.* It is *that* notion that the Qur'an abhors and excludes. No man may, according to the Muslim view, redeem the sin of others, or 'take on' the sin of others. The work of invitation (so mission is called in Islam), the Prophet's task in Makka and Madina, is for the sake of the person who invites, and whoever accepts the invitation honors only himself, not the one who invited him.[35] It is in this sense that conversion to Islam is *peaceable*: it involves no breaking into the person, no being 'born again,' it is not a psychological or cultural crisis, but a reminder: the usual Qur'anic metaphors are the opening or enlarging of the breast. For the full Christian meaning of the cross, the divinity of Jesus is also required, which complicates and deepens the mystery and so necessitates still further difficulties of ritual and intellectual initiation. Let me recall only two of the problems posed by this mystery to ordinary, uninitiated understanding: if Jesus was God and man, to what extent did he 'really' experience torture and death, knowing as he did that he was immortal?

Were there two consciousnesses or one? How did the dying of God as man for man's sake, which dying was the last event of an ingression into the temporal, finite world of human history, save those who died before the Redeemer died? There are many such puzzles to engross those who delight in paradox and whose quest for meaning in life is satisfied by conceptual or verbal formulae. For the less rationally inclined, the mystery must suffice as such. The Qur'an abhors all mystery cults and Christianity with them (Christians, let me emphasize, are not abhorred) first because they divide too starkly those who are 'in' from those who are not, and second, because they divide too starkly the condition of being 'in' from the condition of being 'out.' In the orthodox Muslim view such cults are dangerous because they reduce spirituality to psychology and emotion, for, instead of living in relation with God, the individual is living constantly in dread of having ceased to be in relation. If, for any reason, the community collectively panics, the 'saved' start hunting each other instead of themselves in an incredible quest for satans and witches. The relative sanity and calm about religion that followed the Renaissance and the Reformation was, in one respect, what I imagine conversion to Islam must feel like. Every nation has had its Messenger,[36] though since forgotten or mis-remembered — conversion is thus a reminding, a warning, not a re-making of the 'heathen.'

What Dr. Cragg calls the interrogation of God in Christian faith or in European civilization is, from the Muslim viewpoint, a ceaseless interrogation of the will, a ceaseless introspection that nags the individual to seek godlike perfection of will or of knowledge or of power. All three quests are a delusion — there is no god but God. And yet it is because each is a lost cause that the quest seems heroic beside the 'containment,' the 'mediocrity,' the 'Oriental repose' of Islam.

V

Within that questing, not necessarily its goal, is a substantial human claim upon God — in a defiance of given limits or in an accusing of Him (even in petition the hands seem to point so) to provoke His love, and ultimately in the aspiration to 'fellowship.' This last notion is central to the Christianity that Dr. Cragg expresses through his work on Islam. On a matter of such conviction he is properly emphatic, nevertheless meeting its absence in Islam with an impressive restraint: the linked sequence of chapters 5-9 in *The Mind of the Qur'an*[37] should be consulted, "The Trouble of Man" and "The Seeking of Forgiveness" being the most immediately relevant.

To a Muslim, 'friend of God' means 'near servant,' one whose 'surrender' is perfect. 'Fellowship' is a distinctly Christian aspiration — no Muslim could desire to exchange the status of 'servant' for that of 'fellow.' It is not surprising that a faith first readily welcomed by Hellenism or Hellenized Judaism should have elaborated a monotheism in which God and man are of one family. The Heavenly father is apprehensible to man because He has an inner life analogous to the inner life of man — and vice versa. God is a person, has a psychology, feelings and cares. He can, therefore, be represented in a voice or look or features that become 'vital' in caring response to man. What He cares for above all else is that man sins and, in response, He *yearns* to forgive. The positive reaching out of Love to sin is demonstrated in the crucifixion of the Son, ritually renewed in the sacrament: God dies so that man can be reborn, washed of his sin, potentially of the 'saved.'

In the Qur'an, God gives to man life and caliphate, a fixed term of trial or 'respite,' a lordly freedom to serve or sin, and, after trial, absolute justice. That individuals or communities sin is a self-wronging, they do not wrong God.[38] In judgment, a man's soul accuses himself, his limbs and organs, the very ground he trod upon, his book, bear witness so that he stands self-condemned.[39] God, argues Dr. Cragg, remains aloof, 'immune.' The Qur'an does refer to the liability to sin as a 'sickness,' and to the Revelation as a 'healing'[40] for the breast. But these metaphors are not exploited in the Book whose dominant mood is impatience with the wrong-doers. God is too highly-placed, too sovereign, to be touched by the sufferings that men inflict and undergo. This is a focusing of Dr. Cragg's general argument that Islam is too eager to win the day, to naive about sin, to walk long in the valley of the shadow.

A Muslim can answer this criticism negatively by pointing to the achievements of Christianity's version of the 'rule of Mercy.'

That God is represented is objectionable; also how He is represented. God readily represented is as readily worshipped in the representations of Him so that religious emotion can be had separately from any active religious experience: it is easier to be 'uplifted' by a piece of religious music than truly to seek mercy, and easier to do that than rid oneself of the advantages of sin or to locate its causes and eliminate those. Of God known or longed for (missed) in human form it is as logical to conclude that He is dead as that He is living. Confronting the atrocities of human sin or the apparent injustice of different beginnings and ends, it may well be logical to conlcude that God is inhumane, which is logically insupportable so that one must deny that there is God or that He is of the least interest, either way.

More specifically, the Christian representation proclaims that God is Love, that His Mercy is the First and Last Word. If abused, this representation encourages the presumption of salvation. A crude instance of this is exploited in *Hamlet*: the Prince comes upon his uncle, Claudius, kneeling in prayer, and decides not to kill him there and then because his revenge would be thwarted — Claudius would go to heaven whereas his (Hamlet's) father, murdered unprepared, had been made to suffer purgatory. There are several ironies here — in the play of medieval and Renaissance attitude to the 'hero' and the 'villian,' in the audience's knowing that Claudius knows his repentance is insincere and that Hamlet knows his reasoning is specious. What the scene plays upon is the notion that God *must* forgive those who repented and *may not* forgive those who didn't or couldn't. It is doubtful that even a medieval 'mechanical,' as Hamlet briefly pretends to be, could so presume upon Mercy, yet in practice the notion that God is Love tempts that way: in daily practice, the prodigal knows he can take his sweet time coming home.

The elevation of Mercy to Godhood puts into shadow (postpones) the other Divine attributes, effectively splitting Mercy from the Unity of God. Correspondingly in man, it splits away the capacity to suffer and forgive the sins of others: it *obstructs* mercy from 'human nature' as well as inviting it. While loving kindness, turning the other cheek, healing, alms-giving, etc. (all aspects of a passive, patient indignation against evil) are of God and have authority in His example in Jesus, active indignation against evil sustained in combat, the forceful organization of resources to prevent evil (a rearrangement of the moneylenders' tables after their overthrow) the raising of taxes, of armies, etc. — all these are not directly of God and so *merely* 'human nature.' There is thus a feeling of arbitrariness about the principle relevant to the inescapable conditions and obligations of 'human nature.' The arts of human mercy are isolated for church, and the arts of human government for non-church, authority. To the extent that they meet (that people seek to enter into the House of the Lord) Mercy may inform government. The fact that church too must have government, lands and properties protected under law, is a complication that surely contributed to the caring, radical anti-clericalism of the past, as to the caring, radical agnosticism of more recent times.

The limitation of the active competence of God in man's affairs (as against Caesar) has had vicious consequences that are uniquely characteristic of the achievements of European civilization: only Europeans could so conscientiously have built the 'land of the free' on slave labor; only in the European Enlightenment was it possible to establish in law that the horrors of war can be mitigated by a civilized use of force for strictly military purposes, with the exception of savages, so-called — against these, wanton destruction of life and property was permitted — not simply practiced — was *permitted under the law*.[41] In our time, the same community, sometimes the same individuals, can be conscientious in the establishment of economic relations that deliberately create poverty and dependence for another community, and then be just as conscientious in disbursing their surplus for the relief of that poverty. The question is not one of hypocrisy, believing one thing and doing another — that is a universal disease; it is a question rather of believing and doing two different things.

The history of the laws of individual freedom (their non-observance is not the question) is largely the history of the laws of property; likewise, international law (its non-observance is not the question) is the history of the shifting military and naval balance between the contracting powers. Neither is a history of the application (steady or fitful) of any religious principle. The achievement in the industrialized West of democracy, of welfare provisions for the needy, of a not intolerably unjust distribution of opportunity, are likewise the result of a fine, lately tuned balance between different power-groups within each state — not the putting into effect of a principle valid for all time or for all races. The achievements may seem all the more secure for that — but if that balance is seriously disturbed — by, for instance, sustained mass unemployment — those achievements will crumble, piecemeal or all at once, or issue in the frank barbarism of war. There is in these countries wealth and leisure enough for private protests on matters of principle.

At the present time the most popular cause seems to be banning the bomb, a difficult cause requiring long, unwearying dedication. But there is little energy dedicated to radically questioning the structure of international relations which makes production of the weapon necessary. But for the embarrassment they cause to Western governments, mass protests could be ignored as harmless. In reality the bomb is a convenient ogre for all parties. The real question, in this case, is which of the superpowers should have the most influence in the non-'developed' world; the principled answer is 'neither,' which is a useless proposition; the real answer is 'our' superpower. When the bomb becomes too expensive, it may be banned; when an alternative, less risky method of deterrence has been developed, it surely *will* be banned. For the same kind of reasons the Western powers effected, many generations ago, the abolition of slavery in their own domains. If the motive of abolition had been religious principle, or if religious principle had been derived from the experience of abolition, would not the children of those slaves (surely now after all that time) be indistinguishable as to rights, opportunities and achievements from their former masters? But they *are* clearly distinguishable.

The self-wronging, in consequence of the *kufr* (in the Muslim view) that Jesus is God, that God is Love, that crucifixion is the ultimate in religious experience, is the expulsion of the sacred from the ordinary affairs of life where alone it properly belongs; and in the failure to give to principles that humanity universally acknowledges any political authority, in the short or long term, until and unless circumstances make those principles synonymous with expediency and necessity. The sacred has *atrophied* in the heart of Europeanized man as completely as it has disappeared from his arts and crafts: truly, God is not mocked.

VI

An adequate *positive* response to Dr. Cragg's complaint that God in the Qur'an doesn't care about 'the trouble of man' would require at least half the number of books Dr. Cragg has used elaborating the complaint. A partial answer will be attempted, however, if only to round out the account of what 'person' means in Muslim terms, and to give proper consideration to Dr. Cragg's belief that ubiquitous Western technology can *compel* a Christian application of Islam to the problems of contemporary man.

Dr. Cragg thinks that where the advantages of science and technology are enjoyed, the precariousness of human life has been banished and the area of the 'unknowable' transformed into the 'as-yet unknown.' Therefore, he argues, primitive dependence upon God (for fear of losing one's securities) is no longer valid. He quotes the terrifying questions put to Job in the Old Testament and comments:[42]

'Have you entered into the springs of the sea or walked in the recesses of the deep?' Indeed, scoured them with submarines, churned them with depth charges and charted them on maps. 'Knowest thou the time when the wild goats of the rock bring forth? Do you observe the calving of the hinds?' We do indeed, and from our telescopic lenses transfer the knowledge to a million television screens.

The scholar's confidence here recalls Gulliver on the King of Brobdingnagg's table, vaunting about European military prowess. Even if the questions had been merely practical ones it would be sensible to resist exulting that we have the answers. The productive potential of an ordinary seed can still put to shame the most committed human enterprize, and the finest delicately printed electronic circuitry can look like stone tools beside the sweetness and functionality of geometrical line of a cactus. And if we take all species together, include ourselves, what immeasurable provision there is in the Creation! Pull down, Paquin. Indeed it was not Europeanized man who made the 'green casket,' though he might well destroy it out of spite or stupidity.

Job would have laughed away discursive knowledge, had it been an available option. In the context, the questions are all religious ones, and Job would not have had our modern difficulty distinguishing them as such. The matter of such questions, the absolute, final relation of a particular to the whole, is, even when the particular is man, the exclusive prerogative of God. The feel and workings of the springs of the sea, the extended organism of animate and inanimate existences that they provision and do not provision, are not and cannot be within the knowledge and experience of man.[43] The proper human response to a religious question is to be sure one knows it, not its answer. Here, Job is being 'reminded' that man is in and of nature, in and of his own experience — his is *not* out of it, and he initiates precious little except impatience and ingratitude. We can easily imagine a goatherd, if bold enough, answering — yes, next week. But the energy of 'Knowest *thou*' is to drive the mind forward to the religious experience (conducive to decency of tone)[44] that knowledge of the *whole* meaning of this incident — each goat's own experience of bringing forth, its bringing forth there and then, and not elsewhere, its purpose in meat and milk, in peopling the wold rocks, its demand in pasture and rain and light — rests with God. It is not within human reach to even list the possible elements of this whole meaning, let alone to possess it (to enter into it) as God possesses it, there and then and in infinite prospect and retrospect. The questions, indeed the whole Book of Job, serve to remind him that man is only man and God is wholly god — the issue between them is settled in patience and faith (*sabr*).

The Unseen and the Unknowable are vital elements of Muslim belief — they do not necessarily indicate an (Oriental) 'intellectual docility' or 'foreclosure of inquiry'; they do serve to keep achievement in perspective and proportion, and to prevent muddling and limiting the kinds of questions it is the gift of man to pose. They are, of course, inadmissible in modern scientific inquiry, which admits only a temporary edge on falsehoods. Its proper domain is the relative and partial relation of a particular to a universal, a relation that, united to technological inventiveness and a surplus economy, is the immediate, reliable cause of the material advantages and monstrous barbarities of 'modern' life. Dr. Cragg, fully aware, is not particularly indignant about its consequences in estrangement and shallowness of experience for the majority of 'modern' lives. He is not indignant, perhaps, because he regards the achievements of technology as the proper climax to the 'personal' freedom enjoyed by Western/Christian man. The father had left the door open to the 'far country' so that the prodigal son should feel free to go.[45] Technology has merely taken the door off its hinges — the son's freedom is absolute, economic or other dependence need not now hold him to his father.

The prodigal did come back, of course, to a welcome and forgiveness. An important aspect of the parable that Dr. Cragg neglects is that he came back because he was broke, sorely in need of the new shoes. He came back unpossessed of his prodigal life with nothing but himself in the status of a son with a hopeful claim upon his father's love. That love was not withheld but given in full measure, much to the bewilderment of the righteous brother who had all along kept the bounds: the greater joy in heaven over a repentant sinner.

Symbolically, the parable makes perfect sense. The son can return because he is sure of the father's fatherliness; the father's love and patience (operative even while the prodigal is away) so transforms him that, once back, he has no desire to leave again. Everything hangs on the pull of the father's enduring love to draw and keep the prodigal home.

Out of its symbolic light, the parable makes less than perfect sense. It assumes, first, that the prodigal is quite unchanged inwardly by his prodigal life, that he has no difficulty recognizing himself as the same son of the same father, and no difficulty recognizing the way home. It also assumes that he made no associations in the 'far country' of the kind that would keep him there even after he had realized the error of his ways. Suppose, to make up the simplification of the parable, the son, having returned and been welcomed, did go away again and again. The father would surely still wait, welcome his return again, and so on, until death made repentance and return impossible and then, no loving welcome but fatherly justice. In real terms the 'far country' is of wide extent — it includes the father's house — and it is not passive ground to the traveler but actively penetrates and changes him, as it changes his perception of himself.

Islam's sharpest reproach to Christianity is that it contents itself with moral presence, willfully blind to the fact that its presence (truly moral or not, actively preached or not) subsists in and on the very means it seeks to correct; that, figuratively speaking, it claims to have conquered Rome, when the actual, historical truth is that it compromised with Rome. 'The fault, dear Brutus,' says Dr. Cragg, 'that we are coarsened things, lies not in our cities but in our souls.' In the Muslim view, our cities are (to adapt George Herbert's line) the paraphrase of our souls, an opening out to the senses of what it is our souls contain, what they are made of. The inner life does not, it is true, crudely repeat what is out there, but it constitutes itself, inventively, from that. If the structures outside are powerfully vulgarized, the inner life also will be powerfully vulgarized. Mercifully, human inner life always retains a link, however feeble, with some religious or cultural tradition, some habits of contemplation, so that the inner life, at the same time vulgarized, is also powerfully, though uselessly, uneasy. That is why, in Islam, migration and rebuilding are commanded, necessary, at some points in human history; staying put and being or feeling crucified are not enough. It is in the Hijrah, in contrast to the Christianity Dr. Cragg expresses, that the care of God for 'the trouble of man' is tended to us. We are capable of repossessing our cities and making them holy; our formal devotions and our citizenly duties can be harmonized; even, to a degree, our cities can be our prayers.

Madina is not the whole Qur'an, there are the Makkan passages also; they are meant to interpenetrate, the two cities represent a single, inclusive prophethood, a single, comprehensive Revelation. The appeal of the Qur'an rests now, as it always has, upon that singleness and comprehensiveness: the Unity of God and the spirituality and sanity of the Prophet's example, the Sunnah.

VII

The Unity of God needs no argument, it is self-evident, the category of meaningfulness within which all discourse, all doubt, have place; it is the assumption of law and order in the universe. Logic is not religion, however, nor does it lead to it. Meaningfulness is presupposed in any quest for meaning but is not itself a meaning. The Unity of God has to mean *some*thing.

What it means is constantly on the lips of every devout Muslim. It is in the reiteration and recitation of the Divine Names that the One God is known and felt. Of these, Mercy, Justice, Compassion (or Forgiveness) have logical priority. The Mercy of God is Creation/Revelation, with man in it, for man: beauty, variety, order, awesomeness, softness, usefulness — Dr. Cragg has picked out very capably the Qur'anic imagery and explained the responsibility (privilege) of man to nature. The contrast in the Scripture is absolute between nothingness and life, for only when life is vivid to the mind can it become a religious fact. It is commonplace to hold in mind the notion of life being over, but the Qur'an invites first to the fact of birth. Being alive is a powerful feeling of location in time and space where an emptiness and nothingness would otherwise be. Proper concentration on that fact forces the question, why? Indeed, the question is simply the fact itself (prehended merely in breathing, moving, needing, providing) taken up into conscious reflection. The miracle of birth comes before all others; it is a meaningfulness, for why, otherwise, should the void lump or wrinkle or prick itself at just this point? Being alive is, for the Muslim, at every moment originated and sustained by Divine command. Not so for the non-believer. I am alive and there it is, he will say, why should I attribute it to any Cause?

It is easy to pretend to accept this view, it is quite another matter to live it out. Really accepting it means that being alive is just ordinary and the impulse to sustain life forward, rendered mechanical or accidental, is instantly annulled. The first condition of faith in Islam is the conceiving of life as *important*, for its importance is the energy, the suspense that sustains and carries it to its conclusion.[46] But for the non-believer life just 'is' — he has no conscious intention of being or doing anything important, he will make the most of what there is before it passes.

But man is not created 'unremembered,' Creation is in the same instant also Revelation;[47] consciousness and conscience are innate simultaneously: if not, there is no difference between a drop of liquid or of blood and *man*. There is no way that a man can avoid reflection — he is in the stream and may 'plunge and play,' but he is at the same time created in signs and structures, and must step in twice, reflect, relive even as he lives. Though it may be wilfully refused, the seriousness of life to the person living it cannot logically be denied. As the sole motive for keeping alive and active, pleasure is, at bottom, a morbid preoccupation with the succession of time, which weighs heavily because the moments in succession are not distinguished, or because the moment which is vivid is so by virtue of its transitoriness and so succession takes it away. In theory, the passive (least committed) pleasure-seeker is rewarded by a panorama of inexhaustible variety; in practice he has to see it actively, purposefully, preparedly, or miss the reward. The importance of life thus reasserts itself, though unawares, though received without gratitude. Further, no individual, however non-religious, can refuse the notion that his life *is* his and therefore, if he means only to have pleasure, *he* must decide (within forms defined by convention) what it is, recognize it positively when he 'has' it or its absence when he is disappointed. The importance of being alive, and the inescapability of importance, can be formulaically rendered: Creation is Revelation, Creation is not in jest.

The Divine Justice is the necessary bound to the variety (abundance) of Creation, the limits of it as these touch the individual life. The non-believer will take as much as he can, and pay no *zakat* on his surplus. But 'as much as he can' cannot satisfy a *committed* non-believer. The infinitude of what is available is oppressive, the variety of those who have more intolerable. The non-believer is thus constrained to improvise some limit, to aim provisionally at what he 'likes' or 'needs,' or (with some relief) at what 'they' allow him, what he can 'afford.' He is constrained to do this if only to confirm the feeling of progress. The notion of containment is irresistible. Whether by personal choice or by convention or by external constraints, some limit, some 'enough,' must be determined. The non-believer is, of course, free to refuse every limit as it is attained — there is no compulsion in religion — he can, if resolute in avarice, worry himself to death. If the limit is derived exclusively from what human capacities enable, it will never be something welcome, but something to be endured, an external imposition or series of such impositions concluded by the 'accident' of death. For the pathetically-minded non-believer, endurance is some degree of resignation to his part in a chain of events over which he has no control. For the heroically or tragically-minded non-believer it is defiant and energetic, some degree of vaunting that he is in control of his own will at least, that he need only 'get up and go' to make the most of his life. Both responses are lyrical gestures, exaggerating negatively or affirmatively the role of individual will, both anxious, since neither has considered that the person is located finally in the achievements of the will, not in the will's consciousness of itself as either powerful or powerless. Human purposes, for believers and non-believers alike, are seldom wholly achieved. Ordinary experience confirms that the will is tempered by what turns out at the beginning or end of any venture: living is suspenseful, the person grows into his own meaning or his own absurdity. We act in substantial ignorance of the wider consequences of our actions and in partial ignorance of our motives: good turns out bad, and bad good. The Divine Justice is the experience, solid as any table, that the Mercy of God is not distributed according to any plan that satisfies human expectation or human reason; not only is there immeasurable variety given in the world, but there is a variety inevitable, and seemingly unjust, in human taking from it.[48]

The Justice of God would truly be (as it is often felt to be) arbitrary benevolence or malevolence but for His Compassion or Forgiveness. Without Compassioin, Justice would be merely inevitable fate, inviting human defiance or defeatism; with Compassion, Justice is welcome to the intellect as finitude (relevance), to the emotions as satisfaction, to the spirit as trial, and to the soul in Certainty as peace. In worldly existence it is the only means of a peaceable continuance of any individual life, given that Justice puts definite bounds upon it. Received and directed outward by the individual (toward the future or toward God) Compassion is hope. The limit, the bounding line at any moment, is 'enough' only if it is also 'right': the Creator does not wrong us, it is we who wrong ourselves. Whatever I acquire is 'enough' so long as it answers the purpose for which I acquired it; but if I have no purpose in mind, if I acquire only because I can, then the thing itself is an *irrelevance*, a nuisance, which I must get rid of. It is the Compassion of God that makes His Justice relevant. In human life it is the hope that Justice deserves the name, that fate — not only in the final outcome but even as life is lived — is destiny. It is the most pressing of all human needs, the deepest craving, the hope that I belong to my life *as it is*: its opposite is the despair of wishing to be somebody else because I do not recognize my life as mine. The moments when the hope is gratified can hardly be put in prosaic exposition. But a practicing Muslim will know what is meant in the feeling of uprightness and dignity approaching as he prepares for *salat*, when the body feels 'right,' when cleanliness and purification are identical, or in the quiet between the two prostrations when he prays for forgiveness and wellbeing. Belonging to one's life (thus caring for it) is its utmost value: the 'importance' of life would be a frigid thing without this sense also that it belongs — that is why the Qur'an calls the Creation 'Mercy.' The non-believer, by contrast, must live in a world he doesn't accept, in a life he doesn't recognize, conscious of nothing except his own mastery or subjugation in some particular sequence of circumstances.

No being is without parentage, a past and a place to be in, however grand or restricted. The Qur'an addresses the individual directly and as participant in a community — since he cannot very well be serviceable, even to himself, without community. Salvation is individual certainly — nobody can carry another's sins — but there is, emphatically, no private road to it. Human life is constituted in responsibilities and needs, expressed in social relations; more important, it is constituted by them. To say 'he is a father' implies a separable identity for 'he' and 'father'; the Qur'anic view is a reminder that, in actuality, he is *as* a father, the potentiality and the achievement together make up the being, the one Mercy, the other Justice. The Qur'an and Sunnah, the teaching and the teacher, reveal clearly the directions and the bounds by which and within which the God-fearing man may conduct his life to its just end. No Muslim has the excuse that Islam is an otherworldly idealism or a grandiose conceptual system, impenetrable to ordinary human experience. Nor that it is an overly rigid system leaving him no space to be busy and inventive, to renew and refresh personal communal behavior: there is no necessary opposition between Islam and 'dynamism' in any field of human activity — there are centuries of evidence.

Since, for the non-believer, life simply 'is,' since life is not a religious fact for him, bounds and directions cannot be either. Life is nature's improvisation according to certain rules of environmental pressure that will (the non-believer is sure) one day be fully described and perhaps governable. Laws are human improvisations in response to patterns of power relations between people at any given moment of history, and as these patterns change, laws change. This argument supposes that self-interest (of any individual or group) is the only principle guiding human improvisations in law. The best set up, the most stable system of law, is that which permits the widest possible freedom to the individual's private interest in flexible association with the same freedom for other individuals in the same group. But this argument allows that there is nothing wrong, say, with theft within the law, nor anything that needs doing for those who are just too poor or too far away to ever conceivably be of use.

The committed non-believer works excessively hard to keep his surplus higher than another's, for it is by the Divine Compassion alone that he may desire and recognize 'enough'; without Compassion there is no 'enough' for him, no stopping, only an intermittent loss of breath, of crisis and boom. But the typical non-believer works only as hard as he has to; 'enough' is determined by local convention and practical constraints. He neither believes nor disbelieves; he just wants to be left alone, to get what he can without obviously hurting anyone, though he allows that somebody somewhere may have less because he has more. The Divine Justice is for him only fate — it happens to happen to him, it could happen to anybody — he accepts it sleepily, sullenly, occasionally surprising himself by impetuous, tyrannical bursts of compassion, of being *very* nice to somebody or other, by having a good time sometimes, by sharing that good time with others. If the confirmed non-believer lives, as it were, only in his 'will,' his headquarters, his own central switchboard, sending out commands and getting back 'results,' 'facts,' 'the goods' — the typical non-believer lives just off-center, in an under-department, mostly sinned against, practically innocent, legally spotless, by and large a nice person. His daily needs are supplied effortlessly by technology; any superstitious dependence upon the Creator is out of the question; nature holds no terrors that the magic of science cannot uncover and control. What has Islam — in which remembrance of God is a ceremony of gratitude and praise, in which he must pray five times a day, and which forbids him intoxicants and the convenience of usury (the inconveniences are always piled downwards onto the poorest people) — what has Islam to offer such a man?

Islam has in the past, spread — albeit very slowly — to the peoples of existing civilizations in some cases more, in some less, technically advanced than itself, without smashing them up first: Christianity is a fearsome contrast. But modern Western unbelief (quite common in Muslim countries) is different — it is post-belief, skepticism in theory as well as practice, blindingly successful at organizing its needs, defined in its own terms. Religion is regarded as either a kind of primitive technology for keeping people in order or as a repository of symbols whose maintenance is necessary to individual and community life in the same way that dream sleep is necessary to coherence and co-ordination in waking hours, the precise relation being as yet imperfectly understood though solidly demonstrated. In either case, religion is a means of social or psychical 'health.' Regarded thus, religion can be packaged and marketed. Orthodox Islam cannot be packaged in this way; there is no equivalent of the God-session, for it abhors (as I have explained) cultism, any kind of religion disembodied from the mainstream of life. Prayer is distinct from the daily round of work but, where the community is strongly committed, the daily round of work is fitted to prayer, not the reverse. Prayer reminds the Muslim of the need to pray, and may also supply the need — *wudu* enables *salat*, *salat* enables *du'a*. Without this regular sequence, *du'a* is uneasy and overly introspective; the individual petitioning God 'chokes inwardly'[49] because he is not convinced that he is carrying his daily acts with him into that petition, nor that he will carry the meaning of a petition of God forward into his work with others. The characteristic posture for *du'a* is with the hands held forward, palms open, to receive in patience. Thus, while it is true that Muslim worship commends and generates sanity, poise, inner peace, it does so only to the extent that these are corroborated and established to Muslim practice — the distance between is the vigilance of *jihad*, and dependence on the Forgiveness of God.

Whether Islam may draw and rescue Western non-belief (no longer confined to the West) is not an easy question. It depends upon whether non-believers will feel drawn to the way committed Muslims actually live, which means getting to know them. Islam does draw Muslims to itself — I wonder that the same can be said of Christianity and Christians. For the individual believer Islam is the means of recognizing his life as he lives it, of belonging to all its detail in alert, grateful acceptance. No image floats before the inner eye of a Muslim when he prays — no suffering hero to lean on or identify with, no bearded, fatherly giant — since the One God cannot be imaged. He has no form, He is known in His Attributes, and to these only the Muslim directly addresses himself. What is vivid to him as he stands or bows, alone or in congregation, is the sense that his life (or himself as the receptacle of it and the bearer of it) is a solid and coherent portion of Divine Mercy, Justice, Compassion in the Creation. The 'other' for a Muslim person is the lived life —the past contemplated, the future invited — seen in the Divine light. The life cannot not be lived but in defiance of Qur'an and Sunnah the light burns, in submission or *islam* it suffuses: the latter is the steeper course, but 'Truly with hardship comes ease.'[50] The only worthwhile approach of Islam to Western unbelief will be through the lived lives, the biographies or autobiographies of serious Muslims, or through personal persuasion. In the meantime, for the majority of Westerners, Islam will be what 'pakkies' or 'ay-rabs,' brown and black people believe, people way behind, in no way liberated.

VIII

'Alongsidedness — in good faith?'

As for intent, yes. But as for achievement Dr. Cragg's alongsidedness is in *bad* faith, he does very ill by the Islam Muslims know, though well enough by the 'Islam' known to the majority of Europeans. It would be very nice to be able to say that this is the inevitable consequence of his not being a Muslim — that no outsider can be expected to give a favorable view or even to organize a favorable approach. But this is not the case. His views are as they are, his approach is as it is, because he is *this* kind of outsider, Christian and European, not because he is an outsider as such. The seriousness of the charge can be understood in the sort of reforms of and in Islam proposed by Muslims themselves who, willingly or unwillingly, are working from the very same outsidedness. Dr. Cragg's chief aim is to bring Muslims through Islam to Christian sentiments. Consequently, he does not seek to get alongside so much as to get on top. This vantage point he obtains with the least moral and imaginative effort by simply ignoring the major realities of what he is studying. He divides Islam into elements of a size that his imagination can handle regardless of what this particular liberty of discourse does to the matter to which it is addressed: the chapter titles of *The Dome and The Rock* will illustrate my point.

No one would accept a catalogue of specific chores as a satisfactory description of nursing unless the idea or caring for the sick enters the description (or is, at least, kept in mind) at all points. The fact that nurses sometimes forget this idea and just do dirty chores lazily and badly is worthy of mention — but not as a criticism of nursing as a vocation. Most of hospital routine, likewise, could be represented as cranky squeamishness but for the ordering concept of hygiene. *All* the general ideas that Dr. Cragg has about Islam are the result of negative comparisons with Christianity. His two major contributions are the two studies of the Qur'an. In the first he focuses on the 'event,' an Arab event in the Arabian peninsula leading to an Arab history of political conquest. In the second he focuses on the 'mind' of the Qur'an, that is, on the specifically 'religious' themes in Islam, like 'sin' or 'forgiveness,' or 'worship,' etc. For Muslims themselves, however, Islam is a single unity (in European terms) of the 'secular' and the 'religious' — that is how Muslims feel it, believe it and, if they are serious, how they practice it. There is, alas, no possibility of a third book from Dr. Cragg that will see 'event' and 'mind' together — that is Islam as Muslims know it, and as he cannot imagine a faith to be. I say this with some assurance — Dr. Cragg hasn't finished writing — because, in the first book, Dr. Cragg shows how the 'political' was seen mistakenly as the 'religious' and, in the second, he shows how the 'religious' is inadequately understood in 'political' or otherwise 'social,' 'external' terms. The question is not open for Dr. Cragg. In consequence, he learns nothing from Islam. Instead, he reflects onto Islam the problems of Christianity in history — i.e. in Europe. He claims that Islam is a religion burdened with the problem of power, when in fact — as I have argued, it is Christianity that is so burdened or obsessed, for Islam is burdened with the responsibility of achievement, not power.

The least that could be expected from an outsider is that he understand what it is that Muslims believe, and that he believe that they believe it — for this would oblige him to explain how what is believed could be believed. Dr. Cragg expresses this very nobly, thus:

> .... the Qur'an did not, and does not exist, in order to be 'interesting.' It was, and is, a living summons asking a personal response and requiring a corporate participation. *The first obligation of any study is to be commensurate with that situation.* The Qur'an can never be authentically known in neglect of the sensitivities, the emotions,the spiritual property in it, of Muslims. There have been pursuits of Western scholarship unhappily careless of these courtesies .... To enquire genuinely into the Qur'an is to live with the life of Islam (italics added).[51]

"To live with the life of Islam" has a very special meaning for Dr. Cragg. It does not mean that the critical scholar must begin by asking, "What follows if I believe what they believe?" By no means. He must begin rather by assuming that what they believe is, in fact, unbelievable — they believe it only because, well, they can't help themselves. The Qur'an is the central miracle in Islam, as Christ is in Christianity; its miraculous origin is Islam's central dogma. Self-evidently, what it means to believe this is capable of long and intelligent discussion; but *that* it is believed is not so capable. For Dr. Cragg however, *that* is what needs to be changed about Muslims. This poses a very serious difficulty for scholarly manners — Dr. Cragg negotiates it thus:

> *The reverent reader* ... asks himself whether he may not well come to terms with it [i.e. the divine origin doctrine] as embodying, not the essence of the phenomenon itself, but the form of Muslim security in the sense of that phenomenon, and in the trust of its meaning. It is not seldom that faith erects a dogma where it would better hold a confidence. The *I'jaz* of the Qur'an, its miraculous quality, is then the form by which Muslim conviction possesses its relevance ....
>
> In stating himself this way the outsider will no doubt alarm or dismay the doctrinaire mind. For the latter does not always take comfortably to the distinction we are making between the reality in his belief and the shape of his security in it.[52] (Italics added).

Though he does not explicitly say this, Dr. Cragg rightly grasps here the central fact that for Muslims the Qur'an is divine, whereas for Christians Christ is. But he wrongly supposes that the two 'dogmas' are similarly related to their respective 'core of belief.' Disbelief in the dogma that Jesus was the Son of God need not invalidate the core of belief — that his 'ministry' and his crucifixion made available a certain concept of God's care for the sinfulness of man. There is no parallel in Islam. It is explicitly stated in the Qur'an that the Prophet, upon him be peace, did not forge the revelations; he did not spin the verses out of his own psychological or political or spiritual need as poet or ideologue or theologian might have, nor did he 'assemble' the verses as a gifted mythologist might unify and integrate the diverse, confused legends and beliefs of a people (here of the Arab people, idolators, *and* Jews and Christians). He did not ask for the revelations, the Qur'an says, he did not expect them. I quote Dr. Cragg's quotation from the Qur'an, his own translation of verses whose meaning he resolutely refuses to understand:

> '. . . you never hoped that the book would be inspired within you: it could only have been so as a mercy from your Lord. Have, then, no truck with the unbelievers. Let them not deter you from the revelations of God seeing that these have been sent down to you. Summon (men) to your Lord and on no account be among the idolators. Call upon no other as God beside God. There is no god but He. Everything is perishing except His countenance. His is the judgement and back to Him you will be brought' (28: 85-8).[53]

There was pressure upon the Prophet to, so to speak, renounce the gift of revelation by denying that it was indeed Divine in origin: he could not deny that miracle without denying the nature of God as declared in the revealed (emerging) Muslim perspective. There is both consolation and warning in "Everything is perishing except His countenance." Here, as elsewhere in the Qur'an and in Hadith literature, there is insistence that the Prophet is human, mortal, by no means an agent, save passively by Divine grace, in the miraculous receiving of the Qur'an. Were it otherwise, the Prophet would become an object of worship — Muslims would be 'among the idolators,' calling upon some other as 'God beside God' — whereas he is, upon him be peace, an object of the highest reverence.

Thus it is, that Muslims have for 1400 years believed that God originated the Qur'an — not because this is a means of belief (the shape of their security in it) but because it is of the essence of it (the reality in their belief). Put another way, you cannot hold to the core of Muslim belief without the belief that the Qur'an (and not the genius of the Prophet) is the miracle in Islam: it follows that you have no means of access to that core of belief without the belief (suppositional only for the outsider) that the Qur'an is a Divine miracle and not a human one.

Dr. Cragg makes a mess of this central fact of Islam because he cannot open his mind to the meanings of that fact for believing Muslims — not least among these, the relevance of Divine Will to the detail of human living. For a European, man is the measure of *all* things: thus, a man made the Muslims' Book; revelation must be a pressing psychological-social-historical need, a human claim, before it is met in Revelation from God. These are the presumptions of a mechanical mind. Nothing could be more horrifying to Muslims than the hoisting up of the Prophet onto a Christian pedestal by making him the author of Islam, though only in his great need of Truth. No man is capable of judging who does or does not 'deserve' Revelation: only God is God, man is only man.

If Dr. Cragg were less certain that European ways are, ultimately, the wisest and the most penetrating account of man — an obese certainty fed by the prolonged military superiority of the West — he might appreciate better the quality of human loss and gain mediated by the faith that "there is no god but God." In the *adhan*, peace/prayer, well-being/being well are rhymed with "no god but God." There is a rapturous sanity in this association, a vivid linking in the ear (thus in the whole body) of the finitude of man in contrast to God with the proper response to that relation — namely, self-cleansing. Fragility, transience, finitude are more ancient, inclusive, more shapely categories in which to clothe the dignity of man's sadness, than the modern European idea of 'tragic heroism.' To Muslim ears, there is a rapturous *in*sanity in the Viking vaunting, at the edge of the deep sea or before the open cross of suffering, challenging 'the gods' or God, in a wild, barbarian gesture: "I am the greatest of sinners," "I am dauntless unto death," For all the seductive lyricism that may pad out this gesture, it argues a graceless pettiness, a spirit hooked on its own defiance.

In truth, Dr. Cragg presses the point of the human 'environment' of the Revelation only because he finds fault with that Revelation. If the Qur'an is an arrangement of meanings in a piece of writing (as in the

New Testament) — and not a sacred event in the hearing of the Prophet (a faculty that cannot willfully be controlled) — then it is capable of literary criticism, of being re-worked by each believer, or non-believer. Indeed, agrees Dr. Cragg, there is no 'true' receiving of the Book without this repossessing by reworking.

Let us allow that Dr. Cragg's motives in thus recommending the Qur'an are not to Christianize the way Muslims hear it — finally, to make them anthropomorphize God — but simply to rescue them from a thoughtless, automatic acceptance. Now this is not in itself a bad motive, but it cannot be sustained in an innocent isolation. It emerges as aggressive in virtue of its resources and its origin. The 'single habitat' that the earth has become, that makes Dr. Cragg's enterprise possible — we cannot help but overhear and overlook each other's domains of beliefs and securities — is not a neutral fact like the colour of grass or the weight of lead. It is a European creation, a part (perhaps the climax) of Europe's ambition to reduce, to remake, the world to its own image. There cannot be any authentic European alongsideness with Islam except in scholarly Hijrah, self-exile from the European perspective: Dr. Cragg has not the radical caring in his intentions towards Muslims and their beliefs to be able to do this. The Muslim response should not be vile-mannered or angry; there ought, certainly, to be no surprise and, therefore, a proper composure:

> You shall surely be tried in your possessions and your selves, and you shall hear from those who were given the Book before you, and from those who are idolaters, much hurt; but if you are patient and godfearing —surely that is true constancy.[54]

NOTES

1. *The Call of the Minaret*, (New York: 1956) (Hereafter, *CM*).
Sandals at the Mosque: Christian Presence Amid Islam, (London: 1959) (*SM*).
The Dome and the Rock: Jerusalem Studies in Islam, (London: 1964) (*DR*)
Counsels in Contemporary Islam, (Edinburgh: 1964) (*CCI*).

2. *The Privilege of Man: A Theme in Judaism, Islam and Christianity*, (London: 1968) (*PM*)
Alive to God: Muslim and Christian Prayer. (compilation with introductory essay), (London: 1970) (*AG*).
The Event of the Qur'an, (London: 1971) (*EQ*).
The Mind of the Qur'an, (London: 1973) (*MQ*).
The Christian and other Religion, (London: 1977) (*COR*).

3. *CM*, p. ix: The Christian must move beyond "areas of conscious otherness into an intimacy of attained interpretation where Christ is made known to the heart of the Muezzin's faith."

4. Courtesy counts in the weighing of foreign materials and values because it is a means of receiving information available only through human exchange. Therefore, all gestures should be respectful. But if gestures are all there is (offered in any case with a taint of self-applause), the approach sticks to itself. To pronounce a foreigner's name with precision but then not attend seriously to what he means, to deny that he means what he thinks he means, is not courtesy useful for learning. Thus Dr. Cragg will write 'Muslim' and not 'Moslem,' and never 'Mahometanism' (*CM*, p. x). But in evaluating the biography of the Prophet Muhammad, he confidently reduces his achievement to the political, ignoring the Muslim accent, the Muslim understanding of that biography. Further, he prevents his approach by a gesture that betrays the quality of his courtesy: "To set forth this (Madina) period in the Prophet's career objectively, without offending modern Muslim susceptibilities is difficult in the extreme." (*CM*, p. 84) 'Modern' Muslim susceptibilities are, by implication, the effect of Christian presence amid Islam, meaning (without so many 'offending' words) that pre-modern Muslims can have had few qualms about, e.g. exemplary massacres. The criterion (of 'insupportable contrast') for assessing the deeds of the Muslim community is the sacrifice for man's sake of the Son of God. We may not think this an offensively stupid criterion for Dr. Cragg assures us he is being objective. Interestingly, it is not being objective that is difficult, only being objective "without offending . . . Muslim susceptibilities." If it is impossible for a Muslim to be objective, why is it possible for a Christian to be so? Ultimately Dr. Cragg has it in mind to put Muhammad in Muslim belief on the same level as Christ in Christian belief, each determining the inner/outer shape of his community. Which returns us to the label 'Mohammedanism.' Muslims themselves refuse to do this, not because they have thought out its spiritual dangers, but because they have not had the intellectual courage to be 'theological' about the Prophet's role rather than merely 'legal' (*CM*, p. 57), or to be 'metaphysical' rather than merely 'practical.' (*CM*, p. 100)

5. *DR*, pp. 11-19.

6. *MQ*, pp. 82-3.

7. *CM*, pp. 48-9. This view is expressed, in different words, in all of Dr. Cragg's books on Islam: God teaches "by word, rather than by travail, by ear rather than by thought, by audition rather than by anguish."

8. In *CM* and *AG*.

9. *DR*, pp. 17-18.

10. *Qur'an*, e.g. 35:16: "O men, you are the ones that have need of God . . . ." All references to the Qur'an are to the most readable English translation *The Koran Interpreted*, by Arthur J. Arberry, one volume ed., London, 1980. This edition combines two volumes (Suras I-XX and XXI-CXIV) which are separately paginated pp. 29-350 and pp. 17-363. Hereafter references will be given as follows: Qur'an 35:16 (Arberry II, p. 140). In this instance the relevant verse will be found on p. 140 of the second volume.

11. *Qur'an*, e.g. 10:99 (Arberry I, p. 236).

12. Dr. Cragg prefers to believe that inwardness of devotion was added by the mysticism of later centuries. He has great difficulty in understanding how formative Islam, with its external concerns with making laws and liquidating idolators, could have at the same time generated inner devotion and peace — to match outward conformity and security. Hence his perverse historical view, e.g. *MQ*, p. 164.

13. I have deliberately confined myself to Dr. Cragg's own notes, to distinguish the quality of his interpretation of them. He omits many things — most importantly that, in each occasion of *salat* there are *sunnat* prayers — offered individually, not in congregation, in reverence for the Prophet's example — and *nafl* prayers which are wholly voluntary. There is a rhythmic movement from 'I' to 'we' in each prayer-movement, as between obligatory and voluntary, that balances the whole occasion so that the concluding *du'a* is not overly egotistic nor overly communal. A satisfactory explanation would require more detail than is here possible. It is difficult to find an excuse for Dr. Cragg's particular selectiveness.

14. *PM*, p. 126.

15. *MQ*, pp. 90-91. This argument is everywhere in Dr. Cragg's work. The references pick out only a particular striking statement of it. See also *EG*, p. 79: "The Prophet of *Allah* must succeed in Mecca as surely as the Prophet Jesus must suffer in Jerusalem," and again *EQ*, pp. 66-67.

16. *PM*, pp. 147-8. Islam in the Shi'a form is exempted from this particular criticism.

17. *SM*, pp. 130-136. This is the best condensed account of the failure of Islam vis-a-vis Christianity.

18. *PM*, p. 146: ". . . the Christian faith is pledged and bound over to the conviction that the personal must be paramount. . . ."

19. Though he has reflected upon the problem (*PM*, pp. 7-14) he concludes too easily that "The fault, dear Brutus, is not in our cities that we are coarsened things, but in our souls." Nevertheless, the dimensions of the problem are fairly grasped: the paradox of growing impersonality . . . as the price of an increasing human attainment . . . Alienation derives from the same factors that spell an external competence. The lack of the self appears to be the contradictory climax of the possessing of all things, an over-simplified anti-Western anti-materialism Dr. Cragg does not approve: see *COR*, pp. 85-6 and *AG*, p. 42: ". . . it is all too possible for the inner travail and stress of the Western soul to be misconstrued or unrecognized."

20. In *PM*, pp. 16-25, 150 *seq.*, and in *AG* pp. 40-47.

21. *MQ*, p. 129.

22. *MQ*, p. 23.

23. *PM*, p. 157: ". . . it takes the religious mind to redeem the religious form . . . the supreme lesson of Jeremiah . . . ."

24. PM, p. 147.

25. *PM*, p. 123.

26. *AG*, pp. 22-29, discusses the extent to which this is possible.

27. *PM*, pp. 145-6.

28. *DR*, p. 184. The whole section, pp. 184-8, is relevant.

29. As noted in parenthesis above (p. 16), there was no state religion in Rome until Constantine gave Christianity that responsibility. By contrast, there *was* a state religion in Persia. In both places the Christians resisted idolatry and refused the manners and habits of mind associated with it — hence their unpopularity. But Christianity did survive the persecutions of Rome, it did not survive those of Persia, nor the quarrel between Rome and Persia. Centuries of missionary ardor failed to establish Christianity in either India or China. The social-political-cultural context (or the urban centers particularly) in the Roman Empire did matter — it was not peripheral but formative. There is no adequate acknowledgement of this fact in Christian consciousness of itself. Dr. Cragg writes as though the Roman context were *any* context, Roman persecution *any* persecution by political authority opposed to radical anti-paganism; it seems more likely that it was the only context in which Christianity (as we know it now) could have taken shape. These observations are not based on any Muslim account but drawn directly from: *A History of the Expansion of Christianity:* volume 1 *The First Five Centuries*, by Kenneth Scott Latourette, Harper and Row, Michigan, repr. 1980; see Chapter VIII, pp. 363-369, for Latourette's own summary.

30. Qur'an 6: 59-61 (Arberry 1, p. 155-6). Also, 41:53 (Arberry II, p. 191): "We shall show them Our signs in the horizons and in themselves, till it is clear to them . . . ."

31. *DR*, pp. 217-18.

32. Qur'an, 10:61 (Arberry I, p. 232).

33. Qur'an, 30:32 (Arberry II, p. 107).

34. *CM*, p. 75: "It was not . . . a Christianity calculated to present Muhammad with a fully authentic picture . . . docetism and monophysitism . . . ."

35. Qur'an, 35:18 (Arberry II, p. 140): "No soul laden bears the load of another . . ." Also, 17:7 (Arberry I, p. 303).

36. Qur'an, 10:47 (Arberry I, p. 230).

37. *MQ*, pp. 75-145.

38. Qur'an, 10:43 (Arberry I, p. 230).

39. Qur'an, 41:20 (Arberry II, p. 186).

40. Qur'an, 10:57 (Arberry I, p. 231).

41. Because the law was pragmatic not principled: 'savages' would not reciprocate.

42. *PM*, p. 174. Cf. Qur'an, 17:36-8 (Arberry I, p. 306): "thou wilt never tear the earth

open, nor attain the mountains in height."

43. Qur'an, 14:34 (Arberry I, p. 278): "If you count God's blessing you will never number it." Also, 11:6 (Arberry I, p. 239): "No creature is there crawling on the earth, but its provision rests in God."

44. Qur'an, 31:18 (Arberry II, p. 113): "Be modest in thy walk, and lower thy voice."

45. The parable is explained in *PM* pp. 140-3, pp. 144-9.

46. Qur'an 31:34 (Arberry II, p. 115): "No soul knows what it shall earn tomorrow."

47. Qur'an, e.g. 30: 8 (Arberry II, p. 105): "God created not the heavens and the earth . . . save with the truth and a stated term."

48. Qur'an e.g. 39:52 (Arberry II, p. 171): 13:4 (Arberry I, p. 267): "and palms in pairs . . . watered with one water and some of them we prefer in produce above others."; 10:99-100 (Arberry I, p. 236): "And if thy Lord had willed, whoever / is in the earth would have believed . . . It is not for any soul . . . save by the leave of God."

49. Qur'an, 68:47 (Arberry II, p. 295): "So be thou patient under the judgement of thy Lord, and be not as the Man of the Fish, when he called, choking inwardly."

50. Qur'an, 94:5-6 (Arberry II, p. 343): "So truly with hardship comes ease, truly with hardship comes ease."

51. *EQ*, p. 20.

52. *EQ*, p. 21.

53. *EQ*, p. 38.

54. Qur'an, 3:183 (Arberry I, p. 97).

9

BERNARD LEWIS AND ISLAMIC STUDIES: AN ASSESSMENT

Sulayman S. Nyang and Samir Abed-Rabbo

I n the history of mankind there have been a number of instances when two great civilizations coexisted while developing along separate and different lines. When these two centers of civilization are at relative parity with one another, as we now witness in American-Soviet relations, the two peoples of such civilizations learn to live with one another without yielding any major political, intellectual or cultural advantages to each other. In cases where one great civilization is militarily superior to all others, as we have witnessed until recently in Western attitudes towards non-Western societies and peoples, the cultural balance is tilted in favor of the dominant civilization, and the militarily and politically defeated or subjected peoples and societies find themselves imitating the lifestyles and other behavioral modes of the dominant civilization.[1]

Under conditions of political and military domination or dependence, one finds a segment of the intellectual class in the dominant civilization assuming the role of cultural/intellectual interpreters of the human condition of the peripheral, dependent societies and peoples. With this attitude and orientation such an intellectual class of the dominant civilization usually becomes a dangerous purveyor of truth or falsehood about the dominated people. It is indeed in this context that one relates to the development and uses of the social and human sciences in what until lately were called the colonies of Europe. What is being argued here is that colonial domination is not restricted in its impact and effects to the military, political and administrative realms; rather, it manifests itself most devastatingly in the intellectual and cultural domains of life of colonized or dominated peoples. By imposing a new alphabet and a new imperial language through the creation of a reward system which benefits most handsomely those indigenes who have developed perfect mastery of the foreign language, the promoters of the ideas, wares and cultural products of the dominant foreign civilization soon plant in the native soil a new generation of natives whose world view and outlook on life are the results of their education in a foreign tongue. Such cultural creatures, as Frantz Fanon argued long ago, become

259

men who wear masks. They become alienated from their own cultures and societies. In the language of some of the perceptive observers of the cultural scene in the developing world, such people become the victims of cultural schizophrenia.[2] Yet, in describing this deviant pattern of cultural change and development in the Third World, we should hasten to add that the evidence seems to suggest that area specialists who are without conscience and have no interest in listening to and understanding the perspective of dominated or dependent peoples and societies tend to fall under the category of scholars and intellectuals who cast themselves in the role of interpreters of the dominated or dependent societies.[3] In many instances, some of these students of foreign and comparative civilizations become some sort of cultural psychiatrists who can assist those westernized individuals in dealing with the trauma of the passing of traditional society.[4] Though there is now ample evidence that the earlier formulations of Western scholars regarding the nature of traditional societies have to some extent proved to be incorrect, there is reason to believe that misunderstanding still exists. The persistence of such misunderstanding can be attributed to two important factors. The first is the nature of instruction and the contents of the curricula for area studies and comparative civilization studies. The second, which in our view is the most important, is the built-in bias in the intellectual tradition of most scholars from the West studying societies other than their own.

It is indeed against this background that one can now examine the writings of Professor Bernard Lewis, one of the most controversial students of Islamic civilization. His controversiality, as we shall see below, is the result of his analytical style, his perceptions of Muslim society and his attitudes towards Islam as an ideology, a religion and a civilization in human history. Our assessment is tentative because of the limited number of works examined, and also because of the fact that Lewis is still alive and can change his views in the future.

Bernard Lewis: A Biographical Sketch

Professor Bernard Lewis was born on May 31, 1916, in the city of London in the United Kingdom, where he received his early education before entering the university for advanced training. At college he obtained a Bachelor's Degree with first class honors in 1936, a diploma in

Semitic Studies from the University of Paris in 1937, and finally a doctorate in Islamic History from the University of London in 1939. Following his graduation he took up a teaching job at the University of London. This was soon interrupted by the call to duty in the British armed forces. Being highly trained in foreign languages of the Middle East and a student of its history, Lewis became an attractive recruit for the British intelligence services. He served for five years before returning to civilian life.

Between his graduation and his induction into the national security forces, Lewis completed a few scholarly works which were destined to add to his reputation and prestige. He published *The Origin of Ismailism* in 1940; his *Turkey Today* in the same year; and his *British Contributions to Arabic Studies* in the following year. After the end of the second World War, he resumed his academic activities. An examination of a full list of his writings shows that two years after the conclusion of the war, Lewis published his *Handbook of Diplomatic and Political Arabic,* a work apparently intended to facilitate the work of European diplomats and politicians trying to find their bearings in the newly emerging world of Arab nationalism. This work was soon followed by his edited volume entitled *Land of Enchanters* (1948).

By 1950 the Arab League was a reality and a renascent Arab world was beginning to feel its way along the corridors of international diplomacy. To keep up with the times and to bring his fellow Europeans up to date on the new Arabs, Lewis published his *The Arabs in History* (1950), a work which has shed some light but at the same time put forth interpretations of Islam, Muhammad and Arab history which many Muslims and Arabs would come to perceive as deliberate distortions. Often, the criticism directed at Lewis is not for what he reads Islam to be, but rather his manner and idiom in portraying and explaining Islamic and Arab experience. In other words, Lewis is seen as a historian whose Western origins, coupled with his own perceptual idiosyncracies, combined to make him singularly incapable of relating to and understanding the Arab-Islamic perspective. Instead of developing a more sophisticated modern methodology of historical and social science analysis of Muslim society, past and present, and instead of trying to relate to and understand the style of thought of the Muslims of centuries ago, he persists in the traditional mode of narrative historians, whose generalizations were invariably the offspring of their prejudices dressed in the royal garments of scholarship.

This criticism we are making of Lewis and Orientalism is now widely shared in the Muslim World and is beginning to be accepted even among some Western academics working in the Middle East. Apart from the scathing and bitter attacks of Lewis *et al* in the now widely known works of Edward Said,[5] there have emerged in the last decade not only some forms of self-analysis and self-criticism among the Orientalists, but also some serious attempts to find alternative methodologies in Middle East studies. This search is fiercely pursued by Marxist or neo-Marxist scholars writing on the Middle East. Feeling a sense of inadequacy in the field of methodological development, these young Turks of Western academia are now putting forth their views for consideration. Bryan S. Turner, author of *Weber and Islam*, published in 1978 his *Marx and the End of Orientalism,* where he argues that "what is required fundamentally is a demonstration of orientalism and its replacement by a theoretically valid alternative."[6] Turner believes that Orientalists (such as Bernard Lewis) have accepted uncritically the mosaic theory of the so-called "Islamic Society." Such a conception sees Arab/Muslim society as "a mosaic or a patchwork of tribes, religious minorities, social groups and associations, socially divided vertically (not horizontally as in class society), yet held together by the shared beliefs and values of Islam and all too often by the tyrannical rule of an oriental despot."[7] Although Turner prefers the Marxist method over the traditional Orientalist method, he does not hesitate to point out that Marxist analysis would have to strip itself of the Orientalist elements which have somehow permeated it. Given this situation he calls for a new approach that goes beyond the limitations of the three dominant approaches to Middle Eastern studies, namely, the conventional Weberian sociology, the historicist Marxist, and Orientalism.[8] This work of Turner's is undoubtedly a prompt response to the words of the contributors in Talal Asad's and Roger Owen's *Review of Middle East Studies 1.* In that volume the editors as well as their contributors charged Orientalism and Orientalists for failing to improve their studies methodologically, and for defending their parochialism against what they perceived as the dangers of materialist analysis.

This approach, criticized by young Marxist 'Orientalists' in the West, has been Bernard Lewis' guiding light. During the early period in his intellectual development Lewis became very much enamored with

Turkish studies, necessitated perhaps by the creation of Israel in 1948. One of the most promising of British Middle East experts, he soon focused his attention on the political experiment in Turkey. Drawing on the vast resources of his alma mater, where he had served as a professor since 1949, he began to tap the Turkish research documents. As a result of his efforts, he completed his *Notes and Documents from the Turkish Archives* (1952). This was widely lauded in the councils of Orientalists and this further fired Lewis's enthusiasm to deliver more intellectual goods to his Western audience. One of the journal articles that dates back to these days of Lewis's love affair with Turkey was his "Recent Developments in Turkey," a paper published in the Chatham House publication, *International Affairs,* and offering his readers his analysis and interpretations of postwar political developments in the Republic of Turkey. At this time, he apparently was collecting materials for the book later known as *The Emergence of Modern Turkey* (1961). In the years between the publication of his "Notes and Documents from the Turkish Archives" and the appearance of the book, Lewis wrote a number of journal articles on Turkey, the Middle East and on Islamic Society.

In retrospect, one can now argue that during the early period of the cold war, Lewis was emerging not only as a Turkish expert but also as an Arabist who wished to survey the entire region and offer analysis and prognosis for events and problems affecting the fortunes of Britain in particular and the West in general. One of the articles written at this time was his "Islamic Revival in Turkey."

Another piece of interest was "Sources for the History of the Syrian Assassins." This article, published in October 1952, was the harbinger of what Lewis later published in 1967 as *The Assassins.* This work was well received by his reviewers and Lewis' fortunes increased sharply in the eyes of his fellow Orientalists. In the Arab and Muslim world, however, Lewis's works began to attract attention and some of the Muslim and Arab intellectuals began to attack him as a distorting scholar.

Another point that deserves our attention is the fact that, with the deepening of the cold war in the West and the growing concern about communist expansion, Lewis and other Orientalists began to examine the religion of Islam and its relationship to communism. Working on the assumption that Islam and communism share certain attitudes towards social life and towards the relations between individual and community, they dissected the faith of the Muslims in the arrogant hope of figuring out the essential elements likely to make Muslims willing or unwilling collaborators of communism. The explanations given by Lewis are certainly provocative to Muslims and perhaps satisfying to a Westerner bent on finding a communist skeleton in the Islamic closet. In his 1954 article, published in *International Affairs*, Lewis wrote about "Communism and Islam." In this piece, reprinted in Walter Laqueur's *Middle East in Transition*, Lewis identified two categories of factors which he believes to be crucial in the Muslim world's reaction to communism. Under the category of essential factors he lists: 1) authoritarianism of Islamic society,[9] tradition and thought; 2) the division of the world into bipolar camps of *Darul Islam* and *Darul Harb*; 3) the collectivistic tendencies and 4) the sense of collective solidarity. Under the category of accidental factors he identifies a) the anti-Western motif which Muslims generally share with the communists; b) the present social and economic discontent in the Muslim world, which in his view stems from "the abject poverty of the masses and the callous irresponsibility of the possessing classes" and last but not least, c) the emergence of the impoverished urban proletariat. In his view, the "centre of danger is not the starving peasant . . . but rather the aspiring mechanics."[10] Using these categories Lewis goes on to make a number of generalizations about Arab and Muslim societies that the train of historical events has proved false. Muslim states not only have steered away from the pathways of communism but have decided, rather, to organize themselves into an international body committed to the protection and promotion of Muslim interests. Professor Lewis can retort that, although Islamic solidarity has progressed significantly since the founding of the Organization of Islamic Conference (OIC) in 1969, Muslim states have not yet desisted from their fratricidal warfare, as in the contemporary Iran-Iraq issue. One Muslim response to such an untrue statement from a skeptical Orientalist would be that the Masjid (Mosque) of Islamic solidarity is still under reconstruction, having been demolished by pre-colonial and post-colonial forces active in the Islamic world. Further, Muslims can reply that most of the internal challenges facing Muslim societies were the creations of former colonial and imperial powers. Having invaded, violently in most cases, the societies of the Muslims, Western cultural powers have created a large number of cultural schizoids whose very life is burdened by the problems of cultural alienation. These assimilated Muslims have in many cases wittingly or unwittingly served as surrogates for one or the other of the two main ideological combatants in world politics. Yet, in no instance have we seen the complete transformation of a Muslim society into a willing bona fide communist one.

The theme of communist penetration in the Middle East continued to preoccupy the mind of Lewis through the 1950s. An indication of this concern was his 1956 journal article focusing on "Middle East Reactions to Soviet Pressures." In studying this period in Lewis's intellectual development, one may hypothesize that, though seriously committed to the traditional British stance against communism, Lewis' resolve to wage intellectual warfare, particularly in the Middle East, was most probably increased by his 1955–56 trip to the United States as a visiting professor of history at the University of California, Los Angeles. Lewis, be it noted, came to the United States at a time when McCarthyism was already a factor in American political life and his brief stay doubtless made him more conscious of, and responsive to, the drumbeat of the cold war.

As we have stated earlier, in the 1950s Lewis' interest centered on the political future of Turkey and the train of events in the Middle East. In 1955 he published his "Democracy in the Middle East — Its State and Prospects." This article was fashionable at the time, for following Nasser's coup in Egypt, scholars and political observers began to express grave doubts about the future of democracy in the Middle East. The Wafd Party, which had ruled the largest Arab democracy in that part of the Arab world for many years, was toppled by army men, and the political stirrings in the Levant and Fertile Crescent did not augur well. Yet, in conceding this fact, we also have to note that Lewis' analysis was suspect to many Arabs and non-Arab Muslims in the Middle East. A non-Muslim writer of Indian origin came to the same position many Muslims and Arabs had arrived at much earlier. Writing on the errors, prejudices, blunders and distortions of several Western Orientalists, including Professors H. A. R. Gibb and Bernard Lewis, he makes the following remarks about Professor Lewis:

> "He is a passionate defender of that country (Israel), to the extent that he has testified in its defence to committees of the United States Congress. Should not this political stand affect our opinion of his scholarly objectivity when he writes of countries that are the sworn enemies of Israel (and with the exception of Egypt every single Muslim state is such)?"[11]

Despite these evident biases in his works, Lewis still writes. His preoccupation with the future of Turkey again led him to write on "Democracy in Turkey" for the February, 1959 issue of *Middle East Affairs*. This article was a current affairs analysis of what was going on in Turkey. His analysis reflected very much the general view entertained by many Western scholars who, by this time, were beginning to be called Middle East experts. With decolonization, first in Asia and then in Africa, many of the traditional Orientalists began to find their intellectual grazing grounds crowded by these new experts on Middle East politics. Not to be outperformed by the newcomers, many of the old Orientalists switched to contemporary analyses. Professor Lewis, who has been lauded for his historical works on Turkey and on the Ismailis and the Assassins, became deeply involved in the fashionable exercise of contemporary history writing.[12] Between 1956, when the Suez Crisis erupted, and 1967, when Israel attacked the Arab states for the third time, he became increasingly emotionally involved with the Arab-Israeli conflict. During this particular period he wrote a number of essays which looked at Arab attitudes toward the Soviet Union, democracy in Turkey, the consequences of the June War of 1967, the UN resolution calling Zionism another form of racism and at the Palestinians and the PLO. In all these essays, which came out in the late fifties through the sixties and seventies, he maintains a consistent bias against the Arab world and the Islamic faith.

One interesting development of this period was the publication of two essays which did not deal directly with the Arab-Israeli conflict, but were destined to have an impact on international public opinion in that conflict. In the late sixties and early seventies, when he was living in both his original home country of England and his new home, the United States, political leaders were faced with the dangers of racial agitation. Writing contemporaneously with Black nationalists like Malcolm X and others who were telling the Black world that Islam is the religion of the Afro-Asian, Lewis told the world in his book on *Race and Color in Islam* that Islam is not color blind. This essay, which was first published in *Encounter* in August, 1970 and has also appeared in Spanish in a major journal in Spain, proved moderately effective as a counter-argument to the Arab-Muslim claim that there is no racism in Islam.[13] Regardless of the

motives which led Professor Lewis to write such an essay, the fact
remains that his book has since provided some ammunition to those
anti-Arab and anti-Islamic elements in the West whose prejudices can
now be rationalized in the name of Lewisian scholarship. What Lewis
failed to realize at the time he wrote that book, and here we are
certainly not questioning his right to do so, is that Afro-Asian Muslims
do not doubt the fact that in Islam color is irrelevant. What Lewis' book
does for them is to point out the danger of racism, which has received
its most universal and blatant application in the Western European
experience with non-Europeans. By training his intellectual guns at
Islam, Professor Lewis is, in the kindest interpretation, really engaged
in the dubious game of the European pot calling the Arab kettle black.

Professor Lewis relocated to the United States in 1974. He is currently teaching at Princeton University where he serves as the Cleve-
land E. Dodge Professor of Near Eastern Studies. He is also associated
with the Princeton Institute of Advanced Studies. His decision to come
to the United States can be attributed to a number of factors, some
personal and others professional. With the limited information available we can speculate that Professor Lewis saw the American branch of
Orientalism as the most promising of all and so decided to change his
locus operandi.

This was a rational decision because, as Professor William Hayter
of Hayter Commission fame recently pointed out, the British departments of Oriental studies since the early sixties were facing a discou-
raging situation. Except for the School of Oriental and African
Studies and St. Anthony's College in Oxford, all others were in a
depressed condition. Professor Hayter goes on to tell us that the
position in the United States was different. The fear of Soviet supremacy in technological development led to the Congressional passage
of the National Defense Act of 1958, which in turn opened the
floodgates to academic research and to the development of centers of
area studies.

According to Hayter, one of the points which interested them in
the American model of area studies was the "concentration on
modern studies" and the emphasis on the social sciences and on
modern history and modern literature.[14] He also pointed out that the
change in British status in world affairs since the end of the last world

war also reduced the significance of such studies in the eyes of policy makers, although he added that the development of such expertise in area studies could put Britain in good stead within the European economic community.[15] Given this background one can speculate that Professor Bernard Lewis' relocation to Princeton was influenced by these considerations.

Since his immigration to the U.S. some ten years ago, Professor Lewis has quickly established himself as one of the leading American Orientalists. He has presented numerous lectures around the United States and abroad. Yet, in saying this we should point out that he is a controversial figure and his writings and lectures have angered many Arabs and Muslims. This opprobrium of the Arab/Muslim community reverberates as loud applause in, naturally, the American Jewish community, where Lewis is highly esteemed as a learned man who uses his pen and tongue effectively in the analysis of Middle Eastern affairs. This view and image of Professor Lewis has contributed to his rise in American academic circles and to his receipt of an honorary doctoral degree from the Hebrew University in Jerusalem in 1974. It also won him the Harvey Prize from the Technion Israel Institute of Technology in 1978. He has been invited to Israel on many occasions and his lectures are widely reported in the Israeli media.[16]

Bernard Lewis and Islamic Studies: An Analysis

After a brief sketch of Bernard Lewis' biography let us now turn to an examination of some of his views on Islam, Muslims and Arabs. We hope such an analysis will enable the reader to see him for the kind of scholar he really is.

Lewis defines the scope of Islam as the "final phase of the sequence of revelations — that of Muhammad and the Qur'an."[17] The scope of Islam, however, combines the history, commandments and religious codes of previous peoples and faiths. The Muslims believe that God revealed His commandments and religious codes to various prophets throughout history for the guidance of the intended peoples.

These commandments and codes, however, do not exist today in their original form. Each message was meant for a specific period. This is evident from the following Qur'anic verses (ayats):

63. When Jesus came
    with clear signs, he said:
    "Now have I come
    To you with Wisdom,
    and in order to make
    Clear to you some
    Of the (points) on which
    You dispute: Therefore fear God
    And obey me.

64. "For God, He is my Lord
    And your Lord: so worship
    Ye Him: this is
    A straight Way."

65. But sects from among
    Themselves fell into disagreement:
    Then woe to the wrong-doers,
    From the Penalty
    Of a Grievous Day![18]

In unmistakable words, the Qur'an reveals,

27. Then, in their wake
    We followed them up
    With (others of) our apostles:
    We sent after them
    Jesus the son of Mary
    And bestowed on him
    The Gospel; and We ordained
    In the hearts of those
    Who followed him
    Compassion and Mercy.
    But the Monasticism
    Which they invented
    For themselves, we did not
    prescribe for them:
    (We commanded) only
    The seeking for the Good
    Pleasure of God; but that
    They did not foster
    As they should have done.
    Yet we bestowed, on those
    Among them who believed,

Their (due) reward, but
Many of them are
Rebellious transgressors.[19]

What Lewis and other Orientalists know but fail to acknowledge is that the present day interpretations of God's commandments and religious codes are only interpretations by the respective followers of the religion. Their views on the rigidity or unchangeability of Islam are really the product of their conceptual creations. Again, the claim advanced by Lewis that Islam treats non-Muslims as "unbelievers" or "the Muslim equivalent of the Greek term barbarians"[20] is wrong. Islam treats Jews and Christians, who are non-Muslims, as the "people of the Book" or *dhimmis*. It does not treat them as barbarians, for Islam grants them rights and privileges and demands that they fulfill certain duties.[21]

Lewis moreover, suggests that Muhammad's message was "brought to the people of his birthplace, urging them to abandon their idolatrous beliefs and practices and to believe in one, single, universal God."[22] The terms "people of his birthplace" and "universal God" suggest a clear contradiction, for the message advocating a universal God can only be directed to mankind as a whole and not to the "people of his birthplace." Islam, from its very inception, was and is a universal religion from a universal God. Muhammad and the early Muslims were aware of the scope of Islam, and as conditions permitted they began dispatching Muslim delegates to foreign lands, (e.g., Ethiopia), bringing the attention of the rulers and their peoples to the new religion and asking them to accept God's message, Islam.

In another argument, he alleges that Islam is a "theocratic faith"[23] without advancing any further explanation or substantiation. In one aspect, Islam is God's given system to mankind as prescribed in the Qur'an and through the practice of Muhammad (Sunnah). God, however, left to the people the right to select their civil rulers. Islam did not empower any particular individual, class or institution with divine authority. Rather, it is the responsibility of the entire community (*umma*). The *umma* possesses the right to select and to dispose of the state's elected officials. All matters that are covered in the Qur'an and the Sunnah (Shari'ah) are final. Others are settled by consensus of opinion among Muslim jurists. On the other hand, any Muslim capable of giving sound opinion on matters of concern to

Muslim affairs is entitled to do so without fear. The mere fact that the Qur'an serves as a guide to the Muslims in their relations to God, among themselves and with others, does not necessarily mean that the Islamic faith, which encompasses the religion and the state, is theocratic in nature. Also, the analogy made by the author (p. 16) that God is Caesar and the head of the Muslim community is His Vice Regent on earth, is just another flagrant misrepresentation of the nature of Islam. This analogy can only apply to the Western situation and not to Islam. God can't be compared to Caesar or to any form or shape (human or otherwise). Also, God does not appoint a vice Regent on earth. Every human being is a caliph of Allah here on earth. The Muslim community selects its leaders according to the norms of the Shari'ah. Lewis is in error on both counts.

Offering the reader a definition of the term Muslim, Lewis states that it means, "one who performs the act of surrender."[24] This definition is incomplete. The term means one who accepts the supremacy of the Shariah and works to implement its provisions in his/her daily life. Thus, a person who surrenders to the Shariah but does not put it into practice or who performs acts contrary to its teaching cannot be called Muslim.

In addressing himself to the character and role of Muhammad, Lewis observes that he *was* a humble and persecuted teacher who ruled on behalf of God. Muhammad was *and remained* a humble and ordinary teacher who was chosen by God, and not to rule on His behalf, but to serve and implement His commands. God outlines the functions of Muhammad, in the Qur'an as follows:

> 56. But Thee we only sent
>   To give glad tidings
>   And abomination.[26]

Or as in

> 45. O Prophet! Truly We
>   Have sent Thee as
>   A witness, a bearer
>   Of glad tidings
>   And a warner.

> 46. And as one who
>   invites to God's (Grace) by His love,

And as a lamp
Spreading light.[27]

Or as in

8. We have truly sent Thee
   As a witness, as
   Bringer of glad tidings,
   And as a warner.[28]

Focusing on the role of Muhammad in Mecca and Medina, Lewis argues that, "In Mecca, Muhammad had been a private person preaching a new faith, against the indifference or hostility of the ruling powers; in Medina he was first a chief and then a ruler, wielding political and military as well as religious authority."[29] Before and after his Hijrah from Mecca to Medina, Muhammad remained a humble and ordinary person. Power did not affect or change his personality or behavior. On the other hand, to the Muslims, Islam in general and Muhammad in particular wielded power and authority from the inception of God's revelations, in consequence to God's promise to protect the Islamic religion:

9. We have, without doubt
   Sent down the Message;
   And we will assuredly
   Guard it (from corruption).[30]

Also, according to the Qur'an and the tradition, Muhammad was able to ask and receive, if desired, from God all means (i.e., wealth, force) to make him more powerful than his opponents in both cities, Mecca and Medina. But Muhammad opted to depend on the modest resources of the Muslims for various reasons, among which was his desire to test the strength of the Muslims' belief in Islam and their readiness to defend and sacrifice for it. In doing so, Muhammad followed the footsteps of previous Messengers who were and remained humble, poor, modest and strong in their belief in God and his message.[31] God, however, interceded on behalf of the Muslims on various occasions as illustrated below:

12. Remember thy Lord inspired
    The angels (with the message):
    "I am with you: give
    Firmness to the Believers:

> I will instill terror
> Into the hearts of the unbelievers:
> Smite ye above their necks
> And smite all their
> Finger-tips off them.[32]

or in

> 82. When our decree is issued,
>   We turned (the cities)
>   Upside down, and rained down
>   On them brimstone
>   Hard as baked clay,
>   Spread, layer on layer.[33]

In offering his reader the simplistic conclusions that he does, Lewis rejects and brushes aside a set of beliefs held dearly by Muslims.

In another generalization, Lewis argues "that the people of Yathrib agreed to welcome Muhammad among them, to make him their arbitrator and to defend him from Mecca, as they would defend themselves."[34] He fails to point out that not all the people of Yathrib extended a welcome to Muhammad; only the Muslims among them did so by accepting God's message and by accepting His Messenger as their leader "to defend him as they would defend themselves."

Lewis, again generalizing, states[35] that "every Muslim is required to go on pilgrimage" and to make zakat (a financial contribution that goes to the needy of the community or to the government). He should, however, have qualified the term "every Muslim." Pilgrimage, zakat and any other obligations in Islam are only requirements for those who are capable (financially, economically or physically) of meeting them.

Islam, ideologically speaking, discourages class and caste consciousness. Thus it does not distinguish between peoples in general and Muslims in particular.

> 13. O mankind! We created
>   You from a single (pair)
>   Of a male and a female
>   And made you into
>   Nations and tribes, that
>   You may know each other
>   (Not that ye may despise
>   Each other) verily

> The most honoured of you
> In the sight of God
> Is (he who is) the most
> Righteous of you
> And God has full knowledge
> And is well acquainted
> (With all things).[36]

The Islamic faith is firmly based on egalitarian principles. Thus the notion advanced by Lewis[37] that the "Muslim Society" was divided into two main groups and that Islamic law "recognized some forms of privileges and differences of status" is a sweeping generalization and quite erroneous. He is doubtless referring to the period in which Islam was not the supreme law of the land. A society which is not ruled by Islamic principles cannot, by definition, be called a Muslim one.

Lewis, moreover, states that Muslim law in theory and practice classified the population of the Muslim Empire into four main groups: *hurr, mawali, dhimmis* and slaves.[38] Islamic law, in fact, recognizes only one group of people and that is mankind as a whole, without division.

> "If you judge among mankind
> Judge justly.[39]

The term "mankind" here means Muslims and non-Muslims. Islam, therefore, calls for the practice of absolute equality and justice for all, regardless of color, religion, race, social, economic and political status. Islamic justice has been practiced by Muslim rulers and implemented by Islamic law. Abu Bakr, the first Islamic caliph said:

> The weak of you is strong in my eyes until I restore his
> right to him: and the strong of you is weak in my eyes
> until I take away from him the right of others.

The author has also claimed that an ethnic order of preference existed in Islam: first members of Quraysh, then the Arabs, then the non-Arabs.[40] He further states that these classes were in turn subdivided. Muslims (Arabs, non-Arabs, relatives or non-relatives of the Prophet) are equal in front of the law and there is no legal or social preference among them except in their devotion to the principles of Islam. The exception crowns the nature of the relation between man (in the general sense) and God. The Qur'an and the tradition address themselves very explicitly to this subject and no person should be able to deny or reject this fact. Lewis, however, simply rejects it.

On the subject of women and slaves, Lewis states that Islam inherited some inequalities from the pre-Islamic order.[41] Women and slaves, in the pre-Islamic era were treated as if they were not human. The Islamic order in dealing with women and slaves, however, provided them with a set of rights and duties and made them equal in front of the law. Moreover, Islam gradually eliminated old customs of killing infant girls because of poverty[42] and the inhumane treatment of slaves. Through a well-structured and decisive program, Islam encouraged the liberation of slaves[43] and restricted the means by which slaves could be obtained for war or through war. The term slave, thereafter, became synonymous with prisoner of war. The Muslim ruler was granted three options in dealing with them: freedom, exchange with Muslim prisoners, or redemption. Slaves were granted the right to buy their freedom. The Islamic program to abolish slavery was effective, and during the reign of Uthman, the third Caliph, slavery was abolished. The most significant aspect of the Islamic program in dealing with the question of slavery was the egalitarian nature of Islam, which is credited mainly with abolishing the system. Slaves, women, Muslims and non-Muslims were treated equally in front of the law. Their evidence was accepted and honored by the Islamic courts and they were called upon to serve in all departments and at all levels of the Islamic states. For example, Tariq Ibn Ziad, who was a slave, led the Muslim Army that entered Spain. Islam inherited the problem of slavery and worked decisively and successfully to solve it.

Therefore, Lewis' argument that Islam inherited (by which he implies 'kept') some of the inequalities from the pre-Islamic era is not quite accurate. Also, his argument[45] that slaves were excluded from any office involving jurisdiction is groundless.

On the question of slave trade, Lewis argues[46] that Muslim corsairs traded in slaves in the Mediterranean. However, a Muslim can only be described as one if he/she accepts and implements the Islamic teachings in his/her daily life. Thus, a person who acts contrary to the teachings of Islam by acting as a slave trader cannot be called Muslim. This generalization, however, is another indication of either lack of understanding or deliberate intention to misrepresent the nature of Islam.

Besides slaves, the pre-Islamic era permitted men to acquire slave women of various ethnic backgrounds. Slave women served as concubines who were customarily at the disposal of their owners. Islam dealt with this problem in the same manner as it dealt with the question of slavery in general. Islam even went further to prohibit adultery, which was a widespread social issue in the pre-Islamic era. Islam realized, however, that after wars the number of women increases and that of men decreases. In order to avoid inevitable social problems, Islam founded a social contract between Muslim men and women prisoners similar to, but less important than, marriage. Women prisoners were: 1) treated justly; 2) allowed to buy their freedom; and 3) permitted to integrate into the society. The Muslim men were required to treat women prisoners justly, to prove that they were financially capable of supporting them and, if permitted, providing them with living conditions similar to those of their own women. This social phenomenon ceased as soon as the state was at peace with its neighbors. Moreover, the evidence of women prisoners was admissible in Islamic court and they were allowed to get married. Lewis's argument that "slave-women of many ethnic origins were recruited in enormous numbers to staff the harems of the Islamic world"[47] is false. The term "recruited" does not indicate the time nor explain the conditions under which this might have taken place. Slavery, in general, can only exist as a result of war and thus the term cannot be so generally used. In Islam, no Muslim may, as a Muslim, go around recruiting women to "staff harems." For Lewis to advance this generalization again shows either his ignorance or intent to fabricate the true nature of Islam.

In the Arabic language, the term *bida* means fabrication, falsehood or innovation for unuseful purposes. Lewis, however, defines it as unqualified innovation.[48] Understanding the proper meaning of the term clearly indicates that in Islam, innovation for the good or interest of the society is not *bida,* and innovation as such is considered to be an important aspect of the Islamic legal system. Innovations geared to serving the people or *ijtihad* were permitted and encouraged in Islam. Positive innovation gave rise to various schools of thought, among which the Shi'a stands as one of the most important. All schools of thought base their interpretation of Islam on the Shari'ah (Qur'an and Sunnah) and, in varing degrees, accept *ijtihad* as a significant supplementary source of Islamic law in areas not addressed by the Shariah. All schools of thought in Islam, including the Shi'a, accept the supremacy of the Shari'ah, and thus the statement advanced by Lewis describing the Shi'a as the "largest dissident group in Islam"[49] is inaccurate. There is no dissent in Islam. Dissent is the equivalent of *Kufr* (atheism) and, certainly, the Shi'a are not *Kufr*. The Shi'a is an Islamic school of thought that subscribes to the Shariah and thus cannot be called dissident.

The role of *ijtihad* in the development of Islamic law and jurisprudence is significant. The process of *ijtihad*, which is carried out by capable and knowledgable Muslim jurists, involves all or some of the following steps: *ijma* (consensus), *qiyas* (analogy derived from preceeding juristic judgement), *istihsan* (deviation from the rule of precedent for a relevant legal reason) and *istislah* (the unprecedented judgment motivated by public interest). To date, all Islamic schools of thought subscribe, in varying degree, to this system. Lewis argues, however, that the Sunni jurists of all schools around A.D. 900 closed the gate of *ijtihad*.[50] Moreover, he states that the Shi'a did not accept the Sunni doctrine, thus creating an important distinction between the Sunni and Shi'i Ulema. The gate of *ijtihad* is still open and if it was closed, as argued, it was because the Islamic legal system failed to develop the concept of a "corporate personality" and it was illegally interrupted by the political leadership. A consensus exists among Muslim Ulema that Islam is dynamic in nature and thus the gate of *ijtihad* must continue to be open. They also realize that any attempt to close it is a violation of the nature of Islam.[51]

Professor Lewis also indicates that a division between the Caliph Uthman (who according to Lewis was the first Caliph) and Ali (who was the second) led to the creation of the two religious parties which still exist — the Sunni (who go back to Uthman's followers) and the Shi'i (who go back to Ali).[52]

This statement is historically wrong. Uthman was the third caliph, and not the first, and Ali was the fourth, and not the second. Moreover, Muslim historians do not accept the idea that a division between the two caliphs led to a greater division among Muslims. They point out that Muslim disenchantment with some aspects of Uthman's behavior in managing the state's affairs led to his killing by angry delegates from Egypt and eventually to the selection of Ali as the new caliph. Ali began immediately responding to the demands of the Muslims by correcting the wrongs done by the appointees of Uthman. In doing so, his administration was opposed by an organized group from Bani Umayya, led by Muawiah. Consequently Muawiah was able, illegally, to take control of the Islamic state from Ali, who was killed as a result of the dispute, and to move the center of government to Damascus. During this period and especially after the death of Ali, Muslim opposition to Muawiah strengthened and eventually emerged as a distinct political force. Thus the argument by the author that the division was a result of conflict between Uthman and Ali is inaccurate. Moreover, his definition of Sunni Muslims as the followers of Uthman is ridiculous. Sunnism means, historically, the school of thought in Islam that accepted the validity of the teachings of Holy Prophet Muhammad and the legitimacy and fidelity of all the four rightly-guided caliphs who came after him. Such believers also embrace the position that the Sunnah of the Prophet, together with the Qur'an, constitute the two most important pillars of the Muslim belief system.

The primary goal of the Islamic caliph and the state that he represents is to implement Shari'ah and to legislate in matters not covered in Shari'ah after hearing the opinions of learned Muslims. He is to lead the *ummah* and to manage its affairs. There is no limitation on his tenure as long as he is physically and mentally fit and governs justly. His role, in some aspects, is comparable to an elected statesman in modern political systems. Lewis indicates, however, that the caliph's primary task is to maintain and spread Islam.[53] Muslims believe that this task of maintaining Islam is vested in God:

> 9. We have, without doubt
>   Sent down the Message;
>   And we will assuredly
>   Guard it (from corruption)[54]

Moreover, the task of spreading Islam is vested in the *ummah*, individually and collectively. Thus, Lewis' argument is inaccurate.

Islam respects and protects private property. The Islamic notion of ownership, however, vests the ownership of all natural resources, including land, in God. The use of such resources is for all Muslims regardless of social, economic or political status. The acquisition of land by a Muslim was based exclusively on his/her ability to utilize it. After the spread of Islam, various lands came under the jurisdiction of the Islamic state, thus initiating a debate on the future use and ownership of the land. The Maliki school of thought advocates that mines and agricultural land that come under the control of the state are for the use of all Muslims. The Hanafi school of thought suggests that the land should be left to the original owners, in return for a fifth of the produce. This opinion was called *rekaz*.

Professor Lewis claims that agricultural land acquired as a result of conquest was given by the first caliphs as grants to large landowners, who were normally Arab conquerors.[55] The facts indicate that Umar, the second caliph, refused to distribute the agricultural land of Iraq and Iran among Muslims on the ground that if distribution was to take place among existing Muslims, future Muslims would have no land.[56] Instead, he opted to leave the land with the original owners, as in the case of Egypt, Syria, Palestine, etc., but asked them to pay *rekaz*. Lewis' argument is therefore false.

Conclusions

In concluding this study we can say that Bernard Lewis is a product of the British experience of empire and that his works can never and should never be taken at face value as objective studies. Even though he has written that Orientalists were motivated by scientific curiosity, he himself recognized the political and economic interests behind their curiosity. In his own case we can only say that he is a biased writer with an axe to grind. While at London University he operated as an intellectual agent of the British Foreign Office; at Princeton his works seem to be designed to generate and sustain support for Israel. This is a fact which an investigator willing to trace Lewis's biographical steps will see for himself. There is overwhelming evidence, some of which we marshalled above, that each of Lewis' articles or papers betrays a hidden or discernible motive. He writes either to guide policy or to influence public opinion. A cavalier James Bond instinct for scholarly manipulation through effective cultivation of verbal skills, analytic power, and sophisticated casuistry and political hide-and-seek facilitates deception and distortion.

In a world where wars are unwillingly fought because of the destructiveness of our conventional weapons and the awe-inspiring nature of our thermonuclear monsters, intellectual warfare and verbal games seem less physically torturing and mutilating and hence acceptable, even

attractive. Yet, in saying this, we hasten to add that the intellectual
warfare in which men like Lewis are engaged has the minds of millions
as its battleground. To let Lewis go scot-free is dangerous and unwise.
In the name of international peace and security, and in the belief that all
human groups and civilizations deserve fair and objective hearing and
coverage, we encourage Orientalists and their students to read the
original texts of the Muslim world again and reconsider the errors and
blunders of masters whom they now lionize without tracking down
their footnotes and sources.

NOTES

1. Ibn Khaldun in his *MuQaddimah* made mention of this aspect of subject people imitating the language and culture of the victors. Indeed, there is the general tendency among defeated people to attribute their defeat to the institutions and culture of their conquerors.

2. See, for example, Renate Zahar's *Frantz Fanon: Colonialism and Alienation* (New York & London: Monthly Review Press, 1974), chapter 4.

3. For a very critical assessment of Western social science and its application in third world countries, see Thomas Gladdin and Ahmad Saidin, *Slaves of The White Myth* (Atlantic Highlands, N.J.: Humanities Press, 1980), pp. 149–176.

4. Daniel Lerner, *The Passing of Traditional Society: Modernizing the Middle East* (Glencoe, Ill.: Free Press, 1958).

5. See his *Orientalism,* (New York: Vintage Books, 1978) in which he questions Lewisian scholarship because of the Englishman's arrogance towards Arabs and Islam and also because of distortion of history to advance his causes, including Zionism.

6. Bryan Turner, *Marx and the End of Orientalism* (London: George Allen and Unwin, 1978).

7. See David Seddon's review of Turner's book in *Gazelle Review* (London: 1977), p. 20.

8. Turner, *Marx and the End of Orientalism,* p. 6.

9. This view is shared by almost all Orientalists. The orthodox Muslim certainly does not deny the fact that Allah's will is supreme here on earth and in the Hereafter. What is questioned by Muslim scholars in the writings of Orientalists is their unwillingness to allow for some latitude in Muslim interpretations of Qur'anic verses emphasizing man's free will here on earth. For some discussion of the Orientalists' view of the place and role of Allah in Muslim Society, see Elie Kedourie, "Islam and the Orientalists: Some Recent Discussion," *British Journal of Sociology,* 7:3 (September, 1956), pp. 217–255.

10. See Lewis's paper in Walter Laqueur, ed., *Middle East in Transition* (New York: Frederick A. Praeger, 1958), pp. 316–17.

11. See G. H. Jansen, *Militant Islam* (New York: Harper & Row Publishers, Inc., 1979), p. 83.

12. Professor Abdul Latif Tibawi has identified this phenomenon of contemporary history analysis, which manifests itself in the form of "factual studies," "surveys" and the "appraisal essay," with the rapid development of studies of contemporary political affairs and with the invasion of the preserves of scholarship by journalism, radio and television. See his critique of English-speaking Orientalistism in *The Muslim World,* 53:4 (October 1963),p. 306. Lewis' "studious" association with Israel continues. See, for example, Bruce Lawrence's review of Joel L. Kramer and Ilai Alon, *Religion and Government in the World of Islam* in *The Middle East Journal,* 31:1 (Winter 1983), pp. 161-162. Unfortunately Lewis' "stimulating" words to the Tel Aviv colloquium in June 1979 were not printed in the proceedings as published in Kramer and Alon's book.

Shortly after returning from the Tel Aviv conference, Lewis perhaps because of his earlier interest in Ismailism and the Assassins as well as his continuing interest in the potential threat of communist penetration into the Middle East, turned his attention to Iran. At a conference at the Woodrow Wilson International Center for Scholars on December 9, 1980, he suggested "There may be some possibility that the Soviet Union and Tudeh [the communist party of Iran] will cooperate with the leftist Mujaheddin-i-Khalq party, which is much larger at present than Tudeh." Quoted from Thomas T. Hammond, *Red Flag Over Afghanistan: The Communist Coup, the Soviet Invasion, and the Consequences* (Boulder, Colorado: Westview Press, 1984), p. 213, ff. 17.

13. For an American Muslim response to Lewis, see Akbar Muhammad, "Images of Peoples of African Descent in the Arab world," (a paper presented at the African Studies Association Meeting in Philadelphia, 1980).

14. See his "Future of Asian Studies after the Hayter Report," *Asian Affairs*, XII (old series volume 68, Part 3, October 1981), pp. 246–247.

15. *Ibid.*, p. 252.

16. For more biographical details, see *Who Is Who in America* (Chicago, Illinois: Marque's Who Is Who, 1980),p. 2017; *The Academic Who Is Who: University Teachers in the British Isles in Arts, Education and Social Sciences* (London: Adam L. Charles Black, 1973); *Who Is Who in America*, 2, 42nd edition (Chicago, Illinois: Marque's Who Is Who, 1982–3), p. 1998.

17. Bernard Lewis, "The Faith and the Faithful" in Bernard Lewis, ed. *Islam and the Arab World* (New York: Alfred A. Knopf, 1976), p. 25.

18. A. Yusuf Ali, trans. *The Holy Quran* (Washington, D.C.: The Islamic Center, 1978), chapter XLIII:63–65.

19. *Ibid.*, LVII:27.

20. Bernard Lewis and P. M. Holt, eds., *Historians of the Middle East.* (London: Oxford University Press, 1962),p. 181.

21. Under Islamic Shari'ah the non-Muslims are treated as *dhimmis* or 'People of the Book.'

22. Bernard Lewis, ed., *Islam and the Arab World*, p. 11.

23. Bernard Lewis, *The Arabs in History.* Revised edition. (New York: Harper Torchbooks, 1966), p. 16.

24. Bernard Lewis, ed. *Islam and the Arab World*, p. 12.

25. *Ibid.*

26. *The Holy Qur'an*, XXV:56.

27. *Ibid.* XXXIII:45.

28. *Ibid.* XLVIII:8.

29. Bernard Lewis, ed. *Islam and the Arab World*, p. 11.

30. *The Holy Qur'an* XV:9.

31. *Ibid.*, XI:50–102.

32. *Ibid.*, VIII, 14.

33. *The Holy Qur'an*, XI:82.

34. Bernard Lewis, ed. *Islam and the Arab World*, p. 17.

35. *Ibid.*, p. 26–27.

36. *The Holy Qur'an*, XLIX:13.

37. Bernard Lewis, "Faith and the Faithful," in Bernard Lewis, ed., *Islam and the Arab World*, p. 33.

38. *Ibid.*

39. *The Holy Qur'an* IV: 58.

40. Bernard Lewis, "Faith and the Faithful," p. 36.

41. *Ibid.*, p. 31.

42. Kill not your children
    For fear of want: we shall
    Provide sustenance for them
    As well as for you.
    Verily the killing of them
    Is a great sin.
    (XVII: 31)

43. But those who divorce
    Their wives by Zihar
    Then wish to go back
    On the words they uttered
    (It is ordained that
    such a one)
    Should free a slave
    Before they touch each other:

44. This are ye admonished
    To perform: and God is
    Well-acquainted with (all)
    That ye do
    (LVIII: 3)

45. Lewis, "Faith and the Faithful," p. 34.

46. *Ibid.*, p. 35.

47. *Ibid.*

48. *Ibid.*, p. 29.

49. *Ibid.*, p. 30.

50. *Ibid.*, p. 37.

51. M. S. Madkour, *Manahij Al-Ijtihad Fi Al-Islam* (Methods of Ijtihad in Islam). (Kuwait: Kuwait University Press, 1973), pp. 203–408; especially in this regard see George Makdisi, *The Rise of Colleges: Institutions of Learning in Islam and West* (Edinburgh: Edinburgh University Press, 1981).

52. "Faith and the Faithful," pp. 10–13.

53. *Ibid.*, pp. 31–32.

54. *The Holy Qur'an,* XV: 9.

55. "Faith and the Faithful," p. 38.

56. R. Jillian and O. El-Durzi, *Ossont Al-Din Al-Islami* (The Basics of the Islamic Religion). (Baghdad: Dar al-Hurriah, 1977), p. 22.

APPENDIX I

Bernard Lewis: Selected Bibliography

"History-writing and National Revival in Turkey," *Middle Eastern Affairs,* 4 (June-July 1953), pp. 218-227.

"The Ottoman Empire and its Aftermath," *Journal of Contemporary History,* 15 (January 1980), pp. 27-36.

"Nuzarelti in the Sixteenth Century, According to the Ottoman Tapu Registers," in George Makdisi, ed., *Arabic and Islamic Studies in Honor of Hamilton A. R. Gibb* (Cambridge: Harvard University Press, 1965), pp. 416-425.

"Communism and Islam," in Ruth Nanda Anshen, ed., *Mid-East World: Yesterday, Today, and Tomorrow* (New York: Harper, 1956), pp. 303-315; and also in Walter Laqueur, *Middle East in Transition* (New York: Praeger, 1958), pp. 311-324.

"The Contribution to Islam," in John Richard Harris, ed., *The Legacy of Egypt* (Oxford: Clarendon Press, 1971), pp. 456-477.

"An Anti-Jewish Ode, The Qasida of Abu Ishaq against Joseph Ibn Nagressa," in *Salo Wittmayer Baron—Jubilee volume on the Occasion of his Eightieth Birthday,* ed., Saul Lieberman (New York: distributed by Columbia University Press, 1975 for the American Academy for Jewish Research in Jerusalem, volume 2), pp. 657-668.

"The African Diaspora and the Civilization of Islam," in Martin C. Kilson and Robert Rotberg, eds., *The African Diaspora* (Cambridge: Harvard University Press, 1976), pp. 37-56.

"Recent Developments in Turkey," *International Affairs,* 27 (July 1951), pp. 320-331.

"Sources for the History of the Syrian Assassins," *Speculum,* 27 (October 1952), pp. 475-489.

"Islamic Revival in Turkey," *International Affairs,* 28 (January 1952), pp. 38-48.

"Communism and Islam," *International Affairs,* 30 (June 1954), pp. 1-12.

"The Middle Eastern Reactions to Soviet Pressures," *The Middle East Journal*, 10 (Spring 1956), pp. 125-137.

"Democracy in the Middle East — Its State and Prospects," *Middle East Affairs*, 6 (April 1955), pp. 101-108.

"Democracy in Turkey," *Middle East Affairs*, 10 (January 1959), pp. 55-72.

"Cold War and Detente in the 16th Century," *Survey*, 22 (Summer/Autumn 1976), pp. 55-56.

"Anti Zionists Resolution," *Foreign Affairs*, 55 (October 1974), pp. 54-64.

"Ali Pasha on Nationalism," *Middle East Studies*, 10 (January 974), pp. 77-79; and (June 1974), pp. 77-79.

David Rokeck, *Arad* (poem) translated by Bernard Lewis, *Times Literary Supplement*, 72 (June 1973), p. 610.

"Study of Islam," *Encounter*, 38 (January 1972), pp. 31-41.

"Russia in the Middle East," *Round Table*, 60 (July 1972), pp. 257-263.

"Race and Color in Islam," *Encounter*, 35 (August 1970), pp. 18-31.

"Friends and Enemies," *Encounter*, 30 (February 1968), pp. 3-7.

"Assassins," *Encounter*, 29 (November 1967), pp. 34-49.

"Consequences of Defeat," *Foreign Affairs*, 46 (January 1968), pp. 321-335.

"Great Powers, the Arabs and the Israelis," *Foreign Affairs*, 47 (July 1969), pp. 642-652.

"State of Middle Eastern Studies," *American Scholar*, 48 (Summer 1981), pp. 365-381.

"Turkey Turns Away," *New Republic*, 178 (February 1978), pp. 18-21.

"Is Peace Still Possible in the Middle East," *Commentary*, 66 (July 1978), pp. 37-45.

"Palestinians and the PLO: A Historical Approach," *Commentary*, 59 (January 1975), pp. 32-41.

"The Return of Islam," *Commentary*, 61 (January 1976), pp. 39-49.

INDEX

Abbasids, 17, 38, 140, 145
Abdarrizaq, Ali, 74
Abduh, Muhammad, 64, 74, 81
Abed-Rabbo, Samir, 4, 259-280
Abraham, 53-55, 187, 233, 234
Abu Bakr, 181; quoted, 274
Abbot Joachim, 151
Abdel-Malek, Anouar, 120n, 121n
Adams, Charles, 101, 121n; quoted, 101
adhan (prayer call), 253
agnosticism, 154
Ahrends, W., 57, 59
Al-Ashari, 143
Al-Azhar, 138, 160
Al-Azmeh, Aziz, 3, 89-118
Al-Biruni, 185
Al-Fadil, 184
Al-Farabi, 112, 123n, 143
Algar, Hamid, 21
Al-Ghazzali, 136, 138, 145, 149, 153, 159
Algeria, 11
Ali (fourth caliph), 277, 278
Ali, A. Yusuf, 282n
Ali, Kurd, 74
'alim (knowledgable person), 183
Al-Jabiri, M.A., 123n

Al-Kinda, 37
Allah (also see Christianity, comparative analysis, Islam, Orientalism), 44, 106, 129, 134, 135, 140-144, 146-148, 150, 152, 156-157, 206, 209, 212
Al-Mawardi, 180
"alongsidedness," 203-254
Althusser, Louis, 36, 41n, 122n, 202n
al-ummah al muhammadiyah, 186
Ambercrombie, Nicholas, 41n
American Institute of Iranian Studies, 18
American Research Center, Egypt, 18
American Research Institute, Turkey, 18
American University: of Beirut, of Cairo, 18
amin (faithful), 188
Amos, 156
Anderson, J.N.D., 22, 66; quoted, 15
Anderson, Perry, 41n
Andrae, Tor, 14
anicca, 144
Anquetil-Duperron, Abraham-Hyacinthe, 8

287